CW00953579

Memoirs of an
Aide-de-Camp
of Napoleon
1800-1812

Memoirs of an
Aide-de-Camp
of Napoleon
1800-1812

General Count Philippe de Ségur

Translated by H.A. Patchett-Martin

NONSUCH

First published 1896
Copyright © in this edition 2005
Nonsuch Publishing Ltd

Nonsuch Publishing Limited
The Mill, Brimscombe Port, Stroud, Gloucestershire, GL5 2QG
www.nonsuch-publishing.com

All rights reserved. No part of this book may be reprinted or reproduced or
utilised in any form or by any electronic, mechanical or other means, now
known or hereafter invented, including photocopying and recording, or in any
information storage or retrieval system, without the permission in writing from
the Publishers.

British Library Cataloguing in Publication Data.
A catalogue record for this book is available from the British Library.

ISBN 1-84588-005-6

Typesetting and origination by Nonsuch Publishing Limited
Printed in Great Britain by Oaklands Book Services Limited

CONTENTS

INTRODUCTION TO THE MODERN EDITION

Philippe Paul, comte de Ségur, was born in 1780, the son of Louis Philippe, comte de Ségur (who, like his son, was an army officer and a historian), and his wife, Antoinette d'Aguesseau. After witnessing a cavalry parade in Paris in 1800 he was inspired to join the army as an ordinary recruit, but quickly afterwards obtained a commission. After serving under General Étienne-Jacques-Joseph-Alexandre MacDonald in the Grisons in 1800–1801, of which campaign he published an account in 1802, Colonel Geraud Duroc, later the duc de Frioul, an aide-de-camp to Napoleon Bonaparte, found a position for him on the personal staff of the *Premier Consul*. In early 1807, during Napoleon's campaign against the Russians in Poland, de Ségur was taken prisoner, but he was exchanged after the Treaty of Tilsit. The following year, his participation in the cavalry action at Sommo-Sierra in Spain during the Peninsular War earned him the rank of colonel, although wounds sustained during the engagement forced him to return to France.

By 1812 he was a general of brigade, and he took part in Napoleon's campaign against the Russians, facing the horrendous conditions of a Russian winter and witnessing the annihilation of the *Grande Armée*: of the more than 500,000 men who set out, fewer than 20,000 returned. Having survived this expedition, he fought throughout 1813 and 1814, distinguishing himself at Hanau, near Leipzig, in 1813, when France's ally Bavaria turned against her, and at Reims in 1814. He continued to serve in the army after the restoration of the French monarchy in 1815, but, when Napoleon returned from exile on Elba and resumed power during the so-called 'Hundred Days,' he accepted a commission, and, therefore, when Napoleon was exiled again (and permanently) to St Helena, he was retired from active service until the 'July Revolution' of 1830. During his retirement he wrote *The History of Napoleon and of the Grande Armée During the Year 1812*

(1824); the book portrayed Napoleon in an unfavourable light, which resulted in General Gaspar, Baron Gourgaud challenging him to a duel, in which de Ségur was wounded. In 1830 he was elected a member of the French Academy; in 1831, after the 'July Monarchy' of King Louis Philippe had come to power, he was promoted to lieutenant-general and created a peer; and in 1847 he was awarded the grand cross of the Legion of Honour. He retired permanently after the establishment of the Second Republic in 1848 and died in Paris on 25 February 1873.

De Ségur's *Memoirs* covers the period from the author's entry into the army up to his return to France after Sommo-Sierra. These years saw the acme of Napoleon's achievements across Europe and the rise of France as the major European power of the time. It was during the first decade of the nineteenth century that Napoleon's army defeated Austrian, Prussian and Russian forces leading to French puppet rulers being installed in the German states and forcing Russia, after the battle of Friedland, into the Treaty of Tilsit, which effectively split the continent of Europe between these two great powers. Napoleon also consolidated his own power at home, creating himself Emperor in 1804 and King of Italy in 1805. As well as seeing action at many of the major battles of this age, including Ulm, Austerlitz and Jena, and taking part in diplomatic missions, De Ségur, as aide-de-camp firstly to MacDonald and then to Napoleon, was privy to the innermost deliberations and decisions of those two great generals. *Memoirs* records his experiences of both battle and diplomacy in these turbulent times, as well as providing a unique personal insight into the personalities of some of the most important men in history.

EDITOR'S PREFACE

COUNT PHILIPPE DE SÉGUR, GENERAL of division, Peer of France, Academician, was born in 1780 and died in 1873. He lived for the greater part of a century, and cut a brilliant figure in war, politics and letters. A private in 1800, he became a general in February, 1812, and fought continuously up to the end of the Imperial era. He served through all the wars of the Empire on the staff of Napoleon or at the head of picked troops.

With an equal passion for literary and for military glory, he occupied his leisure after the peace in writing numerous works, and published in 1824 his famous narrative of the Campaign in Russia, which was talked of all over Europe. His most important work entitled *History, Memoirs and Miscellanea*, in eight volumes, appeared in 1873 after his death. It comprises the entire history of Napoleon, and the author's personal reminiscences. As the title indicates, the book is in two parts: on the one hand we have the principal events of that incomparable epoch related and appreciated from the high standpoint of an eloquent and conscientious writer; on the other, the personal memoirs of the General, the account of all he had done and experienced.

It is this intensely attractive and dramatic personal record which we publish for the first time in a separate form under the title of *Memoirs of an Aide-de-camp of Napoleon I.*

The author first devotes several pages to his father, Count de Ségur, a celebrated ambassador of the great Catherine, who concluded the first treaty between France and Russia, was one of the French combatants in the War of Independence of the United States, a Councillor of State, and Grand Master of the Ceremonies of Napoleon the First, Academician, and lastly a Peer of France. His name will often crop up in the Memoirs of his son. In this introduction the reader will also find narrated several events of the life of the great grandfather of General Philippe de Ségur, Marshal de Ségur, the hero of Laufeld and of Clostercamp, War Minister of Louis XVI during the American war, who received numberless wounds in the most famous battles of the eighteenth century.

The writer also recounts the first years of his impoverished and proscribed childhood, in the midst of the whirlwind of the Revolution.

INTRODUCTION

I BEGIN THE RECOLLECTIONS OF MY life by speaking of my father. Together with a cultivated, lively, copious, acute, and profound intellect, he possessed an unfailing benevolence, a candid honesty, and the gentle gaiety of a happy nature and a pure and satisfied conscience. But whatever might have been his perspicacity, it was impossible for so loyal, so gentle, and so loving a being, precipitated, as it were, from another world, from the court of the great Catherine, where he had been Ambassador, into the midst of our Revolution, to understand its passions until after he had himself suffered from them. The Queen had made him the confidant of her wishes, he believed in them, he had been deeply moved by her sorrow: she had persuaded him that she was open to reasonable concessions.

In the first instance, he endeavoured to make use of his ties of friendship and relationship with the heads of the various innovating parties to draw them towards this princess. But it was an impossible attempt. In their rivalry for popular favour not one of these chiefs, carried along or outstripped by those around them, could answer from one day to another for his own promises or his intentions of the day before. It would have meant isolation and deposition from all that constituted power, entailing on the one hand the animad-versions of one's own party, while, on the other, there would be no chance of regaining the favour of a Court and an aristocracy implacable in their indignant pride and wounded interests.

The Queen herself, surrounded by distrust and conflicting passions, was no longer mistress of her own decisions. So that from the very outset, although my father had only undertaken these conciliatory steps towards the liberal chiefs at the desire of this princess, he became the object of her mistrust. It was at the same time a sorrowful surprise to him to find himself suddenly exposed to the malignant rebuffs of those amongst his former friends who, hankering after everything and anxious to grasp back all, appeared to the Queen her most trusty and faithful partisans.

It nevertheless happened several times that, in the midst of this whirlwind of antagonistic passions, my father's reputation for ability, moderation, and loyalty, dawned on these unfortunate princes as a means of salvation. On three special occasions amongst others, in their ever-increasing distress did they avail themselves of it; first, when they chose him for their ambassador to Rome, secondly, by offering him the Foreign Office Ministry which he was unable to accept, and lastly by appointing him their Minister Plenipotentiary at Berlin.

My father did not even start for Rome; the Pope refused to receive him; all union on this side had become an impossibility. As for his mission to Berlin, I had it from himself that he would receive no instructions save from the King and Queen exclusively. Unfortunately this precaution was useless. These instructions were entirely of a pacific nature, but whether through dissimulation on the part of our princes towards their Plenipotentiary, or that after his departure they had been drawn into another line of policy, the fact was that his devotion was turned against himself and he was sacrificed to it. After having worn himself out in vain efforts, perceiving that he had been tricked and calumniated by those whom he was endeavouring to help, or rather by their blind advisers, he was forced to renounce the attempt to avert the peril which he foresaw would soon overtake them.

The catastrophe of August 10th and the September massacres were then imminent. At the time when this disastrous epoch had actually arrived, disheartened and discouraged by the mistrust of the very Government which he had vainly endeavoured to succour, he had for two months past withdrawn himself seven leagues from Paris, and was at Fresnes, in the home of his brother-in-law, M. d'Aguesseau, where the news of the demagogical profanations of June 20 and the cruelties of August 10 reached him, not as a surprise but as an aggravation of his sorrow for the misfortunes of the vanquished, and his horror at the revolutionary excesses. Soon the atrocities of September 2 and 3 invaded even the retreat where his energies were solely directed towards the preservation of his wife and his three children from this irruption of barbarians. A band of these demagogues were in pursuit of a well-to-do farmer of the neighbourhood, suspected of royalism, and denounced as a monopolist because he was wealthy; these miscreants had caught him, and without any kind of trial, were proceeding to make an end of him when my father came to the rescue, haranguing them with such success that in a sudden transformation, these wretches passed from a murderous frenzy into a no less exaggerated transport of humane enthusiasm. In this fresh outbreak they made the unhappy farmer, still pale, and trembling in every limb, drink and dance with them around the tree of liberty from whose branches they would pitilessly have strung him up only a moment before.

On his return to Paris during the sinister winter of 1792 to 1793, he found installed that Reign of Terror, which stained and dishonoured France, and disgusted her for so long with liberty. It was a style of government for which our new historians who happen to be admirers of Danton, should give him the entire credit, as we shall see. In fact that political invention which he so audaciously boasted of dates specially from his Ministry of Justice and the massacres which he avowedly organized: here is a proof.

A few weeks after this massacre of priests, women, and inoffensive old men and prisoners, my father happened to meet him. Danton accosted him and entered into conversation, and my father challenged him concerning the horrible events of these two days, saying that he failed to see their motive or their aim, and that he could not understand how he, a Minister of Justice, could neither have foreseen, nor at any rate have checked them. They were at the time walking side by side: stopped short, looked my father straight in the face, and with his too well-known cynicism, replied: 'Sir, you forget to whom you are speaking; you forget that we are the riffraff, that we have issued from the gutter; that with your opinions we should soon fall back into it, and that we can only govern by the law of fear.'

It may well be believed that after such a declaration, conversation was cut short and that my father hastened to leave a monster who was capable of boasting of a system of the most odious crimes which have ever sullied the pages of history.

A few days later my father was arrested on two occasions. The first time he was torn from the hands of these terrorists by the agency of one of those tender friendships which he so deservedly inspired; on the second it was his own courage alone that saved him. Brought before the revolutionary committee of the section for having refused to mount guard at the doors of the Temple where the King was a prisoner, he nobly decided on explaining his invincible repugnance in the plainest language to this assembly of ignorant and infuriated men: 'Was it for him, a former minister of this prince who had often showered benefits upon him, to join the ranks of his gaolers, and even possibly find himself some day in the position of being forced to arrest with his own hand the unfortunate monarch whose confidence he had once possessed? Were there not a thousand other posts in which he could be useful to public order without exciting the deserved mistrust of his fellow-citizens? In any other position he would be able to fulfil his duty without doing violence to sentiments which the consciences of those around him would enable them to realize, and which in his place they would have felt themselves!'

Fortunately the courageous frankness of this declaration awoke an echo in all hearts. There was a general acclamation; the spy who had denounced him, perturbed and taken aback, was ignominiously expelled, and my father was brought home in triumph.

The Girondins, however, already so far removed from their starting point, and guilty withal, were ignorant that in a spirit of faction, and through fear, they were on the eve of being drawn into the commission of the most cowardly and heinous of all crimes.

It was the beginning of January, 1793, and my father, in the attempt to save the unfortunate Louis XVI, was taking steps which he had no reason for supposing would be fruitless. Indeed, on the very eve of the fatal judgment, he received most reassuring promises from one of the most eloquent of the judges. Vergniaud especially went so far as to indulge in certain unbosomings of conscience.

'What! he, vote for the death of Louis XVI! It was an insult,' he exclaimed, 'to dare to suppose him capable of such an unworthy action!' He descanted on its awful iniquity, he pointed out its uselessness, its danger even, and there is no doubt that for the time being this Girondin believed himself incapable of it. But only a few hours after his disavowal, he found himself under the necessity of committing this odious crime, owing to fatal engagements with his party and the terrible impulsion of a revolutionary tribunal. This wretch, after having voted for the death sentence, even voted against any reprieve.

It was impossible for my father to think of returning to Fresnes whither his brother-in-law, M. d'Aguesseau, had retired. This family gathering on a large estate would have excited the ferocious cupidity of these who levied blackmail in places of public resort. Prudence counselled dispersion. He therefore bought near Sceaux and in the village of Châtenay, at three leagues distance from Paris, a little property which became our family retreat. It was there that he gave shelter to my grandfather, Marshal Ségur, who had been denounced and proscribed on account of his record of glorious deeds of arms, and of a seven years' wise, economical, and beneficent administration at the War Office.

Very soon the commissaries of the Committee of Public Safety appeared to drag him from our arms. But their brutality faltered at the spectacle of this old warrior covered with wounds! One of them, however, attempted to lay a hand on him; but the astonishment of the illustrious veteran, and his resolute, cold, and imposing glance arrested the ruffian who drew back and maintained a respectful demeanour during the remainder of his unworthy mission.[1] He refused, however, to accept my father's self-sacrifice, who offered himself persistently either to take my grandfather's place in prison, or to share his captivity.

It lasted six months: he had been incarcerated in La Force and placed in a dungeon where his only bed was a mattress on the ground laid on some stinking straw. The unalterable calm and constant serenity of his mind preserved his health in this cold and wretched prison where he was respected and even tended by his fellow captives, workmen of the lowest class of the people, for there was no distinction of persons among these victims. Fortunately the impudence of the Terrorists stopped short at actually leading to the scaffold an old impoverished man who had been maimed in his country's service and on whose possessions there was nothing to confiscate. Not withstanding which, the impatience of one of these scoundrels, whose cruelty dishonoured his great ability, had already fixed the date of execution when the revolution of the 9th Thermidor settled that of the wretch himself.

As for us, who had remained at Châtenay in a state of consternation, we received the daily list of the atrocities of the members of the Convention with the names of their victims. Each day brought us news of the agony of the sweetest, the most beautiful and inoffensive of women, even of children and venerable old men: suffice it to name the Vintimilles, the Malesherbes and that Duchess of Ayen, my mother's sister, herself a mother to the poor, whose death warrant was clamoured for and obtained by Fouquier-Tinville!

There were our relatives, our connections and a thousand others, for there were whole sections of suspected persons.

We were in constant affright. One night at the bottom of our garden we heard the drums beat to arms in the village. The instinct of danger caused us to rush back to the house, and we were not mistaken, consternation was depicted on every countenance. Two commissaries of the Committee of Public Safety had just arrived in the commune. They lost no time in seeking my father. One was a little fair, insipid weakling; the other a great, tall, swarthy scoundrel in carmagnole garb, with the red cap on, a long sword trailing at his side and a pair of pistols in his belt. His mean countenance bore the imprint of coarse and violent passions. He began by brutally telling my father that 'he had come to arrest him and fling him into one of the Paris prisons where he would not remain long enough to rot!' He added that the first thing to be done was the examination of all papers, a task, which he left to his colleague, as this worthy commissary of the existing government was not able to read.

Luckily it was already late, our grand commissary was hungry, above all thirsty, and was not such a bad fellow in his cups. So that while his colleague was hunting through the drawers of every cabinet in the house, we were plying our *sans-culottes* with drink, and as he appeared to be yielding to our instances, we at last succeeded in mollifying him by representing the despair of our poor mother, and persuading him that an indisposition from which our father was suffering was so serious an illness as to render his removal to Paris an impossibility. This man, who was better than he appeared to be, or than his employers really were, feigned to believe us and even ventured on leaving my father amongst us, under arrest, with two peasants to mount guard over him and answer for his person. This kindly impulse saved us; our commissary justified. his action in Paris, and my father passed out of notice with no further ill-effects during the continuance of the Reign of Terror than the ever-increasing alarm which the daily reports caused us.

Later on, when matters returned more or less to their normal condition, our protector, the *sans-culottes*, became our protégé! But neither money nor work sufficed for him; he stuck to nothing. It became an impossibility to follow him through the various vicissitudes of his fortunes, which were worthy to be chronicled like Vidocq's Memoirs. I believe, however, that they ended on a house-top where he was wounded while trying to escape from a constable whose bullet did him a cruel though necessary service.

The first Terror was followed by a second, on 18th Fructidor. It was then that Napoleon appeared on the scene. As soon as my father discerned this bough of laurel in the midst of the shameful and terrible shipwreck, he seized it and clung to it, and by using every effort, first as a man of letters, then as a legislator, finally as a Councillor of State, succeeded in attaching the whole of France to it. It was he who broke through the silence imposed on the Legislative Body by proposing a ten years' Consulate. His work in the home section of the most learned, the most illustrious of State Councils, past or present, and probably future, was immense! In this department he co-operated with the whole force of his mind and his experience toward the formation of our Codes.

From that time, proscription being a thing of the past, his merits raised him everywhere to the highest positions. We witnessed him in succession a member of the French Academy in the Republic of Letters; Grand Cross of the Legion of Honour; Grand Officer of the Crown at Court, and finally Senator in the first of our political bodies.

After the fatal day of Waterloo, and his devoted offer to accompany Napoleon into exile, being forced to fall back on his writings as a means of livelihood, our youth owed to this last vicissitude the best Ancient History that the University of France had ever put into their hands, the history of France up to the reign of Charles VIII; three library volumes worthy of a place beside the moral works of Plutarch, and his Memoirs, which in spite of their success and our earnest wishes, his great age, his sufferings, and above all his reverence for the sad fate of Louis XVI and Marie Antoinette did not admit of his completing.

In the midst of these labours his excellent reputation was the cause of his recall to the Chamber of Peers where all parties welcomed him, and where he endeavoured to render feasible that form of government which Tacitus had indicated and believed possible. In July, 1830, his dying glance witnessed for the third time the fall from the throne of the elder branch of Kings of our third race. General La Fayette, his nephew, being near to him on his deathbed received his last prophetic words which I also heard, and which events have only too well justified; but the first misguided raptures of this popular Revolution were still at their height when my father expired.

Now for my turn!

II

I had been brought up at home till 1790; then in England up to the beginning of 1792; on return whence, as I have already related, we had to seek an asylum at Fresnes, where the echoes of the saturnalias of June 20th, the excesses of August 10th, and the massacres of September, had invaded our solitude.

We have seen that with the rise of the revolutionary whirlwind, my father, being forced to consider our personal safety, had taken refuge at Châtenay, near Sceaux, three leagues from Paris, with my grandfather, my mother, and three children, of whom I was the youngest. Voltaire, it was said, had been brought up there; I remember that the Abbé Raynal used to come there to see my father. The theories of this historian had just been put into action, to his apparent disgust. I have heard him regret the exaggerations of his philosophic writings; reproaching himself for having fed the flames of this horrible bonfire by placing torches instead of lanterns in brutal hands which only made use of them to consume and destroy everything! This eloquent octogenarian voice pleased my childish ears; I was then unaware that three years previously the same voice had acclaimed and encouraged the young artillery officer who was destined to become our Emperor; but who could have predicted that I myself, twenty years later, after having devoted fourteen of the best years of my life to the service of this great man, should perhaps leave on record to posterity some of the features of his history.

I was twelve years old; the Reign of Terror was beginning; we were poor and proscribed; everyone had abandoned us, including masters and tutors, and my father remained our sole teacher. It was too much for me; there was too great a disproportion between the pupil and the master. At this early age which is that of new sensations, and in the midst of tragic scenes surrounding my weak and sickly existence, my heart alone had singularly and precociously developed itself at the expense above all of my mind, which had remained in its first infancy. The emotions which are often secretive at this age were with me acute, profound and tenacious; but my intellect distinguished or understood little, and worked mechanically. I neither grew in body nor in mind. So that instead of being a source of consolation, I only added to the troubles of my family up to the age of seventeen.

At this epoch, which was that of the Directorate, some remains of the brilliant world of the 18th century had survived. Many then of talent, of letters, and of pleasure, had devoted themselves to these relics of the most charming society of modern times. Saved from the shipwreck, they tried to console each other by bringing into this new world, in the midst of the still sanguinary ruins of the old one, the manners of other days, the love of pleasure adorned by a gallant or romantic sentimentality, that of a light and graceful literature, above all of a mordant and mocking conversation, that puerile weapon of ridicule, the only one that remained to serve our hate against the revolutionary giant. With it we made a mad onslaught against the axe hanging over our heads and still dripping with our blood, against the scandalous good fortune of boorish *parvenus* even against the glory of its armies, then victorious over the whole of Europe!

In this society, my uncle, the Viscount de Ségur, was one of the men most noted by the light graces of his mind. It was he who had initiated me into it. My father was of it, but only by one side of his nature—that of a man of the world and a man of letters; the other side, that of a statesman, a publicist and historian, bound him to political society. Both of them lived by their pen.

As for me, suddenly transplanted into the seductions of the amiable and joyous world in which my uncle reigned, I was dazzled by it, I was seized with the ambition of sustaining the reputation of wit, of courage, and of gallantry of my family. This ambition took possession of all my adolescent faculties: I could see nothing beyond. So that, when at the age of seventeen I was quoted on account of some songs, a duel, and other society successes, I fancied myself to be a complete man of the world, having done all that could be expected of my age and my capacity.

My education had not been subjected to any method. Accustomed never to begin anything at the beginning, in the same way that I wanted to write books before I had read enough of them, and to be a philosopher before having left the sixth class, I formed my own political opinions on hearsay; I followed the lead of example and sentiment. I shared the hatred by which I was surrounded for a revolution which had ruined and desolated us, and which would even still proscribe us! There was nothing in this but what was natural, all the more so that it was not the more thoughtful opinion of my father, and that there is often a spirit of contradiction between the pupil and the master. From that time, without examination and confusing all in my indiscriminating aversion, I refused to accept anything from the present time, I clung blindly to the past, childishly displaying in the streets the black collar of the Vendeans, and calling the hero of Italy Monsieur Bonaparte.

However, considering all things, good and bad, I was better than the vain and sterile reputation which was the object of my ambition. It was a favourable symptom of my youth that I sought and liked the conversation of serious men older than myself, attaching much value to their esteem. As to women, I addressed myself to those whose qualities of heart and mind were the most exacting. However distinguished they might be, my imagination placed them still higher! I religiously worshipped in them the type of ideal perfection which I had created for myself, and it was in spite of the strict conditions which this type imposed, that I endeavoured to please them. I applied myself to the task without respite, without relief, taking everything seriously; my mind and heart always on the strain; playing the lover fervently, laboriously committing many follies, and fancying that my whole future lay in the most ephemeral of successes.

This exclusive circle, beyond whose limits I seldom passed, was not altogether useless to me. It was dominated by delicate taste, noble and polished manners, benevolence, and the most exalted sentiments; by these alone could one hope to please. Everyone spoke in turn, there was very little scandal, no chatter upon dress or domestic economy, one had to contribute an opinion on the news, the plays and the books of the day, on the actions and sentiments of the hero of whatever literary work happened to be in vogue. These judgments were controverted neither in haste nor with pedantry, but more or less developed according to their relation with the condition of heart or mind mutually existing between the interlocutors. In short, I was living in the very midst of one of the most select sets of this celebrated society, which the man of the world and the man of letters of a former day frequented by way of completing himself.

Too prematurely launched into this career, and proscribed from any other, and at the age of eighteen being incapable of producing anything beyond light verse and vaudevilles, its drawback was its futility from this my disposition saved me, but at my own expense. We have seen that by nature and education I was of a serious turn of mind; I therefore rhymed without a vocation, laboriously, expending in the polishing of my couplets the few resources of my mind, and succeeding but poorly. The remembrance of the distaste with which I regarded my sterile vein, that of the *ennui,* which I experienced above all in summer, lounging in Paris, then empty of my set, wandering without aim or money, badly dressed and worse fed, this remembrance of want of occupation, of privations, of discontent with myself and my wasted time, long remained in my memory as an unbearable weight.

The second Terror, that of the 18th Fructidor was then rampant. Prudence as well as poverty kept me at Châtenay where at least I found the necessaries of life. There, in a neglected but still elegant abode, in the midst of a well-filled and well-selected library, with no society but my own, my enfranchized imagination took fresh flight, and a thousand ambitious dreams in this isolation where nothing disturbed them, carried me out of the real world and transported me into that of illusions. Then with a stick in one hand and a bundle in the other, I took the road or rather the by-way towards the capital; for it was always across the fields, or in the direction of Fontenay-aux-Roses or of Châtillon that I wended my steps, carefully avoiding the high road, habitations, passers-by, and all that might interrupt the charm of my solitary reveries.

Oh! how relieved I felt when no longer dreading a chance meeting, an interchange of greetings or even a glance, I had passed the last house in our village! With what a transport of joy I at once let loose the reins of my wild imagination! With what promptitude it carried me off into the world of enchantments, and how in this two hours' journey, it bore me on from one glorious success to another to the very summit of the most brilliant and diverse careers! I can still look back on those moments as amongst the most fortunate of my existence! The illusion was at times so complete that I no longer knew I was on the tramp, cold or heat, fatigue or poverty, were all alike forgotten. But when the hero of so many enchanting adventures arrived unexpectedly at the real end of his journey, the frontier of Maine was the fatal landmark where so many ravishing illusions suddenly jostled each other, were shattered to atoms, and fell to dust. Then, alas! brought face to face with sad reality, the irresistible Alcibiades, the millionaire Crœsus, the Olympian winner precipitated from his triumphal car, found himself on foot, bathed in perspiration, and covered with mud or dust! Everything then became an obstacle to be avoided, a brutal waggoner perchance, or a suspicious official. Lucky if he could profit by some assemblage in which he might pass unperceived, to slink away as a suspect, and escape the ever risky necessity for an ex-noble of exhibiting his passport.

On my return home, the downfall would become absolute and complete. To the transitory, tender joy of these fleeting moments succeeded the discouraging question:

'What is to become of you?'

I

MY VOCATION

I WAS NINETEEN YEARS OLD, BUT it seemed that I was not fit for anything, not even to be a clerk in an office, for my writing was too bad.

Yet that was my last resource. Time pressed, and it was humiliating to remain a burden on my family. I was on the point of resigning myself to my fate; already I was sadly striving to become a very poor copyist when a last journey brought me back to Paris. Directly I had passed the suburbs I noticed that day a singular emotion on the countenances and in the attitude of all the persons I met, which inspired me with a vague hope.

Revolution was then following revolution; I foresaw one coming. In my destitute state, and in the midst of the ever-increasing proscriptions, any change could but be a change for the better, as far as I was concerned. Disenchanted of my dreams and thrust back by my misfortunes into the world of reality, I for the first time felt one of the great public. Curiosity and even a keen interest led me on, drawing me out of my own way, regardless of any risk to myself. Not being able to be an actor in this new agitation, I at any rate wished to be a witness of it. I knew nothing; I did not dare to ask anyone, but was led on by a powerful instinct, which guided me straight towards him whose destiny was soon to control my own.

It was the very moment when Napoleon at the Tuileries, elected by the Council of Ancients, was commencing the revolution of the 18th Brumaire, and haranguing the garrison of Paris to make sure of it against the Directory and the other Council.

I was stopped by the garden railings. I leant up against them and gazed eagerly upon this memorable scene. Then I ran around the enclosure trying all the entrances; at last, when I had reached the gate of the draw-bridge, I saw it open. A regiment of dragoons came out, it was the 6th; these dragoons were marching on towards St. Cloud with their cloaks rolled around them, their helmets on their heads, sword in hand, with that warlike exaltation, that proud determined air which soldiers wear when they approach; the enemy, resolved to conquer or perish! At this martial apparition the warlike blood, which I had inherited from my forefathers, coursed madly through my veins. I had found my vocation; from that moment I was a soldier, I only dreamt of combats, and disdained any other career.

Nevertheless, however carried away I might have been, thoughtful, dreamy, and melancholy by nature, I reflected on my own enthusiasm, carefully keeping, to myself a resolution so opposed to the whole of my preceding life. Hitherto, in the exclusively aristocratic and anti-revolutionary society which I had frequented, my words and feelings had been full of horror and disgust for all that appertained to the revolution; I proscribed it as it proscribed me; I did not except the army itself from this blind aversion.

I held such a false and sorry opinion of its composition that I remember in a duel, two years previously, with young Verdière, son and aide-de-camp of the General-Commandant of Paris, whilst waiting for weapons, I had not chosen either to give my name, or to sit down at night on the parapet of the Quay Voltaire beside one of his seconds, for fear that officer should treacherously throw me into the river! I was, however, so little suspicious by nature, that when the quarrel had broken out a minute before in the Vaudeville Theatre, when it had been a question of choosing seconds, I, alone against three, had asked one of these gentlemen to act as mine. I was ignorant at the time that they were officers, but as soon as I knew it I distrusted them.

However, these worthy young men, who were older than myself, insisted that all should be in regular form; they even had sufficient confidence and patience to wait in the Champs Elysées, while I went to seek a second among my acquaintances. The meeting took place in the Avenue Marigny, by the light of a gas-lamp, which, before the revolution, my uncle, the Viscount le Ségur, happened to have erected on that spot. It was only after having narrowly escaped killing my adversary, and being twice slightly wounded myself, that our duel, which had been interrupted by officers of the police, came to an honorable conclusion. Notwithstanding which, this proof of the loyalty of these military men did not alter my state of feeling. I even congratulated myself on having concealed my name and that of my second, having insisted that I should be allowed to go and fetch him by myself; so as not to expose his household to some infamous denunciation.

This odious prejudice will show the pronounced tone of my mind. How, then, could I possibly follow the vocation for which I felt this sudden call? How could I conciliate this love of arms with this aversion for the army, this passion for glory with the hatred for the sole flag under which it could be won? But the sight of this regiment on the march had transformed me from a young dreamer into a man of action, without separating the two in my personality. The first smoothed for me the entrance into the world of reality by adorning it with illusions. My imagination, fertile in projects, immediately conceived the idea of implanting my own royalism in this thoroughly republican army. I even ventured to think that I might lead a good number of my fellows to imitate my example; that this germ of an anti-revolutionary army might take root; and that as one revolution had hitherto trodden on the heels of another, judging of the future by the past, I imagined another might soon take place by which our party might profit. This idea, wild though it might appear, did, however, bring forth something; that is why I speak of it, because I soon gained proselytes for its execution. This was some months later in Switzerland, when I had already gained my step as an officer; conspiracies were then in the wind, they cropped up on all sides; ours, indeed, was almost a conspiracy, but set on foot by a pack of thoughtless young men whose dream, when discovered, was treated with contempt, which was quite right; it only left us the poorer by our expenditure of money and ideas, to which we resigned ourselves.

It may seem almost ludicrous, that having entered the army in the hope of persuading it to embrace royalism, it, on the contrary, drew us into its cause; and having left Paris warm royalists in 1800, we were almost as warm republicans when we returned to it in 1801. This new transformation was due to fraternity of arms and an appreciation of the true state of things on the one hand, and, on the other, to the rebuffs which we experienced at the hands of our former set. A year sufficed to bring it about. But I will return to the order of events which will explain this inconsistency.

I had imagined that the day of my public enrolment would be that of my departure, that at least the explosion which I dreaded would take place when I had gone, so that I should not hear it; but it happened quite differently. The appeal, rather perhaps political than military, to a picked class of young men who should provide their own arms and horses and equip themselves, had just appeared. General Dumas, who was a friend of my father, was to organize this body; I was the first to go to him and at once inscribe my name, but under promise of secrecy. It was only when I had taken this first decisive step that I confided it to my father. He approved of it, which is what I had expected. He did more; he was kind enough to keep it a secret whilst smiling at my weakness.

I nevertheless, on the eve of being severely censured, felt very uncomfortable in those salons where I was still so welcome. It was even worse when I realized that our organization would be set on foot in Paris, in the very midst of this dreaded society. From that moment my anxiety daily increased; I could not sleep, I was in a perfect fever. At last the fatal moment arrived when I had to go to the Town-hall publicly to sign the act of enlistment.

It was the 24th Ventôse of the year VIII (February 1800) when my father took me there, or rather dragged me to the Place de Grève as if to execution, such was my dread of the commotion which was sure to follow. My return to the Fauburg St. Honoré which I, as well as the best people of my own set, inhabited, was even worse. The nearer I approached, the greater became my anguish, until, at last, feeling on the verge of giving way, I grew so terrified and indignant at the extent of my own weakness that this fresh shame somewhat restored my courage. A reason for thus losing it when great resolutions have been taken, arises from a natural inclination to see them only on their worst side; one forgets the other, the very cause of one's determination, when on the contrary that is the moment one should turn entirely towards and hold fast to it. My father recalled my wandering wits, one of the greatest services he ever rendered me, without which I do not really know what would have become of my poor head. Anger brought me back to my senses, for I was not spared. One of my nearest and best-loved relatives was the first to pronounce the word *dishonour!* The excess of severity set me in revolt; I accepted war. I gave back scorn for scorn; I shouted louder than my adversaries, even enlisting several of my friends in my cause. These young noblemen, less earnest than myself, or simply following the natural impulses of their age, successively answered to the same call. They were then to be reckoned as of us, and instead of attacking us they had to defend themselves. This was the beginning of the first amalgamation of the old society with the new. We should remember it was not five months since the one had finally proscribed the other.

However feeble and imperfect this first fusion might be, it was not without importance; which fact must reflect some importance on the account of it. Doubtless this happy reconciliation would have taken place without me, but it was through me that it began. That is the reason why Napoleon made me a sub-lieutenant on the 9th Floréal of the year VIII after I had served only a few months as a private of Hussars in the volunteers styled '*Bonaparte's.*'

I had not only bearded my own set, but I had to return to my family at Châtenay to answer for my desperate action to my grandfather the Maréchal de Ségur. Arriving in the early morning,

I drew near to his bed in the most respectful attitude, 'You have been guilty of disrespect,' he said severely, 'to all the traditions of your ancestors; but the thing is done; remember that. You have of your own free will enlisted in the Republican Army. Serve it frankly and loyally. You have made your choice, and it is out of your power to go back on it.'

Then seeing me bathed in tears he was a little moved, and with his only remaining hand he took mine, and drawing me to him pressed me to his heart; then giving me twenty louis which was nearly all he possessed, he added: 'Here, this will help you to complete your equipment; go forth, and do your best bravely and faithfully to maintain under the flag which you have chosen, the name which you bear and the honour of your family!'

Fifty years have passed since then, but I never think of this noble and sad farewell, of this manly and touching blessing, without being moved to the very depths of my being!

II

MY DÉBUT

At the beginning of the year 1800, the time when I enlisted, our frontiers were on the point of invasion; and from the Helder to Genoa, all the efforts of Bonaparte had only succeeded in bringing about 150,000 men to oppose 300,000 of the enemy.

It was then that, in the midst of numerous cares of all kinds, steadily following his aim, which was to rally all to his own fortunes, he had made to a hitherto proscribed party of the youth of France that appeal to which I had been the first to respond. It had not been directly addressed to them, it is true; but it was evident that his protection was offered to them, that it opened the ranks of the army to them; and that by calling upon them to equip and mount themselves in a select new corps, he offered them in return the gratitude of the nation. Nothing had been left undone that might draw and appeal to us. General Dumas, who had been proscribed by the terrors of '93 and of the Directory, had been entrusted with our formation. This general dated from Louis XVI; he was possessed of the pleasant wit, the benevolent disposition and the gentle and attractive manners of the ancient order. It was the same with the chief who was immediately over us in command, Colonel, formerly Count, de Labarbée, a former officer of the royal army.

Some weeks were necessary for the Paris recruitment of our corps, which was first called *Volunteer Hussars*, then *Bonaparte's Legion*, and which only numbered two or three squadrons and a strong battalion. As for our duties, whilst we were waiting to go into barracks, they consisted, besides a little sentry duty, in writing and carrying out the orders of General Dumas and in following him. This last service, insignificant though it might be, did me a good turn. It happened in this wise.

Our general, having business to transact with the Director Carnot, a former member of the Convention, at that time Minister of War, happened that day to select me for his orderly. Arrived in the court-yard of the War Office we dismounted, and my duty was to wait there with the horses; but as General Dumas, when starting, had ordered me to follow him, fancying that I must not leave him, I scrupulously dogged his every step in my anxiety to carry out my orders to the letter. In consequence, when he went upstairs I did the same; I also followed him through the ante-chamber and the reception room step by step, walking immediately behind him, and even into the Minister's study. Preoccupied with the business which had brought him there, and having no cognizance of my blunder, he immediately entered into conversation with this personage. General Dumas was between the Minister and myself, with his back towards me; being taller than he, my head rose above his, so that Carnot, astonished to see in the inner privacy of his study a young soldier standing like a post behind his interlocutor, was not listening to him at all, and with an air of utter astonishment appeared to demand the explanation of such an unheard-of proceeding. The General, on his side, surprised by the Minister's reception of him, and noticing that he appeared much more taken up with something that was going on behind him than with the affair that he had come to discuss, turned back. On seeing me: 'What the devil are you doing here?' he exclaimed. I replied by alleging the orders which I had received: then both of them burst out laughing, and gave me the first lesson in my duty by sending me back to my humble post. But as soon as I had gone, this prank of mine naturally brought about an explanation, in which General Dumas expatiated upon my voluntary enlistment, the first which had taken place, and on the usefulness of the example which I had set.

My ingenuous action brought about speedy results; I had attracted attention; my name was favourably noted, and the rank of sub-lieutenant which I obtained on May 1st, 1800, was the happy consequence of this adventure.

Such are the caprices of Fortune. Her first favour was bestowed on me for a blunder; a brilliant action would perhaps not have done so much for me. I certainly have no cause to complain of Fortune; but since then how many difficulties and dangers have I faced without obtaining as much from her!

We were soon sent from Paris to Compiègne, then to Dijon, the meeting-place of the second army of reserve. Napoleon reviewed us there on his way to cross the St. Bernard. From Dijon we went to Carrouge, near Geneva, where we were quartered, the victory at Marengo having interrupted our march. There I met Madame de Staël at a ball where, in remembrance of my father, she was kind enough to dance with me, entering at once into a political conversation which she soon abandoned; then, remembering my early efforts, she asked me what I had done with my pen (*plume*). Absorbed as I then was in the career I had chosen, I pointed to the plume in my shako, lightly saying that I had placed it there, and that I did not think I should ever feel inclined to use it in any other fashion.

I might even have added that at that moment the thing I feared the most was that I might be forced to take the quill once more into my fingers and again become a man of letters. During our stay in this cantonment, the news of the armistice of Varsdorf and the thunder-clap of Marengo came to vex and damp our ardour; it seemed as if the war would come to an end without us.

III

MY FIRST CALL TO ARMS

SINCE MAY 6TH, THE DAY on which the First Consul reviewed us at Dijon and classed us into the second army of reserve, we had, as I have said, advanced as far as Geneva. There, whilst constantly receiving accounts of the glorious deeds which were being accomplished in Italy, we envied the fate of the most humble private who could boast that he had taken a part in them. We looked upon each one of them as a hero. What were we in comparison? When should we be able to recount our exploits and cut a figure in our turn? These laurels disturbed our rest. After so many wars and so many victories we seemed to think that the race had been won, that we had arrived too late, and that there would be nothing but leavings for us, if any remained!

We were quartered near Geneva, at Carrouge, when on some pleasure excursion or other, we committed the unpardonable impertinence of harnessing some of our troop horses to a brake. Returning to our quarters at night through a narrow street, we suddenly came upon our Colonel! It was impossible to go back. Had we either stopped or passed on our way with a salute, our lapse of discipline must have been taken note of and met with exemplary punishment, and we were hesitating in face of the approaching difficulty when one of us, who afterwards became a General, cried out: 'Leave it to me, we must bewilder him, I take the responsibility of it!' And immediately seizing hold of the reins, he whipped the horses up to their greatest speed, galloping straight towards our chief with such impetuosity that there was hardly time for him to lean close up against the wall so as not to be run over. 'Devil take the young fools!' exclaimed the colonel; but every one of us, horses and officers, were already out of his reach before he had time to recognize us.

It might be useful to recall a more serious adventure of another kind, which will show the danger of making rash acquaintances. While passing through Switzerland, we had in my company a non-commissioned officer, son of a widow who afterwards married a nobleman of one of the best old families in France. This cavalry sergeant was a man of ready wit, without any morality; he always had a string to his bow ready for an emergency, without seeming to know that in justice he deserved it should be drawn against himself, and this is just what would have happened to him, had it not been for me, as we shall see.

From one vice and another he had dropped into crime; I knew he was a man of no reputation, but beguiled by the charm of his intellect and believing that he had abandoned the error of his ways, I had been led into much too great intimacy with him. On our arrival at Coire, we were quartered in the environs when I was warned by a letter from our colonel that a burglary and the murder of a jeweller had been planned in the very village which we occupied, that this non-commissioned officer was the originator of it, and that the police were on their way to seize him.

On receipt of this news, partly from fear that the honour of my company might be stained by a criminal sentence upon him, partly from pity for the wretch, I made up my mind to warn him, so that he might go and get hanged elsewhere, and otherwise than in the uniform which I was wearing. I went off at once to his lodging, which was on the first floor, in a big room furnished with two benches and a long and narrow table.

The scene which took place there, which was for a moment very critical, made a deep impression upon me. I found him alone, and immediately, without preamble, informed him of the fate with which he was threatened, warning him that there was only a moment for escape if he meant to avoid it. But dreading a snare, with one bound he leapt over the table which he put between himself and me, and seizing his pistols, raised the trigger and pointed the weapon at me, exclaiming that 'I had doubtless come to frighten him, to drag a confession from him, to arrest him. But that if I made the slightest movement he would kill me on the spot!'

The smile of pity which he saw on my face, and the tone of my voice when I impatiently repeated that he was losing his sole chance of escape, must have been very convincing, for, transformed all of a sudden, he threw down his weapons, came close to me and took my hands, which he pressed against his heart, swearing eternal gratitude; then putting together a few belongings, he disappeared out of sight so completely that none of us ever heard anything about him afterwards, neither did the officers of police, whom I found in my rooms when I got back: they had only missed him by five minutes. God grant that the dangers he ran may have brought about his reformation, without which I should have on my conscience all the crimes which, thanks to me, he may have committed since that day!

I myself was at that time denounced and reprimanded on account of a very different plot, a result of the disorder and the agitation of these revolutionary times. I have already described the kind of royalist Utopia by which, after my voluntary enlistment, my conscience, tormented by the change of flag under which I served, had endeavoured to reconcile the contradiction of my aristocratic rancours with the instincts of my warlike humour.

With this thought ever before me, I had associated myself with some comrades in my regiment, mostly Vendeans, who were animated by a similar spirit. We had initiated a kind of conspiracy whose object was to royalize the army. As to the means to be employed, the least ridiculous of them consisted in a project that the most enterprising amongst us should make an offer to the First Consul to levy a voluntary corps of 6000 Vendeans, in which we had already assigned our individual positions. We made our accomplice Piré, now a lieutenant-general, leave Lausanne for Paris.

This young Breton who was devoid of scruples, was very proud of his brilliant wit, his charming face and figure, and of having escaped the massacre of Quiberon! He had arrogated to himself the principal part in this adventure, and, curiously enough, was at first favourably received by Bonaparte; indeed, had it not been for audacities of another nature, such as offering himself as a candidate for the hand of Mademoiselle Hortense de Beauharnais, he might have succeeded! But he had taken away with him on this mission the whole of our money. We had filled his purse to the extent of leaving nothing in our own; so that, a week after, when we had to dine at Lucerne, we spent our last halfpenny in the worst eating-house of the whole town. It was not the custom then to receive daily pay or rations, so that we started off famished the next morning, without the least idea how we should get through the long day without bite or sup. But Fortune protects us in certain phases of life. When we had arrived at our destination and after having had our billets allotted to us, we were, not withstanding our difficulty, on the point of dispersing, when we were ordered to form in circle around our colonel, who announced to us that, acting on orders that moment received from headquarters, men and horses henceforth should be fed by those on whom they were billeted. We all rushed off at once, and if these poor Helvetians did not find us difficult to please on the point of quality, they must have been rather surprised as to the quantity of our demands, and the haste in which we had at once availed ourselves of this thrice-welcome order.

We thus traversed Switzerland by long and short stages: it was a fortunate commencement of our travels. But the drawback of a too ardent nature is that one imagines beforehand everything grander and more beautiful than it can possibly be: so that, however admirable nature may be in reality, its most remarkable phenomena appear inferior to the enchanting visions by a too warm and vivid imagination. This is an unfortunate disposition which destroys the charm of travel. It did not, however, affect me, when, from the summit of the Jura, I suddenly perceived the imposing mass of the Alps and that towering Mont Blanc whose wonders had been so often described to me! But in my subsequent travels I can only remember to have been astonished by the dome of St. Peter's at Rome, the fine works at Cherbourg and the burning of Moscow!

When, before reaching Coire, we for the first time crossed the Rhine not very far from its source, although then under the fascination of another influence, the narrowness of its stream at this point, the suspension of arms which still lasted, and our distance from the enemy, did not even moderate my wild enthusiasm at the aspect of this famous river; I felt transported with martial pride; I crossed it proudly, with my head held high and my hand on the hilt of my sword, and when on the other side I felt myself another man; it seemed to me that I had taken a great stride onwards in my heroic career.

A little further on we found ourselves at the extreme limits regulated by the armistice and I placed my vedettes at the foot of the glacier named the Splugen. Going up to the source of the Rhine from that point, other sensations took possession of me. Beyond Thusis a deep gorge brings one to the rather wide but not deep bed of a torrent whose transparent waters, flowing over a slaty bottom, appear black as those of the Styx. This forms the approach to the Via-Mala, a kind of gate or entrance to Hell, a gigantic relic of chaos, where, for about two leagues, the road runs along by an abyss. This road is cut out, partly on one side and partly on the other of the two flanks of an immense rock separated in half, forming an enormous narrow opening at the bottom of which the compressed waters of the Rhine precipitate themselves with fearful clamour. Very often the cornice narrows off on account of the steepness or of some abrupt turn of the rock. It is then necessary to cross from one side to the other on narrow bridges formed of trunks of pine trees thrown across the abyss: worm-eaten, gaping apart, and trembling under the horses' feet, swayed about by the leaping torrent which roars as it breaks on its bed of rocks. Its course is so impetuous, its bounds so violent, that, notwithstanding the depth of the gulf, the water dashes up in a mist which envelops the traveller, who is almost deafened by the tumult of these cataracts, although they are too deep and almost too narrow to be seen.

It is by this long opening that the village of the Splugen is reached. It was late when I arrived at this poor hamlet; I should have stopped there if only out of curiosity, so as not to lose this opportunity of climbing to the top of the Alps. But I was seized with an unaccountable disgust; the poverty of the inhabitants, the barrenness of this uncultivated country, the isolated appearance of these regions almost lost in the clouds, several weary days of travel and the oppression of these upheaved masses, the very sky itself darkened by a coming storm, all conspired to repel me. I was wrong, as a traveller, and, above all, as an officer of the advance-guard, whose object should be to see everything, and carefully reconnoitre everything, to consider in their different relations every means of entrance and exit, and to acquire every possible information concerning the country through which he is passing.

But I only remained at Splugen long enough to place my picket; after which, in spite of the storm the rain, and the gathering darkness, followed by an orderly, I took a half turn and re-entered the Via-Mala in spite of the remonstrances of the inhabitants who warned me in vain of my imprudence. I was only too well aware of it, after a quarter-of-an-hour's march, when I was quite deafened by the wind, the tumult of the storm, and the roaring of the torrent; when, in addition to the icy rain falling from the sky which one could hardly perceive between the two rocks, the lowering clouds which enveloped us, and the thick mist which rose up from the depths of the precipice, the darkness of night came on and we were forced to dismount so as to know where we were going and not to fall back into the gulf. We stopped short in consternation; it would have been wiser to have returned to Splugen, and we hesitated, but vanity and a love of sensation prevented me from retracing my steps.

The only thing we could then do was to walk on slowly with the bridle over our arms, one hand on the rock and the other hand feeling for the ground at each step. But words cannot depict the anxiety of the moment whenever the road failed us, and we had to guess at these bridges thrown across from one rock to another, to avoid the crevasses and thus to cross the gulf. Every moment we stopped to call out to each other, fancying that in the midst of the tumult of the torrent and the tempest, we had heard the sound, of a fall into the abyss Frequently our hand and our feet touched nothing but space. Then, throwing ourselves back against the rock, we remained in a state of terror, dreading our next move- ment, almost motionless on the ledge, and nearly determined to remain there until day-light should show us the way out of this peril, which we had braved without rhyme or reason, and which could only have entailed blame and ridicule upon us had it come to a fatal issue.

Then recovering our courage, pressing close to the rock, and leaving our horses to find their own way, we would make fresh attempts in different directions; the one who had the best luck would call to the other, and thus we got on little by little. At last, after four hours of mortal anguish, the storm having gone down, the sky being lighter, the air fresher, and the roar of the cataracts sounding further off, we found ourselves on more open ground. We had left the Via-Mala behind us; our horses had followed us, and a faint but welcome light revealed to us a humble chalet, in which we took refuge. The next day we got back to Coire, whence, Moreau having exchanged our regiment with Macdonald for a battalion of greater use in these mountains, we pursued our way by Feldkirch into Suabia, and having there rejoined the army of the Rhine, we were reviewed by our new and celebrated general- in-chief.

IV

HOHENLINDEN

T HE ARMISTICE HAVING, HOWEVER, BEEN extended, Macdonald, general-in-chief of the army of the Grisons, and General Dumas, the head of his staff, had taken advantage of it to come as far as Augsburg to confer with Moreau. Fortunately for me, my regiment was passing through the town on the very day of this meeting, and General Dumas detained me, presented me to the two generals-in-chief, and got Moreau to invite me to the dinner which he was giving to Macdonald; a splendid banquet with covers laid for fifty guests, a repast of the conquerors served by the conquered at the enemy's expense, to the sound of martial music, in a palace of which we had taken possession, the guests being the most celebrated generals of the day in the full splendour of their youth and ardour, dazzling with gold and glory. I had never seen anything like it before and was quite fascinated. I began to understand that to the illustrious memories of our old aristocracy had succeeded other glories and other memories, which would be ineffaceable from that moment; that we should date afresh from a new era which had left its stamp on the age, and had already laid the deep foundations of a new society. I learnt later that this meeting had not been altogether devoid of political motives: one of the principal being the jealousy which the ever-growing power of the First Consul inspired in these generals. Napoleon's own anxiety was aroused by it; for he had learnt that in the midst of the banquet this distrust had found vent in a biting sarcasm against one of his sisters; he had even been informed that this sally of one of the generals-in-chief had been well-received and loudly repeated and commented upon by his colleague.

Besides an ambitious rivalry, there was a feeling of sincere republicanism at the bottom of this spirit of opposition, although but a pale reflection and an almost worn-out impression, it is true, of the former proud and patriotic traditions of this army. There might still be found amongst them some of those Spartans of the Rhine, as they were then called, volunteers of the early years of the republic, martyrs to the cause of liberty and national independence, for which they had sacrificed themselves with a devotion free from all personal ambition, or hope of fortune, or advancement, or even of glory. After having braved every danger, they had been known hundreds of times to refuse the highest positions, to reject them one after the other, and proud of their rigid republican probity, to pursue their way in nakedness and hunger, enduring the most cruel privations, and, even as conquerors, remaining poor in the midst of all the rewards which victory offered; an heroic war of citizenship which was very far from being a mere calling, in which these elect few, privates, officers, generals, warriors by patriotism and not merely by profession, had no other thought than to spend themselves altogether to ensure the public safety, and to return to their homes poor and simple citizens.

But after 1796 and 1797 when in this very army of the Rhine the spirit of conquest had succeeded to this former exaltation of the defensive virtues of the country, it had all become modified by the continuance of war, by the fascination of celebrity, and the contagion of acquired fortunes. Even in 1800, at the time when I entered it, there remained but few of these primitive men who were so entirely patriotic and devoid of private interest: they might be recognized by the simplicity of their attire and their manner of life, by the independent and austere seriousness of their attitude, as well as by a certain air of haughty, bitter, and contemptuous surprise at the sight of the growing luxury and ambitious passions which were taking the place of the ingenuous and disinterested devotion of the early republican enthusiasms.

The luxury of this dinner, which I had recently attended, and of the greater part of the uniforms worn, contrasted strongly with these austere remembrances, and yet in the body of this very army some traces of them might still be discovered in its honest discipline, especially opposed to every kind of pillage, in the simple and popular manners, in the good fellowship and tone of equality visible not only amongst comrades but also towards the general-in-chief.

Without effort, and without even being aware of it, I had impressed Macdonald favourably, but the impression might only have been a transient one without General Dumas, who turned it to account, as we shall see presently. After the cessation of the armistice, about a month later we left our cantonments to assemble under the command of d'Hautpoul. This general had become famous through a thousand dashing actions in the midst of which a short and sublime harangue of his was frequently quoted. When his division was on the point of rushing on the enemy he dashed past it at a gallop, exclaiming: 'Carabineers, brave carabineers, pierce their ranks! Cuirassiers, drive through them! Hussars, hack at them!' and giving at the same time himself the order and the example, he was obeyed instantly.

His intrepidity, however, must have been rather more habitual to him than his eloquence, for with us his inspiration was less happy. 'Hussars,' he said, 'we're going to march upon the enemy. Forwards and let not one of you turn tail, otherwise'—his anger at this very supposition having made him lose the thread of his discourse, in order to give himself time to pick it up again he began a string of such hearty and sonorous oaths that, seeing us all burst out laughing, he turned his back abruptly on us, with this fine conclusion: 'otherwise, otherwise he will be too late for the wedding!'

A few days after we arrived at the outposts through a long file of men, who had been wounded in the early actions which had preluded the battle of Hohenlinden.

As for me, my campaign was to come to an end at Hohenlinden. We had just arrived on that snow-covered field which was on the point of becoming so famous, when, conjointly with the news that Macdonald had chosen me for his aide-de-camp, I received the order to join him in Valteline. Thus to leave my regiment and the army on the very eve of a great battle was an impossibility: I obtained an extension which the vivacity of my colonel very nearly caused rue to repent.

Our chief was then M. de Labarbée, a man of fifty or thereabouts, perhaps less, for at my age, that of a mature man always strikes one as more advanced than is really the case It was that former captain of the Rochefoucauld Dragoons, renowned for his wit, his height, his martial bearing and his herculean strength, above all for an unexampled dexterity in all bodily exercises, and for a temerity on all occasions and in all places which was as audacious as it was lucky.

It was well known that before the Revolution and the war, he had braved the anger of a whole band of officers, and had extricated himself brilliantly from the quarrel; it was a garrison dispute which occurred in a café that had been taken possession of by their set, who had made a regulation that officers of any other corps who should go there would not be allowed to pay for anything they ordered.

M. de Labarbée, feeling insulted by this pretension, refused to submit to it, and as no one dared to receive payment from him he began to break everything in the place; then, ordering a bucket of lemonade to be brought to him, he gave it to his horse to drink, saying: 'As it was the officers of the king's regiment who paid; there was no reason why he should stint himself.' After which, he had quietly awaited the result, following it up by several duels, which all ended favourably.

Then came the Revolution, then the emigration and the war which rapidly gained him a colonelcy. It was at this time, finding himself one day in presence of the Austrian cavalry, he ordered the line which he commanded to remain motionless, and springing forward, sword in hand, rushed on the enemy's line which he broke through, then turning back, and making a path for himself through the ranks of the enemy, returned, covered with blood, to his own men, and calmly again took up his position at their head.

It may well be believed that a warrior of such a character and of such vigour would submit himself with difficulty to any discipline, above all to the rules of military administration. Thus it happened that when on leaving Dijon, a member of the commissariat who was inspecting our humble corps, had disapproved of a certain conveyance which the colonel had ordered for the baggage, we saw him, for all reply, seize hold of the commissary, lift him in the air and turn him round like a feather and then deposit him head-foremost in the waggon, saying: 'that he would now be in a position to appreciate its usefulness'; then, dropping him on his feet, 'that he hoped he might always be able to get through his inspections as quickly and easily.'

In another review that took place at Lucerne, when our then general, an unfrocked monk whom he despised, passed before him, instead of saluting him with his sword he provoked him by brandishing it around his head in a menacing fashion.

Such was our colonel! Amongst us youngsters, our beardless youth reminded him of his own mature years. This displeasing comparison very often annoyed him, a fact which I perceived on the eve of the battle of Hohenlinden, when we met the enemy and heard their bullets whistling round us. I was the youngest of them all, and, proud to be at the head of my platoon, exclaimed, on perceiving me; 'Ah! ah! M. de Ségur, you hear those bullets, they will teach you that there is no difference between you and me here, and that to-day we are all of the same age!'

Moreau had made our division, which was d'Hautpoul's, pass over rapidly from right to left in a forced night march of great cold and severity. We formed the left flank of the centre of the army, on which side the great day of the morrow was, as far as concerned our division, of little importance. But it was not so for myself personally. When we were encamped at the close of the day, our colonel, who was better lodged, and who had presumably

dined better than we had, came to visit us on horseback. I got in
his way without knowing it, and he roughly thrust me aside with
a kick. I protested at this treatment, but he continued his course,
without looking back or stopping, and without condescending to
make the slightest apology!

As for me, almost rooted to the spot and speechless at such an
unexpected aggression, my imagination was all the more active.
I passed the night partly in fits of rage and partly in helpless
outbursts of tears. Towards daylight, happening to see the colonel
walking alone across the plain, I hastened onwards and offered
him my resignation, explaining that as that would put me on
an equality with him, I should then make use of my right to
ask satisfaction for the insult which he had offered me. Either
M. de Labarbée did not remember anything about it, or had not
recognized me when he pushed me away the evening before. He
seemed so utterly surprised, and looked me over from head to foot
with a glance of disdain so eloquent with the exclamation of the
Cid: 'To seek a quarrel with me! What has made thee so vain?'
that, could Daguerre have fixed that glance instantaneously by
his new method, I think he would have been able to reproduce
the verse word for word on my feeble body. He, however, said
nothing more than this, that I could not resign without dishonour,
in the face of the enemy. I retorted that I considered myself already
dishonoured by his violence, and that as soon as I had satisfied
this urgent need of reparation, I would again enlist as a private
under another chief.

But he had too good a heart and too much sense to take advantage of his position and did not carry the matter any further, but
called around him several officers, to whom he nobly related the
inadvertence of which he had been guilty, begging them to bear
testimony to his confession, and making this generous and complete reparation in the most honourable and flattering manner.
There I recognized at once the officer of the ancient régime; for
nobody was better or more pleasant company when he chose;
he was only otherwise by fits and starts. The rest of that day was
given up to an engagement which was decided by the centre. As

for us, our poor part in such a great victory only consisted in a few manœuvres and skirmishing, followed by camping-out on the ice; after which, having been sent to take Moreau's orders, and breakfasting with him at Nymphenburg I returned by long stages, alone and penniless, but at the country's expense, to join General Macdonald in Valteline.

During this journey I again revisited Suabia, Coire, the Via-Mala, and that Splugen which I had so little appreciated. Indeed, I had almost passed it again without seeing it; it was apparently my fate, whether by my own fault or not, to lose the opportunity of noticing this gigantic land-mark between the north and the south of Europe. But I had been ill for several days, and my weary eyes almost overlooked it; I was in such a weak condition that after having fastened me on my mule, I heard my travelling companions say to each other that the journey over the glacier would make an end of me, and consider what they should do with my remains when on the other side of the mountain. But the very reverse happened; the air of the glacier renewed my strength, the crisis was a favourable one. When we had reached the other bank of the Lake of Chiavenna I was hoisted up on a waggon horse whose horribly hard trot, which would have killed me nowadays, set me quite to rights again. Such is the privilege of youth! And thus I arrived completely convalescent at Macdonald's headquarters.

V

THE CAMPAIGN OF THE GRISONS

MACDONALD WAS AT THAT TIME a prey to great anxiety. The hard task which he accomplished in the midst of these glaciers was that of overcoming the severity of the season, the dangers of these regions and the resistance of the enemy. His army hardly numbered 40,000 men, and it had to scale the triple summit which separated it from the valleys of the Adda, the Oglio, and the affluents of the Adige; whence falling on Trente, it should take possession of the upper course of this stream and that of the Brenta itself.

The armistice was on the point of termination, when, starting from the valley of the Grisons, Macdonald began by throwing out across the still practicable Splugen, 3,700 men under d'Hilliers in Valteline. He himself took up a position at Rinecks, thus drawing the attention of the enemy to this opposite side, as much by his own presence there as by the important entrenchments which he extended from Constance up to Feldkirch, their object being at all risks to cover his retreat into Switzerland.

At the same time he pushed on reconnoitring bodies towards the sources of the Adda and the Albula, to Bormio, Avos and Lenz and all the issues of the Engadine.

Having thus protected his left flank, he quickly turned back towards the right with the residue of forces which he could dispose of; and remounting the Rhine up to its source, he rapidly passed through Coire and Thusis, entered the Via-Mala, road of ill-luck, and arrived at the foot of the Splugen. This meant braving the very heart of winter, the very stronghold of famine, and all the horrors of Alpine chaos on the mountain-tops in the very worst season of the year.

It is fourteen leagues distance from Thusis to Chiavenna, but this short journey necessitated one of the most formidable conflicts with this cruel country in the whole of the war. All necessary precautions had been taken, sledges were sufficient for the dismounted guns; but there were no baggage mules for the stores, so that it was necessary to load every soldier, already more than hampered by the weight of his knapsack, his cartridge pouch, and his arms, with five days' provisions and ten packets of cartridges.

This attacking party was divided into four columns. For several leagues beyond Thusis the first defiled between two high rocks so close to each other that the men could hardly see the sky; there was no foot-hold but an ice track, a dark, narrow, and slippery ledge cut out of the rock on the edge of a gulf, intersected in several places by rickety wooden bridges, by which they crossed from one side to the other of these two masses, with an abyss of 300 feet beneath them and the double mountain over their heads. Torrents rushing down the precipices, icicles of a thousand shapes, and avalanches which broke down the infrequent pine-trees and the insufficient railings, were the least of the obstacles on this Via-Mala passage to Splugen. The column arrived at Splugen on November 26th, having to scale the glacier in front of them, which ascent was begun on the 27th. In the good season three hours are sufficient to reach the hospital, but at this time they did not know whether it might not take them the whole day. During the first hour, the left bank of the torrent which they were following was a guide to them and the fatigue was endurable; but when they had reached the head of the valley, an ascent of 60 degrees in the gradient, which took an hour-and-a-half, exhausted their strength. The top was reached, however, the mountain was conquered and they found themselves at the parting of the waters of the north and of the south of Europe! The cold drove them on, and having recovered breath, they resumed their way through two glaciers separated by a space of 400 metres: guides placing land-marks in the road which the workers swept for them, sixty dragoons of the 10th, with General la Boissière at their head, trampling down the snow.

It was hoped that before night they would reach the hospital where the highest plain begins, when suddenly the wind rose in the east. They were immediately enveloped in thick clouds of snow and pulverized ice, but persevered on their way until an enormous avalanche about a hundred feet in diameter detached itself from one of the summits with the rumbling and velocity of a thunder-bolt. It carried off the head of the column. Thirty dragoons disappeared with the horses which they were leading; they were borne down into the torrent, flung against the rocks and buried under the snow. The general was marching on a little distance ahead, which saved him; he was almost the only one left, and half-frozen, and in a fainting condition, was carried by the mountaineers to the hospital. As for his column, which was almost entirely separated from him, it had to stop short; a mountain of snow had filled up the path, and being unable either to advance or remain stationary they retraced their steps towards Splugen.

On the next day, the 28th, the remainder of this cruelly muti-lated company of dragoons with Cavaignac, colonel of the regi-ment, were the first to offer to start anew. But the storm continued, and this tempest even lasted to December 1st, the guides declaring that the glacier would be rendered impracticable for a fortnight. Macdonald, however, who was still at Coire, sent word to hasten the march, for the provisions were giving out, and it was necessary to get on as quickly as possible to avoid famine and stoppage.

But on December 1st, a fine frost having set in, General Dumas, the head of the army staff, took advantage of it, overcoming the opposition of the mountaineers and the mountain itself. The account of his arrangements is remarkable; under his orders the best guides with four of the strongest oxen of the country walked abreast, breaking a way through the snow, which forty labourers, who followed, cleared away. After them a company of sappers continued the work which was finally accomplished by two hundred foot soldiers marching in solid ranks of six abreast. Then came the cavalry, then the artillery, and lastly the baggage animals with their escort.

Silence had been enjoined, and was observed as strictly as at manœuvres. Thus they advanced through this deep cutting, but the progress was so slow that it was nearly night before they reached the hospital. Several men were frozen; some soldiers and horses went beyond the track and were buried in the snows which hid the precipice. A sea of snow a quarter of a league in depth had then to be crossed, on which the least wind might raise waves capable of burying the whole column. After this there was another danger to brave in the descent of the Cardinel, a road winding on itself and precipitating itself by a spiral and almost perpendicular zigzag into an abyss 600 feet deep; then came the little plain of Isola, and Campo Dolcino, when night fell and arrested further progress.

During the descent several men turned giddy and several mules lost their footing; they rolled mutilated from rock to rock, their cries being audible for a few moments, and then they disappeared.

During the two following days the same weather favoured the march of the second and third columns. On December 5th it was Macdonald's turn, and the fourth and last passage, but the evil genius of these high places had regained his sway. A deluge of snow filled up the cutting that General Dumas had opened up, and the numerous landmarks that had been placed there were hidden or carried away by the storm, which the mountaineers refused to face. Macdonald, however, grew angry and obstinately resumed the march. His guides, and even his grenadiers, were several times daunted and retraced their steps, but he persisted, walking at their head, with the plummet in his hand, insisting on the great masses of snow being opened up as he passed through, and the guides and soldiers in spite of the increasing hurricane were forced to follow him.

He succeeded at last, but his column was on several occasions cut in two at various points, and separated from him by banks of snow. The 104th half-brigade which had been entirely scattered took days to reunite. Many sledges and their burdens were abandoned, indeed on this last day many soldiers were maimed by the cold: a hundred and ten men and more than a hundred mules and horses perished altogether.

On December 6th, two-thirds of the army of the Grisons had passed the flow of the German waters up to the sources of the Italian waters. They filled the Valteline.

But there still remained the passage, from glacier to glacier, of the valley of the Adda into that of the Adige. First came the ascent of Aprica, which is perhaps less elevated, but more winding, steeper and more rugged than even the Splugen. Not so many men perished there, but more horses, especially the baggage animals; hampered by their burdens they could not turn round with sufficient quickness in the sudden bends of the path, which, rising and descending almost perpendicularly, wound in steep zigzags between the rocks; many of them rolled down the precipices. Having reached the valley of Camonica the advance-guard attempted the Tonnal. But the passage was defended by 50,000 Austrians who had intrenched themselves behind the ice, and twice in spite of the most determined and intrepid assaults, our Generals Vaux and Vandamme, were obliged to give way after having reddened the glacier with blood needlessly spilt. On his side Macdonald vainly endeavoured to turn the left flank, and to arrive upon the Sarca beyond one of the forts of the Tonnal. Here it was nature alone, unaided by the enemy which opposed them; for no passage could be found practicable.

Then, reinforced by 2,000 Italians, the general-in-chief descended the Oglio as far as Visogne. The news of the passage of the Mincio by our army of Italy had rendered him most impatient. When he announced it to us, he asked his soldiers, now almost equal to mountaineers, if they would allow themselves to be passed by their comrades, who had been victorious in the plains, and, with an unerring instinct, judging our ardour by his own, he carried us straight on to the San-Tyéno. This mountain is unapproachable by artillery, and even the cavalry had to turn back by the Lake of Iseo. As for us, even after the Splugen, the glacier astonished us: it is so elevated, so steep, so full of the rudest difficulties, that even for infantry it is necessary to open a passage through enormous blocks of ice by hewing out steps with axes. We were obliged to make use of our hands as well as our feet and to hold on by the tails of our horses to reach the summit. At last, from crest to crest, from ravine to ravine, crossing without stopping night or day and at a quick march, twenty-five leagues of slush and ice, we passed the enemy, the advance posts, in short everything; and on January 8th, 1801, ascending the summit of the Michelsburg, we flung ourselves on the Adige, forcing the passage, and snatching from the Austrians the town of Trente.

Without taking breath, Macdonald, at Levico, seized on the one hand the sources of the Brenta and on the other, pushed forward towards Pietra the vanquished who were descending the Adige.

Here we witnessed the audacious and even haughty spirit of Macdonald, and his frank and proud glance, which was often tempered by satirical gaiety become transfigured by keen delight, when the south wind brought us the sound of firing which appeared to respond to the volleys of his advance-guard: this could only be the firing of Brune's army.

The enemy which we were following, however numerous it might have been, was thus surrounded in the narrow and deep valley of the Adige, between Macdonald who was descending, and the left wing of the army of Italy which was mounting it. Thus so many difficulties, so many obscure and inglorious conflicts with nature, were at last to be crowned by one of the most striking acts of this war; for, in fact, the cannonading we had heard came from General Moncey, the commandant of Brune's left wing. The enemy between two fires comprised Laudon and those very 200,000 Austrians who by the efforts of the front of Macdonald's left wing on the upper Inn and the upper Adige, and his rapid manoeuvre on the right, had been forced to abandon the Tyrol. They hastened to take refuge near their army of Italy, and found themselves surrounded and attacked in front and at the rear at the very moment they had hoped to reach it.

But Moncey, who was a kind-hearted man, was also of too anxious a nature. His responsibilities excited him too much. This disposition of mind had no doubt been aggravated under the odious government of the Terror which insisted on its generals being victorious, under penalty of losing their heads. Laudon took advantage of it; feeling himself caught as it were in a trap, he had recourse to stratagem. He announced to Moncey the false news of an armistice. Moncey hesitated; on the one hand, the position of the enemy, retrenched within the Pietra seemed formidable to him, on the other hand, the same south wind which had borne to us the sound of his firing had unfortunately prevented him from hearing ours; so that not knowing we were immediately behind Laudon, he was unaware of the full extent of this general's difficulty, and did not sufficiently distrust him. Moved at the thought of the bloodshed which would ensue, and having obtained all that he had desired, the conquest of Pietra and cession of Trente, the unfortunate general hesitated no longer, but signed the suspension of arms which was demanded, and the too-lucky Laudon, at the very time when he would have been forced to lay down his arms, profited by this respite, escaping from the valley of the Adige into that of the Brenta, through an almost impracticable defile.

The Pietra being thus abandoned and the enemy dispersed, the astonished advance-guard of the army of Italy found itself face to face with ours. Moncey, at one and the same moment, perceiving Macdonald, and recognising that he had been the victim of a stratagem of war, that his credulity had caused him to lose one of the most important results of the campaign, and that he would become the laughing-stock of three armies, was confused and humiliated and utterly crushed by his mistake. The same disposition of mind which had led him into the error almost caused him to kill himself in despair. This mystification had entailed on Macdonald the loss of the entire fruits of his adroit and difficult man yet he forgot it all to console him. As for Brune, who still openly proclaimed himself a Terrorist, he was less generous: in his anger he replaced Moncey by Davout in the command of the left wing, but Davout nobly refused to take advantage of his misfortune; under the necessity of obeying, although he came to Pietra it was only to place himself under the orders of his unfortunate former comrade.

VI

I RALLY TO THE REVOLUTION

MACDONALD, EITHER THROUGH FORESIGHT, OR on account of his haughty and somewhat suspicious character, accused Brune not only of not having seconded his difficult march with sufficient promptitude, but of having purposely defeated its aim by stealing a march upon him in Trente with his left wing. He was, above all, indignant at having been treated merely as one of his lieutenants when he involved him in his armistice. His displeasure even extended to the First Consul. Why had he deceived him as well as the enemy by only giving him 14,000 men, when he had promised him 30,000? Why had he assigned him the least brilliant and the most trying share in these dangers and struggles with the natural difficulties of the under taking? Why had he, in a manner, placed him under the orders of Brune? What a humiliation it would have been had he not forestalled in Trente by a few hours, the general's left wing! His inadequate and harassed army would have overcome nothing but the glaciers, and issuing forth devoid of glory, would have been forced to receive from the hands of Brune as a reward of so many hardships this rich cantonment won by a last march of almost fabulous rapidity.

With such dispositions on the part of our chief, one can imagine the quarrelsome and hostile spirit which animated our headquarters.

A few days only had sufficed to restore our young troops, when the armistice, a threatening symptom of peace, aroused our impatience, which found vent in a thousand remarks, the imprudence of which at such a time was not sufficiently taken into consideration.

'What could we do with a peace which would only profit the Director? Each army would then only have fought for itself! By what right should his guides, his guards, his armies of Egypt and Marengo with their renown in direct rivalry to ours, blazon it forth on their banners above every other? Would it be permitted that the conquerors of Naples, of Zurich, and of Hohenlinden, that Macdonald, Masséna, and Moreau himself, all our generals-in-chief in short, should become the subjects and the footstool of Bonaparte?'

These sentiments, not openly avowed by all, were fermenting in all hearts, inflamed by the most jealous of passions, the love of glory, and envious equality; and the pride of our generals with whom we all united in a feeling of indignation at enforced submission to another general-in-chief, formerly their companion in arms and their equal.

Such passions menaced the rising power of the First Consul, and were eagerly fed by every breath borne to us from the capital by private letters and a pernicious press, rousing into being a still more violent passion, which, in addition to the others, especially in the army, excited universal discontent. There, above all, the war of the Revolution had been a war of caste and classes. This plebeian army had there attained glory and position in opposition to the French aristocracy and all the foreign aristocracies, whose patrimony these positions had been from all time. Generals, officers, nearly all dated from 1792. The remembrance of their humiliations under the Monarchy was still alive. Whatever pride and strength they might feel in their illustrious acquisitions, these were yet of recent date, and they had been contested and endangered within a year by the triumphs of the Coalition. They knew that in the eyes of the nobility of the whole of Europe, they were considered only as an army of *parvenus*, possessing no other right than that of victory.

This was where the sting lay. In these days when time has confirmed results, when the fusion has taken place, and the decreasing struggle has altered its nature by being transformed from that of the poor against the rich, or rather that of those who possess nothing against those who possess something, there still remains enough of that jealous distrust to enable one to realize how keen it then was.

Into the midst of this burning focus of self-love and self-interest, pride and honour, the news came from Paris of the proposals of the Pretender, the return of the *émigrés,* and their reception at the hands of Madame Bonaparte. There was a general outcry. The feeling of irritation became so strong at headquarters that, for having made an appeal to the national generosity in favour of the most inoffensive of these exiles, I was warned in conversation that I was becoming a suspect, and that my presence in the ranks, of my comrades would be intolerable.

Such was the general perturbation of mind, the germ of which was already perceptible when we learnt the outrage of the 3rd Nivôse followed by the transportation of the Terrorists. This criminal attempt had not met with the indignation which it deserved; it had even been made to appear ridiculous, party spirit being so excited. The independent and jealous pride of the chiefs was aroused by this disposition of mind; it hoped something from it. We know what were the bitter fruits it produced: it was fatal to Moreau four years later; it checked the career of his best lieutenants, and for the space of eight years it arrested that of our general himself. Otherwise this was less serious at Trente than at the headquarters of the army of Germany, thanks to the merry life we led there, to the composition of the army, and also to the refined and elegant habits, the noble sentiments, and the constant cheerfulness of Macdonald's happy nature.

It was then that I understood the Revolution. For the first time I saw its strongest and deepest roots revealed to the light of day. My youthful affections had been wounded by the passions which surrounded me, they thrust me back upon myself, self-contained as I already was by nature, and rendered my position most difficult, but the situation was not altogether unprofitable. In the midst of this plebeian army so justly proud of itself, I was able to gauge the double folly of royalist and above all aristocratic pertinacity: the first under the Republican banners seeming to me a treachery; whilst, as to the second, I felt amongst so many older, more experienced, and wiser warriors than myself, that these exclusive pretensions of birth were not only dangerous, but even unjust and ridiculous. From that moment I accepted the Revolution as an accomplished fact, founded on right, demanding our adherence as a matter of good sense and equity, in the best interests of our country and even those of the old nobility itself.

Having once acquired this conviction, traced out this route, and chosen this part, I remained constant to it; I desired to serve it, by drawing with me old France, that is to say, the greatest number of nobles possible, so as to hasten the fusion, and prevent the possibility from henceforth of any return to the proscriptions of the Convention and the Directorate. This idea took strong hold of me, and from that moment it has persistently inspired my intercourse, my actions, and even my simplest words.

This was especially the case when, by way of encouraging myself in a course in which all the actors had changed parts, I used constantly to count over and recapitulate the names of colonels and generals of the old nobility who, in spite of the proscriptions, were then serving in the line regiments of the army and who should strengthen my position in it. These were Caulaincourt, d'Hautpoul, Grouchy, Pully, Rochambeau, d'Hilliers, Macdonald, etc., etc.; I only forgot one of them, the one to whom I owed my own call, and who was soon to become our most powerful protector. I mean the First Consul! But through the inconsistent impulses natural to my age, blindly yielding to the influence of the atmosphere around me, I saw in him nought but a temporary usurper, my general's enemy and that of Moreau, who was shortly to be overwhelmed by the weight of universal hatred.

For all that, this dominating idea of mine may appear somewhat deep-rooted and tenacious to have emanated from the brain of a young sub-lieutenant of twenty. But it must be borne in mind that I felt isolated and almost a suspect; I was poor, dreamy, and passionate; ultra sensitive as far as concerned both myself and others; constantly observing them and myself, judging them after my own pattern, and fancying that I was much more an object of observation than was really the case.

My mode of life at Trente was economical, prudent, and studious. My inclination to take everything seriously, my deeply impressionable nature which necessitated some management, without causing me to fall out with my comrades, yet kept me aloof from them.

One of them only the other day was reminding me that they had seen nothing in this studiously busy isolation of mine beyond a marked taste, nay, a strange and precocious passion for work, which they respected even while complaining of it; so that in the midst of a thousand pleasures and frivolities which the armistice left these excitable and lively youths—perhaps rather too fond of play—the leisure to indulge in, my only pursuit by day was study, and my only amusement by night was to play chess with a Colonel, an old Pole who was a master of the game and whose sole endeavour was to teach me enough to render me able to hold my own against him. My studies fortunately trended in the right direction, either through the influence of General Dumas and that of my father's letters, or from a feeling of shame at my own ignorance concerning the spirit, the aim, the localities and events appertaining to our campaign.

At that time we were all lodged together in the vast Gothic palace of the Bishop of Trente. I got Macdonald to entrust me with his correspondence, and his instructions to his generals, which I used to carry off to my third story, where, once again fired by my early passion for work (though now for a more positive and useful object), I seriously embarked on my double career of soldier and historian. I used to make extracts from all these documents; I steeped myself in their essence, which helped me to the understanding of the questions I would put to our chiefs, and a thorough survey and study of the plan of campaign. Having got thus far, and our departure drawing nigh, I carefully packed up my precious treasures, little thinking how soon I should have occasion to make use of my work at Copenhagen; that later on it would see the light in Paris, and be one of the very means which caused me to be selected to serve on the special private staff of Bonaparte.

So far was I then from seeking to attach to this great man, that I did not even desire to do so. His actions, nevertheless, should even then have revealed him to me as the protector and reconciler, whose powerful succouring hand might alone draw together and amalgamate the old and new elements of French society. But at my age, without a guiding light or mentor, I could not do otherwise than go astray. Where is the sub-lieutenant of twenty who reads or cares to read the daily publications? Yet at that age one rashly begins to write a literary work without any preconceived plan, in the same way that one forms an opinion, or even takes a part in the politics of the day, on hearsay, without reflecting on the consequences. This study was more difficult in the army than anywhere else. So that when, after the Peace of Lunéville, I, being the youngest, was left behind with orders to escort the guard and baggage of General Macdonald's headquarters to Lyons, across the upper part of Italy, I was in utter ignorance of the events which were even then taking place in France.

VII

I ACCOMPANY MACDONALD
ON HIS EMBASSY TO DENMARK

THE GENERALS-IN-CHIEF WHO had returned to France, at the time of the peace, had been obliged to descend from the heights of command, and could with difficulty reconcile themselves to this species of downfall: they endured impatiently the rapidly growing supremacy of one amongst them who had formerly been their comrade and their equal. They criticised and blamed everything loudly, especially the Concordat. This spirit of revolt was beginning to extend even as far as to the Consular Guard which Lannes commanded. The discontented pride of these generals was ever growing, and it increased by the support of many warriors, whose fame, proceeding almost entirely from the north, felt itself aggrieved by the more popular glory of the south, which clung to those who had conquered under Bonaparte. Thence resulted two rival camps—two armies which were almost enemies. Following on the perils of a foreign war, which had been overcome, arose the necessity of forestalling those of this jealous rivalry in our own ranks—this smouldering intestine war. With this aim in view, especially in the case of Moreau, honours were bestowed, praise lavished, and family alliances set on foot; in fact, every kindly means of conciliation was made use of; but this general's opposition has already been seen. With the others, for instance Bernadotte, St. Cyr, Brune, Augereau, and Macdonald, Napoleon employed more efficacious means. Missions of various kinds, some warlike, others both warlike and diplomatic scattered them abroad. Bernadotte was sent out in command of the armies of the west, and to St. Cyr was given the command in Spain of the French Division which had been sent out against Portugal. Lannes and Brune were dispatched, the one as ambassador to Lisbon and the other to Constantinople. As for Macdonald, whose free and sarcastic speech, whose proud and independent character, and whose friendly relations with Moreau rendered him somewhat of an obstacle, even before his return to France in the early months of 1801, he was destined for Denmark.

Denmark held the key of the Baltic. By virtue of its position as an advance post of the armed neutrality of the kings of the North which was threatened by the English fleet, and determined to defend itself, it demanded a general from us. Macdonald's mission to this distant court was therefore represented to him as being less of a diplomatic than of a military nature. He was to carry to this extremity of Europe the glory of the French arms, and his aides-de-camp, his staff, and his engineers and artillery officers were to accompany him to the spot. Macdonald only accepted this mission on the condition that he should be called back as soon as it ceased to be of a warlike nature, consequently having immediately started from Trente for Paris by way of Verona, Milan and Turin, he left me orders; as the youngest of his aides-de-camp, to bring back to France his headquarters and two companies of infantry and cavalry which were to escort it. Fortune thus favoured me, in that during my first year of service, I had seen the south-east of France, Switzerland, the South of Germany and the whole of the Alps; I was now going to see the north of Italy; I had taken part in a great battle, in the war of the plains, in that of the mountains; finally, I was only returning to Paris to leave it again, and to see, in a two-fold aspect, the east of France and the north of Europe.

On my arrival in Milan I paid a visit to General Moncey who was the commander-in-chief there, and I found his appearance was quite in harmony with his position. He had a grand bearing, was of fine stature, with a noble countenance and grave and stately manners. To this exterior aspect; however, and a noble heart was joined a mind ever over-anxious; caring too much for the praise or blame of others, he over-rated those who opposed him, so that he added to his real difficulties by having to encounter those he created for himself in his adversary.

I am still astonished when I think of the longevity of this marshal, that his anxious disposition and irritable conscience, which the least responsibility excited beyond expression, should not have worn out his life. A breath, a trifle, put him into a fever. He was in that condition at this very moment, notwithstanding the general esteem in which he was held, and the favour of the First Consul; and this was due not only to the recollection of his unfortunate armistice of Pietra, but also, in spite of the Treaty of Lunéville, to the anxieties of a command which, however, had become of quite a pacific nature. A quarter-of-an-hour's conversation thoroughly revealed to me this uncomfortable condition of mind, which never gave him an instant's peace. I was astonished at it then, and forty-one years afterwards, I cannot understand how, perpetually a prey to such wearing emotions, it was possible that he could still be in existence!

A year after my first departure, during the second fortnight in May, I returned to Paris and found myself once more with my family. The return of summer, coincident with my own, had driven my former set out of Paris. This was one difficulty the less for me; the trial, however, would in any case have been of short duration, for on arrival I received the order to be ready to start off again. I heard that Macdonald, on his return to Trente, passing by Nevers, had learnt there the assassination of Paul I, and the disaster of the Danish fleet, burnt by Nelson in the roadstead of Copenhagen, and of the forced submission which had been the consequence; that fancying his mission was then without an object, he had considered himself released from it; but that Napoleon had persevered, alleging as a pretext, the possibility of arousing from this double disaster the armed neutrality of the kings of the North; and that, in order to decide him to go to Denmark, he had held out the

flattering bait, after a short stay in this post, of the ambassadorship
of St. Petersburg. Macdonald already was at great expense, busy
with the necessary preparations for so important a destination. The
First Consul, who never neglected the slightest detail, had remembered the brilliant reputation which my father had left behind him
at the court of the great Catharine: and he insisted that I should
be diplomatically attached to this embassy. On June 1st I received
my nomination; and soon after, in the capacity of junior attaché
and aide-de-camp, I started with Macdonald. It would have been
impossible to present for the first time to the north of Europe a
more illustrious or worthy representative of the pure glory of the
arms of the Republic. This journey was a continual triumph for
Macdonald, in which we had even more than our proper share.
The multitude pressed after us on every occasion; Macdonald
showed himself generous even to prodigality, above all, towards
any needy Frenchman whom he met on his way. We saw Leipsic,
Dresden, and Pilnitz, that celebrated starting-point of the war of
the Revolution. We were presented to the Elector, a worthy prince,
though of a methodical character, so much the slave of etiquette
that it followed him, so they said, into the very interior of his
palace, even into the arms of the Electress! We used to make a joke
of it then: our native revolutionary thoughtlessness and want of
method made merry over the superabundance of it possessed by
this people; to-day, some of us may think it would have been better
had we been more like them. We may even regret that we did not
possess those wise, regular, and orderly habits which the difference
in our national characters does not allow of our imitating.

We were detained some days in Berlin. I there received from the
princes and princesses of this court, and still more explicitly from
many of their followers, much testimony to the deep esteem in
which they held my father, his history of the late King of Prussia
(truthful though it was), and the expression of their regrets that
this prince had followed opposite counsels to those which my
father had tendered him during his last diplomatic mission. It may
be remembered that this mission had preceded the war of 1792,
which it had not been able to prevent.

Concerning the non-success of their first campaign one of the former aides-de-camp of this deceased monarch endeavoured to make excuses for it in this wise: according to him, the orders given to the Duke of Brunswick had not been carried out. Frederick William II had not intended at Valmy to stop short at a mere cannonading. His idea had been to attack and engage the enemy. But the Duke of Brunswick, remembering only too well that the king had been his pupil, had paid no heed to his instructions. This officer also owned to me that, misled by our émigrés, they had only expected a mere military march, in the course of which the various inhabitants, and our army itself, should have hastened to rally round the Prussian flag. He thus accounted for the fatal proclamation of the Duke, the disappointment of this general, and the discouragement which had resulted from it.

Our sojourn in Denmark, lasted for six whole months. But Macdonald in each dispatch renewed the demand for his recall, in the last clamouring for it so imperiously that it was obliged to be conceded.

This sojourn, however, worked for my good; it even exercised over my future a fortunate, unexpected, and decided influence. If I allude to this with complacence I beg to be excused. These details overbalance the futile reputation which I had gained by the songs which I used to scribble heedlessly on the margin of the archives of our legation, and which did not bear favourable testimony to any serious pursuit of study. At the age of twenty, little excuse is perhaps needed for some frivolous amusement in the midst of real work; but my own self love, and the necessity of leaving a good example behind, induce me to say that it would have been wrong to judge by appearances only; that in reality I employed my time satisfactorily, and if the result had been more fortunate than I had any reason to expect, at any rate I deserved it to a certain extent. In the daytime, with Macdonald and elsewhere, at table or in society, I used to seek the society of the most famous people, listening to them, and asking them as many questions as my youth warranted, thus trying to collect as many notions as possible on the country, the things and

the men amongst whom I found myself; then at night, before
setting to work on my summary, I would joyfully enrich my
note-book with the booty which I had been acquiring. I did
even more; having once begun my hoard, I became greedy; using
every effort to add to it. I even dared to carry my ignorance to
the most distinguished savants. The professors, amongst them
a Frenchman and the celebrated Nybourg himself, treated me
with indulgence. This *savant* who was pallid, ill, and enfeebled
by hard work, had already nearly lost his sight; the least light
dazzled him. It was, therefore, when night put a stop to his work
that I used to seek him out to converse with him. I would enter,
groping my way to his inner den, where I could hardly see him
by the feeble light of a solitary candle, in the midst of folios and
dusty MSS. which surrounded him, and with which his room
was crowded. Our conversations would sometimes distract his
attention from them, and this intercourse was good for both of
us; I acquired scientific instruction from it, while he gained rest:
which was what each of us needed.

Up to this time the news of our successes and reverses had
exercised a remarkable influence on this cold and distant people.
The Danish Government had thought it best to give way to it.
Should we succeed, the astute Bernstorf would slightly loosen the
reins on the neck of the people; should the Coalition get the upper
hand, he would gently tighten the curb.

Nevertheless, the taste for our Revolution in this country had
been so keen, and had so blinded their discernment, that during
the Terror, Robespierre, not only in the eyes of the Danish bour-
geoisie, but even amongst the aristocrats and the Duchess of
Augustenburg herself, had passed for a great man! His discourses
had been read with enthusiasm: his victims had been condemned
as justly-punished traitors, his downfall had been lamented!
However gross may have been this error it was a long time before
the people saw more clearly.

In looking over my notes, I find in addition to these observations—several of which are now out of date—some more trivial
anecdotes on the mental state of the reigning king, who, however,

reigned as little over his kingdom as over himself; his senses were not quite adrift, but he had unshipped the rudder which had guided them. His nonsense was sometimes rather funny. It was told of him that one day leaning up against a chair in the family circle, after having contemplated them all in silence, he suddenly exclaimed: 'It must really be confessed that we form a charming party. My daughter is bandy-legged; my son is exactly like an albino; my brother is a hunchback; my sister squints; and I am a madman!' Then extending his observations to the then reigning sovereigns: 'For the matter of that,' he continued, 'my more distant family connections are not much better; my cousin George of England is the most demented man in his kingdom; my brother Paul of Russia has a touch of it, I think; my colleague of Naples is not much better; my little cousin of Sweden promises to be as bad; and to return to myself, I am about the maddest of the lot;' then, noticing that one of his courtiers was clasping his hands and lifting his eyes to Heaven: ' Well, what do you expect from that? You will not deceive the One above and may as well leave Him alone,' he added.

There had been some scandal about the wife of his brother (who was, as we have seen, a puny and misshapen prince) and a courtier of herculean stature. The latter one evening felt a smart tap on his shoulder, upon which he turned round. 'I beg your pardon,' cried the king, bursting out laughing; 'but I really took you for my own brother!'

Other scandal-mongers accused the Prince Royal of sacrificing too much to his military position, but of only bringing to bear on this expensive mania the restricted views of a corporal. It is true that in the frequent reviews which we witnessed we had often seen the prince, who was otherwise very good-natured, get into a rage with his grenadiers, abuse and even beat them, then himself taking a place in the ranks, mark step with his cane over his shoulder, and make himself a perfect laughing-stock. One day when he was submitting to his father's approbation and explaining to him the economy of a plan of financial reform, the king, without answering, got up and began gravely to march up and down with his cane

over his shoulder, saying: 'Right, left! right, left!' then, stopping
in front of his son: 'That's the kind of thing that is too expensive,
sir!' he retorted; however, as the prince insisted, the king gave
way; but recognising that his son was as mad as himself, he signed
'Christian and Company.'

On October 11th, Colonel Duroc, an aide-de-camp of
Bonaparte, arrived. His mission was to Berlin and St. Petersburg
principally, then Stockholm and Copenhagen. My wish to add
to the contents of my note-book led me to seek him out without
any ulterior idea. The young men of those days accustomed to risk
everything for glory, and living in the midst of new and rapidly-
rising reputations and constant illustrious self-sacrifices, either
Royalist or Republican, were not self-interested. I was like them
in this respect, and even more so owing to the family conditions
in which I had been brought up, and had no ambition beyond
that of being highly considered. On this occasion I thought of
nothing but winning the esteem of this individual. His reserved
and scrutinizing attitude gave me little encouragement at first;
besides I looked, and was, so young then that he did not notice
me much amongst so many older people; but it happened fortunately on the second day of his arrival, that amidst a small circle
to whom Duroc had addressed some questions upon the Danish
fleet and army, I alone was able to answer them. Thereupon, either
from curiosity or surprise, he continued by taking me aside and
entering into conversation; when, as may well be believed, I was
not backward in exhibiting my new acquirements. The result was
that Duroc sought me out in his turn; and that, flattered by his
notice, I offered him a note of all the information I had collected
which would be likely to render his mission more effectual, and
which he accepted.

On the day of his departure, October 15th, I guessed by the
manner in which he wished me good-bye, and by the friendliness
of the officer who accompanied him, and who pressed me to join
him very soon in Paris and enter the Guides regiment in which
he was a captain, that I had acquired the esteem and friendship of
the illustrious traveller. I, however, soon forgot this, seeing in the

incident nothing beyond the desire of rendering himself generally agreeable; but I had made more way than I thought, and this interview was fated to exercise the most powerful influence on my destiny. Duroc had carried away a pleasing and even affectionate remembrance of our meeting, a feeling which he lost no time in imparting to the First Consul and which was not to be subsequently effaced. Such is the importance of creating a favourable first impression; a success which a studious youth easily acquires on account of the surprise which is inspired by the contrast of a steady desire for work at an age when pleasure is more attractive, and to the indulgence which is naturally extended to youth.

Not having anticipated any special results, I returned on his departure to my habitual life of quiet observation, without knowing that it had already borne all possible fruit.

My thoughts too, were soon to be entirely centred in the news of a sad and unexpected loss: this was the death of the Maréchal de Ségur, my grandfather, who was taken from us on October 8th, 1801, by a fit of the gout. Macdonald, however, more and more disgusted with his new career, could see no object in his mission but his own removal from the capital; and in truth it had no other. Thus on September 5th, 1801, irritated by the evasions by which Talleyrand responded to his demands for a recall, he wrote him a rude and threatening letter, which needlessly occasioned a complete breach; for the minister, in a dispatch dated the previous night (December 4th) had at last sent him his letters of recall. These he received on December 19th and at once acted on them; leaving Copenhagen on the 23rd he brought us back in the first month of 1802 to Paris, where Duroc had only preceded us by some weeks.

VIII

I AM ENTRUSTED WITH A
MISSION TO THE KING OF SPAIN

I N THE MIDST OF THE first feeling of melancholy pleasure with
which I revisited my people for the second time after our cruel
loss, my six months' absence, and my trying voyage at such a bad
time of year, I perceived that my father, Macdonald, and the First
Consul had determined no longer to look upon me as a soldier. I
saw that my letters, my observations of the country which I had
just left, and, above all, the kind report of Duroc, my rank of
junior attaché, and my father's own renown as a diplomatist, had
caused me to be considered for the future as marked out for that
career. It was opposed to my own inclinations and the general
feeling of the day, to the impressions which I had received from
the example of Macdonald, and the attraction which the career of
arms had always had for me from my childhood.

Having, therefore, made my choice between my two
commissions of junior attaché and sub-lieutenant, when
Macdonald joined us for the purpose of paying our homage
to the First Consul, I begged him to introduce me only in my
position of aide-de-camp to Bonaparte. But he took no notice
of it; and when my turn came I was introduced as a junior
attaché.

This took place in the chamber now known as the Throne-room in the Tuileries. Bonaparte stopped short on hearing my name coupled with the designation of junior attaché and looked at me fixedly and his countenance which was grave that day assumed a benevolent aspect as he answered: 'Yes, I know that he shows much promise.' But although I saw this great man for the first time at close quarters, I was not so dazzled as I might have been, on account of the hostile sentiments held at headquarters, and having made up my mind not to tie myself in any way, I ventured to contradict him and answered, 'Citizen Consul, if I show any promise, it is not for diplomacy, but for the military career.' This boldness surprised and displeased him: being then all for peace and negotiations, it ran counter to his views for me; he resumed his severe aspect and in a blunt and abrupt manner rudely turning his back upon me, answered: 'Very well! you will have to wait for war.'

As may be imagined, I came away from this audience with a very poor opinion of the kind feeling of the First Consul. But that was not all; we were descending the grand double staircase which the Swiss Guards defended on August 10th, now no longer in existence, when Macdonald, who never missed an occasion for a joke, stopped short and turned round to compliment me on 'my successful début with General Bonaparte, and the speedy promotion which such a favourable reception should lead me to expect.' I replied that he was the cause of it, having against my wish introduced me as a junior attaché; but that I consoled myself for this misfortune because it kept me attached to his person. 'Not at all,' he answered, 'I cannot keep you; the regulations only allow me three aides-de-camp, and you make the fourth.' Then becoming serious, as he saw me overwhelmed by this unexpected blow, he added: 'Never mind; till something better turns up I will attach you to Beurnonville.' He was his friend, and I made no objection, but I felt annoyed because I saw in this an underhanded means of binding me to a diplomatic career which Beurnonville himself then preferred to that of arms. In this false position I employed my leisure in the studies necessary to my position, and in correcting my précis of the campaign of the Grisons which I had been urged to publish. On the other hand, finding myself once more amidst my old set, I tried to cultivate it at the same time as the new; but there had never been any real fusion; they were still two inimical camps and more antagonistic than ever.

In spite of the advances of Madame Bonaparte, the generous and conciliatory policy of the First Consul, and our own example, the old aristocracy, still rooted in the past and entrenched in hatred and disdain, only lived on its recollections, and fed itself with vain hopes. Everything was an obstacle, both in form and idea, everything jarred between the world that the Revolution had created and the society of the *ancien régime.*

The latter was accustomed to look upon as paramount all the little refinements of good society, the exquisite politeness of conventional forms and ceremonies, and the urbanity, grace, and indefinable charm, whose distinctive and minute shades characterized the social code of the women of a former day. To these refined manners of the old society, the unformed and boorish ways of the men of the new were alien and intolerable; that alone, without the overturning of rank, power, and fortunes would have rendered any amalgamation impracticable. One should not therefore be astonished that this former society chose to include the First Consul, and the remarkable men with whom he was surrounded, in its general aversion for the revolutionaries whom he had brought to their bearings. The army itself was included. Its immortal deeds were in their eyes but ephemeral accidents or mere triumphs of brute force; a kind of barbaric, false, and illegitimate glory, and the honours acquired by this glory, a usurpation of ancient and imprescriptible rights. These were the very natural sentiments held by the remainder of this cruelly decimated party, which, with no following, was still animated by this spirit of caste, the most persistent of all forms of party spirit on account of its close ties of society and family, its hereditary habits of domination and punctilious code of honour, its pride, and its exclusive pretensions which had become a second nature made up of all those passions which act the most powerfully on the heart of man.

This is not a criticism of the aristocracy; rather would it be its eulogy, provided it were not exclusive and as much as possible kept pace with the times. In fact what other body so old, so cruelly vanquished and dispersed, would have been able to remain as faithful and constant to its traditions, and present so inflexible a resistance to such great misfortunes!

As for me, with the strong conviction that this resistance was as unjust as it was out of place, having broken from them and seeking a standpoint elsewhere I made a very bad choice: whether in my indignation at their rebuffs and at the reception of the First Consul, or from a spirit of military camaraderie, intensified by the republican hostility against Bonaparte of Macdonald and Moreau, under whom I had first seen service, I became almost a revolutionary. Neither the advice of my father, his nomination to the Legislative Assembly on January 31st, 1802, the lieutenant's commission which I received on April 5th, nothing of this could at first win me over again.

Paris was then full of various army staffs, impatient of their inactivity and irritated by what they called the dictation and the usurpation of the First Consul. They dubbed as anti-revolutionary the measures in favour of the *émigrés* and the re-establishment of Catholic worship. I listened to their outcry without sufficiently disapproving its bad tendency; on April 8th, in Notre Dame I witnessed their indignation at the *Te Deum* being sung for the Concordat which had been signed eight months before. I did not sufficiently protest on that occasion against the reply of Delmas to Bonaparte: 'Yes, a fine monkey indeed! It is a pity that it was short of a million of men who got killed to destroy just what you are endeavouring to bring back again!'

The brutal impertinences which several of the other generals permitted themselves to utter in the Tuileries and even within ear-shot of Bonaparte, displeased me to a certain extent, but did not sufficiently excite my disgust; I must admit also that in the cathedral my attitude was not the least irreverent of any; I even remember, on the return of the procession which passed by the Palais Royal near a group of officers amongst whom I was standing, the contemptuous airs with which we acknowledged the many salutations of the First Consul, and which certainly were not calculated to please him.

In my position, and with the aim I had in view, all this was absurd. A coarse remark of Moreau had the effect of first opening my eyes to the false step which I had taken. Calling on him one morning in the Rue d'Anjou-St.-Honoré, when Grenier, Lecourbe, and he were conversing upon the French army in the time of Louis XV, I was listening to his remarks, ordinary as they were, (for his speech, like his manner, was very common,) as if they were oracles, when either forgetting or choosing to ignore my descent, he spoke in filthy and contemptuous terms of all the generals of the ancient régime without any exception. This insulting slight caused me to colour up. I was even then wearing mourning for my courageous grandfather, and retired immediately, all the more indignant because it was impossible for me to make any reply to this abusive brutality.

I never saw this general again until curiosity led me to one of the cross-examinations which he was undergoing at the Temple, but though still very indignant with him, I had sufficient consideration for his disgrace not to let him perceive me.

There was nothing of that kind to fear from Beurnonville or Macdonald, still on my return home I could not help comparing this hostile scurrility with the grandeur of soul of Napoleon, who had taken advantage of the fête of July 14, 1801, to collect the scattered remains of Turenne and celebrate their reception in the Invalides. His efforts to rehabilitate and to rally around him all the proscribed persons who had fallen victims to the revolutionary government were brought under my notice; but even more to the point, I was reminded that during my sojourn in Denmark, having learnt that my grandfather, from whom he had received his first commission, was living in great poverty, he alleviated the hardships of his last days by a pension, and when the old warrior went to the Tuileries to thank the First Consul, he was splendidly received, Bonaparte actually going to meet him. During their short interview he treated him with the utmost deference,

going as far as the head of the staircase with him, and insisting
that the guard should present arms and the drums beat, so that
the full military honours might be given to him which were due
to the then abolished rank of marshal! So great a contrast of petty
meanness and ill-will with the generous consideration and marks
of esteem shown to my grandfather and to our aristocratic renown,
profoundly touched my wounded soul. My eyes were opened. I
recognised in Bonaparte the true support I had been seeking, which
seemed to present itself for the succour and possible rehabilitation
of the remnant of the society of former days. Nevertheless, tired
of my uselessness and feeling myself in disgrace with Napoleon
for my anti-diplomatic prejudices, I had just demanded active
work in my new rank in the regiment of dragoons commanded
by Caulaincourt, when I learnt that the First Consul was furious
against him on account of a plot which had been set on foot in this
very regiment in relation to the Concordat. It was a false report,
but had been received as a true one, in consequence of which, a
squadron of this corps composed of the malcontents was on the
point of being sent to San Domingo.

At that juncture I received a note from Duroc dated the 4th
Prairial of the year X (May 24th, 1802). He begged me to go to
Malmaison at midday as the First Consul was anxious to see me. I
was to be introduced by the aide-de-camp on duty, as Duroc was
sorry that he was obliged to be absent and therefore could not
undertake to present me himself.

Certainly there was nothing in such a communication to alarm
me, but young and vivid imaginations are subject to see things
in a certain light and are not always remarkable for good sense. I
fancied, insignificant as I was, that the coincidence of my request to
enter the 19th regiment with the breaking out of the spirit of sedi-
tion in that regiment had drawn upon me the anger of Bonaparte. I
therefore arrived at Malmaison with the conviction that I should be
severely reprimanded to begin with, and then threatened or ordered
to take my departure for San Domingo. My surprise may be imagined when on the contrary, after a truly paternal reception, I could
perceive nought but the most fascinating benevolence imprinted

on the features of this great conqueror which had appeared to me so formidable at the Tuileries; and when I heard his voice, which had seemed. so rough, say in an accent as sweet as a caress, 'that he was going to give me a mission in Spain in consequence of the satisfactory reports that he had received of me, that I should have ostensibly to deliver a letter to the king from him and one to the Prince de la Paix which should be done in secret, without General St. Cyr, our ambassador, knowing anything about it, these two individuals not being on friendly terms; but for the rest, Citizen Talleyrand would give me all necessary instructions.' Then walking up and down with me once or twice the length of the long study which looked upon the garden and the court-yard of the castle, and ran the entire width of the building, he added several kindly words as to the confidence he reposed in me, and sent me away with the same air of amiability with which he had received me.

On my arrival at Malmaison I was like a hedge-hog, only thinking of defending myself; when I left I was astonished, charmed, and enthusiastic. The next day I was still more astonished when M. de Talleyrand, in giving me my instructions, my dispatches, and my passport presented me with 10,000 francs. I had never possessed more than my month's pay, which had always been anticipated, in spite of the economy which my position imposed upon me.

It was a far cry from Madrid to Copenhagen where I had been formerly. My sojourn in the one capital, however, was the road by which I reached the other. However great the distance and contrast of climate, it seemed to me less than the difference of character and habits in these two peoples. My journey too was full of incidents and accidents which I had no right to attribute to chance alone. We all knew very well that the esteem of the First Consul could only be won on two conditions; success and promptitude. I therefore spared neither money nor health to accomplish my task quickly and well, but at my age and with my character the one was easier than the other. So that if I could not reproach myself on the score of speed, we shall see that as far as concerned the result of my mission, its success was due entirely to chance.

I found Madrid almost deserted; the Court was at Aranjuez on the Tagus. I at once betook myself there to call on General St. Cyr, our ambassador. This general's appearance was in harmony with his already famous military renown: tall, and manly, with a serious and noble countenance, and manners of a calm and imposing simplicity. He received me with cold dignity and presented me the next day to the King and the Queen. Their reception of me was gracious and even flattering on the part of the Queen; and on that of the King, although somewhat measured and studied as well as incisive, just what I should have expected from the good nature of a sportsman King who was, however, a chaste, pious, honest, and benevolent prince, though without any education, and entirely governed by his wife and by Godoï his favourite, an individual who was so obnoxious to the whole of Spain that, from that moment, he and the Queen sought refuge from his hatred in the powerful friendship of the First Consul.

Godoï was not present at this audience, perhaps because St. Cyr was. I had not been informed that this general, of austere virtue, of inflexible principle, and most exemplary disinterestedness, except where military glory was concerned, detested the favourite. For the matter of that, my secret instructions might have told me as much; and Napoleon, who was more politic than his ambassador, was not, like him, above making use of this inevitable intermediary to attach Spain to the destinies of France.

As for me, in haste to deliver Napoleon's mysterious letter to this 'Prince of Peace,'[2] on the very next day I issued forth early from my lodgings, the first which, since my arrival in Spain, I had not found utterly intolerable. But by an unheard-of thoughtlessness, while wishing to accomplish discreetly this secret part of my mission, I chose the very hour, the very place, and garb which could not fail to attract attention to my proceedings. It would have been but a necessary precaution to go at night, wearing a dress coat, at the time when I might find the prince alone; instead of which it was in broad day, in my uniform, and at a public audience that I presented myself at this favourite's residence.

It was only when I found myself in a long gallery, in the midst of a crowd of applicants, that I became conscious of my oversight, but there was no time to repair it. The prince was absent. During a mortal half-hour of suspense I remained there as if caught in a trap, cursing my folly, and trying to slink unnoticed through the crowd; not daring to look anybody in the face and fearing that amongst these strangers some Frenchman might accost me, imagining that all eyes were fixed on the sorry figure which I cut, and on my unlucky uniform. However, what I had so ill begun I finished better, that is to say more fortunately than I deserved. Growing bolder, I slipped through the crowd to the door by which the prince must enter, and seeing a *valet de chambre* there, I decided on announcing who I was in a whisper to him, with the result that as soon as Godoï arrived, I was ushered alone into his presence. I remember that the room in which he received me was bare of furniture, but filled with a remarkable display of boots and shoes of all kinds.

He was a man with a round, good-looking but insignificant face, tall and vigorous in stature for this country, but already tending to fatness. I found very little dignity in his manner, he gave me the kind of reception that one grants to the emissary of a patron. In his lavish civilities, he invited me to dine with him that very day, but being now very much alive to my imprudence, which was causing me inward qualms, I pointed out to him that such an invitation must reveal our interview, and that to keep the secret it would be much better that I should appear to be a perfect stranger to him. Understanding this necessity, he accepted my excuses. As there was no other issue from the room than the one by which I had entered, I was obliged to appear for the second time in the long audience chamber whence I made my escape by quickly losing myself in the crowd and edging towards the door; then taking a roundabout way to get home. I hastened to divest myself of the tell-tale uniform and helmet which I had so imprudently elected to wear.

From that moment and during the whole week that I was waiting at Aranjuez for the answer to my dispatches, anxious and aghast, I do not believe that Machiavelli himself would have thought of so many subterfuges and insidious ways and words by which I endeavoured to find out if our ambassador had any suspicion of my ill-planned visit; with this end in view I used to ask him, or ask others in his presence, a thousand questions about the appearance of this prince as if I had never seen him; I feigned only to know him through the general's eyes, and to share all the aversion with which the favourite inspired him. In this constant state of anxiety, fearing any moment to find that the ambassador had learnt my unlucky interview, I used to come back again to make sure almost as soon as I had left him. This was very nearly the means by which it was found out. One day, while out walking together we met this object of my constant fear riding in his carriage: the enmity between the favourite and the general had then reached such a pitch that they were no longer even on bowing terms, when behold the prince, with his head out of the window, flourishing his hand to me in the most friendly manner! At this, St. Cyr, utterly astonished, eagerly wanted to know what it meant, and I, feigning even greater surprise than himself, pretended and affirmed that the salutation which I took care not to acknowledge, could not possibly be meant for me, inwardly cursing the prince the whole time. After all these hypocritical efforts on my part, my consternation can easily be imagined when St. Cyr the next day receiving me with much composure of manner, began to question me concerning a part of my instructions, which he said, I had kept secret from him.

At these words, fancying that my duplicity had been unmasked and my mission defeated, I felt as if my blood was turning to water. But I managed to contain myself in spite of my extreme anxiety, affecting the most ingenuous astonishment, and begging him to explain himself, as if it were a matter of impossibility to know what he meant. It was lucky I did so, for in reality neither of us had understood the other. I perceived this as soon as he owned that he had suspected me of an understanding with Lucien Bonaparte, and of having been entrusted with secret communications for the secretary of this brother of the First Consul of whose presence at Aranjuez I was completely ignorant. Relieved of an immense burden; and delighted to find the ambassador so far from the right track, I felt so strong in being able to tell the truth, and denied this erroneous imputation with such convincing eagerness that St. Cyr restored me to his full confidence.

It was thus that I atoned for the thoughtless act which I had committed, but my success cost me something, nevertheless. I had been so preoccupied by it, that giving way too much to the discontented ambassador, so as to deceive him the better, I was led to neglect proper forms and ceremonies as he did: consequently he sent me off, not only without taking leave of the Prince but of the King himself, so that I did not receive the valuable present which, according to custom, he would have bestowed upon me. I gave this up without regret; but what was much worse was to have lost such an opportunity of studying this Court, of putting myself into communication with the favourite, of investing my journey with more importance, and of leaving behind me at Aranjuez a better impression of my tact. One of my instructions had thus cost me more than it need have done, but eager minds possess the great drawback that having once thrown themselves into an undertaking they are only able to see one side of it.

But I had unconsciously given myself a great deal too much trouble. My usual good-luck did not need all these out-of-the-way precautions from which my conscience and my self-love still suffer. We are told that there is a Providence for drunkards, the same, I think, holds good as regards youth, which is an intoxication of another kind; my good-luck had served me to the extent that in this great audience of the 'Prince of Peace' I had not been noticed by any agents of our embassy; because the uniform which I had chosen so inopportunely to wear was fortunately a dragoon uniform exactly resembling that of the same branch of the service in the Spanish army; so that with my oval face, and my dark hair and complexion, I had probably been taken for a Spanish officer.

On my return, which was even more rapid than my journey out, I noticed among other things the sensation that the name of Bonaparte produced in this foreign country, the mere sound of it causing all obstacles to vanish, and all gates to fly open, even those of the Spanish custom-house!

In its substance, and its results, my mission had been prosperous, and satisfactory to the First Consul. He asked me very few questions, which was again fortunate, for I had not made sufficient preparation by brief but well digested notes to be able to give my replies desirable weight. This should never be neglected in such cases, as a matter of conscience, for the greater good of the mission in the first place, and one's own subsequently.

However this may be, on the second occasion when I saw Napoleon, at one of those public audiences in the Tuileries which used to follow his frequent reviews: 'You have accomplished your mission well and quickly,' he said kindly; 'take a holiday and don't worry yourself; you shall yet make the tour of Europe!'

I had not long to wait, it is true, for a new mark of his goodwill. But during that short time I was very near forfeiting it by the publication of my Précis of the campaign of the Grisons, my Copenhagen work. This précis, exact in detail, but defective as to style, was a glowing eulogy of Macdonald, in which Brune was not spared. As a matter of policy, I should not have done this, but it would have been ingratitude on my part had I allowed such a feeling to sway me, out of consideration for my new protector and at the expense of the first, so the book appeared. It came to my ears that it had been spoken of ill-naturedly to the First Consul, who exclaimed with some temper in presence of Rœderer: 'What are these young enthusiasts troubling their heads about? the only effect is to revive the quarrels between the generals !' Fortunately Rœderer, who was a friend of my father's, took my part; so highly praising both work and author that he restored me, as we shall see, to a higher place than I deserved in the esteem of Bonaparte.

IX

I AM NOMINATED ORDERLY OFFICER TO THE FIRST CONSUL

AFTER HAVING REFUSED WITH SCORN the offer of the château of St. Cloud as a public gift, to be his own private property, Napoleon spent six millions of francs in restoring it as the property of the nation, and had just taken up his abode there; but we still found it difficult to accustom ourselves to these successive appropriations of royal residences. The sonorous word Republic, under the dictatorship of the man of genius pleased our imaginations, and it was besides an accomplished fact, cemented by victory, peace, and public prosperity; but a usurping king was extremely distasteful to us. Amongst the greater number this arose from pride and a spirit of independence, but as far as concerned myself, these feelings were complicated by remembrances which these signs or preliminaries of usurpation too directly wounded. I had sacrificed them to enrol myself with the nation, and it was repugnant to me to appear to abandon the cause of the whole to take the part of one.

This was the state of things when, three months after my return from Spain, I received a short note from Duroc on October 7th, 1802, ordering me to go the next day to the château of St. Cloud at noon precisely. I do not remember how I learnt that this was with a view of attaching me to the special staff of the First Consul, but I remember very well that my first impulse was to hesitate to obey; but in spite of this swagger, which was a combination of royalist and republican feeling, the fact remains, that with my father's support I found myself the next day at the hour named in the gallery of Mars at St. Cloud, where Duroc presented me to Bonaparte. The much too flattering words which that great man let fall on this occasion, while overwhelming me with astonishment, had the effect of attaching me once for all to his person. 'Citizen Ségur,' he said, in a loud voice, before a crowd of senators, tribunes, legislators and generals, 'I have placed you on my private staff; your duty will be to command my body guard. You see the confidence which I place in you, you will respond to it; your merit and your talents will ensure you rapid promotion!'

As much delighted as surprised by such a flattering reception, in my agitation I could only answer by a few words of gratitude and devotion, which Napoleon received with one of his indescribably gracious smiles; continuing his way through the crowded assemblage of personages of more or less note, he went on to the gallery of the chapel in which he heard mass. Intoxicated with joy and gratified pride beyond the bounds of expectation, and feeling as if I trod on air, I walked up and down these brilliant chambers as if taking possession of them, turning back and again stopping on the spot which even at this lapse of time I can still see before me, the spot where I had just listened to such expressions of esteem and regard, meditating upon them, and repeating them over a hundred times. It seemed to me as if they associated me, as if they identified me, with the renown of the Conqueror of Italy, of Egypt, and of France! I do not know what that autumn day was really like, but it has remained in my memory as the most beautiful, the most glorious day that ever shone upon me in my life. I was nevertheless abashed, and alarmed at the thought of the necessity of justifying the good opinion, however premature, of so great a man. Thus, when I returned to Paris to my father's humble abode, it was only with blushes and under my breath, that in telling my story I could repeat these words of praise which must have appeared almost beyond belief. I considered myself then the sole usurper, feeling how unworthy I was of such praise.

The routine of my new duties was not difficult. It consisted in parading in the courtyard of the Tuileries the relieving guard, in giving it the parole and countersign, and in commanding and superintending for four-and-twenty hours every third day all the guards on duty. But my first contact with these picked troops was not such an easy matter. The guard of that day, men of gigantic stature and great vigour, in the full prime of life, struck me at once with the admiration which is inspired by the fame of irresistible troops, and with the veneration due to soldiers justly proud of ten years of hard work and victory. In the face of such men what was a life of twenty-two, a few missions, and two campaigns? It was not, I confess without a painful effort to overcome my justifiable modesty that, new to the work as I was, I appeared before their ranks and was able to assume that air of assurance and tone of authority which military command exacts.

That first moment once over, the rest was easy enough; I had only to live amicably with the officers, and to control their mess, and it may be believed that I had no difficulty in acquiring their confidence and friendship. The difference of origin and education between us was no obstacle; and I might even remark, in spite of the war of classes which was then in its first heat, I have always felt that with some management, an illustrious name, instead of being a hindrance, becomes an advantage. This, like all others, doubtless possessed its drawbacks, and it was necessary to forestall them. If indeed it be wise and prudent to win forgiveness from one's equals for a superiority acquired by merit, it is still more necessary to prevent the jealousy which is inspired by a transmitted distinction only due to the accident of birth. The best means and the most natural were not to pride oneself upon it and to appear quite unmindful of it; but as those with whom one was brought into relation were constantly thinking of it themselves, if one displayed a kind and unaffected benevolence, and the evidence of an internal conviction that personal merit should always take precedence of other considerations, there remained but one difficulty to overcome; that which has been imposed, from all time, by the possession of a more or less illustrious name, entailing the necessity of proving, that, without priding oneself foolishly upon it, one bears it worthily, and that one is deserving of the notice and the consideration which it attracts.

Deeply imbued with these sentiments which were born with me, being transmitted from my father, I soon made friends with all around me. With regard to the modification of my opinions, and their conformity to my present position, which was a matter of duty, this transformation was naturally effected. Everyone knows how a picture may take different aspects according to the point of view from which one looks at it, and what a variety of opinions and impressions it produces. This influence, brought to bear upon politics, is still more powerful. I was no longer contemplating the situation of public affairs and the great man who controlled them, from a humble and obscure corner, and through the medium of an atmosphere laden with envy and discontent, but from the very centre of attraction of this powerful planet which drew France and the whole of Europe in its wake in a trail of dazzling light. I soon felt myself absolutely under this domination.

Besides, how prosperous had become my position, living an intoxicating life of delight in the midst of glorious trophies, under the eyes of a hero who was an object of continual admiration, in the very aureole of that glory which from henceforth should irradiate my path. Dreams, realities, all concurred to this end. No epoch was ever more splendid for Paris. What a happy and glorious time! That whole year has left on my memory the impression of a realization of the most brilliant Utopias, a spectacle of the finest galas, and that of a grand society restored to all good things by the presiding genius.

The First Consul in his more personal surroundings had initiated many ingenious amusements, and given the signal for an almost universal joy. True, his household was divided into two parties, but, kept in check by the firmness of their chief, they remained in the shade. These were on one hand the Beauharnais; on the other, Napoleon's own family. The marriage of Louis Bonaparte with Hortense de Beauharnais on July 17th, 1802, appeared to have put an end to these differences, so that peace seemed to pervade everything, a domestic peace which was not one whit more durable than the other peaces of this epoch. But at first this alliance, and several other marriages amongst the younger members of Napoleon's family, increased the general cheerful disposition of mind by the addition of their honeymoon happiness. The well-known attractions and wit of the sisters of the First Consul, the many graces of Madame Bonaparte and her daughter, and the remarkable beauty of the young brides who had just been admitted into this fascinating circle, above all, the presence of a real hero, gave an indefinable charm and lustre to this new Court, as yet unfettered by etiquette, or any other tie than the former traditions of good society.

Our morning amusements at Malmaison consisted of country-house diversions in which Napoleon used to take part, and in the evening of various games, and of conversations, sometimes light and sparkling, sometimes profound and serious, of which I still find records in my note-book. The Revolution, philosophy, above all the East, were the favourite topics of the First Consul. How often, as night drew on, even the most youthful amongst these young women, losing all count of time, would fancy they could see what he was describing, under the charm of his admirable narratives so vividly coloured by a flow of bold and novel illustration, and his piquant and unexpected imagery.

One evening at St. Cloud, when he was describing the Desert, Egypt, and the defeat of the Mamelukes, seeing me hanging on his words, he stopped short; and taking up from the card-table, which he had just left, a silver marker—a medal representing the combat of the Pyramids—he said to me: 'You were not there in those days, young man.' 'Alas, no,' I answered. 'Well,' said he, 'take this and keep it as a remembrance.' I need hardly say that I religiously did so, the proof of which will be found by my children after me.

Such was his usual amenity; concerning which I remember that one day when our outbursts of laughter in the drawing-room were interrupting his work in the adjoining study, he just opened the door to complain that we were hindering him, with a gentle request that we should be a little less noisy.

The other amusements of his household consisted in private theatricals, in which his adopted children and ourselves took part. He sometimes would encourage us by looking on at our rehearsals, which were superintended by the celebrated actors, Michaud, Molé, and Fleury. The performances took place at Malmaison, before a select party. They would be followed by concerts, of Italian songs principally, and often by little dances where there was no crowding or confusion, consisting, as they did, of three or four quadrille sets with plenty of space between each. He would himself dance gaily with us, and would ask for old-fashioned tunes, recalling his own youth. These delightful evenings used to end about midnight.

This was the origin of those absurd reports that the First Consul used to take dancing lessons, or strike attitudes copied from various actors. His own personal share in these diversions, on the contrary, would only last for a few minutes, after which, he would return to his work or to serious conversation.

Our morning diversions at Malmaison were the first to come to an end, owing to the license which a distinguished *artiste* introduced into them; the others which were always under proper restraint, went on during the autumn of 1802, and the following winter. They were hardly even interrupted by the journey of the First Consul to Rouen, to the field of the battle of Ivry and on to Havre, which he thenceforth called the port of Paris. But after that, the multiplicity of affairs, and the serious complexion which they assumed by the hostile attitude once more taken up by England rendered these pleasant recreations inopportune. Then ensued the gradual elevation of the First Consul and the increase of his *entourage*, which imposed stricter etiquette, greater differences of position, and diminished the informal charm of the domestic circle.

Another incident cast some restraint on the freedon of our amusements. I am anticipating what occurred in 1803 so as not to come back upon these details. The preparations for an impending war had taken the First Consul to the sea-side in Belgium. During his absence the young people of his household had participated very innocently, but perhaps with too little circumspection, in the pleasures of the capital. Dinners, excursions into the country, and theatre-parties were the order of the day, even including certain thoughtless visits to public balls and dancing places where the presence of young women of such high position could not fail to be remarked and talked of. It is true that these were but giddy escapades of school girls who had only just come out of the hands of Madame Campan; but their husbands were away and they took fright at certain malicious reports, and however false and exaggerated these may have been, they made an impression on the too suspicious disposition of Louis Bonaparte. This was the beginning of his jealousy which existed for a long time without any real grounds. I am ignorant if the First Consul was worried with complaints on this subject, but as a matter of fact, on his return we were at once scattered abroad on various missions, and suddenly transformed from idlers into workers.

A little before the rupture of the Peace of Amiens, the First Consul had invoked the intervention of Alexander and Frederic; he sent General Duroc and myself into Prussia, at the same time as Colbert was dispatched to St. Petersburg. We fell in with Colbert at night on the high road and there our meeting was marked by an adventure sufficiently comical for me to yield to the desire of relating it.

This colonel and the officer who accompanied him had just been left on the highroad by their postilion who, according to German custom, had taken his horses out while he refreshed himself at the inn. After waiting about a quarter of an hour, Colbert's officer, in his impatience, sprang out of the carriage, and a few minutes after Colbert did the same. The two of them thus dashed into the inn, one on the heels of the other, in the darkness; and both in a towering rage happened to meet in a dark passage, swearing in such good German, that each took the other for the tardy postilion. Under this impression, cane in hand, and clutching one another by the collar, they belaboured each other with growing fury till the host and the real postilion rushing to the fray, candle in hand, our two friends, rather the worse for mutual blows, perceived their mistake a little too late.

I now saw Berlin for the second time, but we only remained there three days. Duroc, being very explicit with the king, was successful; but doubtless following instructions, in the quarter-of-an-hour's visit which we paid to one of the ministers whom we knew to be against us, his manner was so cold and silent that, fancying I was in his way, I got up after saying a few words and went to look out of the window. Nevertheless, as the same silence continued with added significance I drew near again, upon which these two personages separated without a word, as they had begun.

One of the remembrances of this short journey which still remains with me is the admiration which I felt for the beautiful and witty Queen of Prussia when I had the honour of being admitted alone to her presence, thanks to the memories which my father had left behind him. I can still see that princess reclining on a costly couch, a golden tripod by her side, and a veil of oriental purple lightly covering, but not concealing, her elegant and graceful figure. There was such harmonious sweetness in the tones of her voice, such winning and sympathetic fascination in her words, such grace and majesty in her demeanour that in my momentary confusion I almost fancied I was in presence of one of those enchanting apparitions depicted in the fabulous stories of ancient times. Could I foresee that three years later this very queen, in warlike garb, would be flying before our squadrons, and that at the close of the battle of Jena, I myself carried on by a last charge into the centre of Weimar, should have been very nearly taking her prisoner?

Since then in 1840 during my last journey to Berlin, as envoy of the King of the French, when I was taken by M. de Humboldt to the mausoleum in the park of Potsdam consecrated to the memory of this princess, I recognised her at once in the beautiful marble monument representing her again in a recumbent position, but on her bed of death, from which my eyes long fixed on her image could not detach themselves without tears.

X

THE EXECUTION
OF THE DUC D'ENGHIEN

Whilst england in terror was exhausting herself in preparations of defence, whilst Pitt clutched back the Prime Ministership, whilst Pichegru, escaped from exile, offered to betray us to him, and Dumouriez to hand over our former plans of invasion; our strongest forces, as if of their own accord, had all massed themselves on the sea-board. The hand which set these springs of war in movement did it with such ease and power, that at the same time it went on with the admirable work of administrative and judiciary regeneration in France, as if still in time of peace. On January 15th, 1804, Napoleon initiated the fifth year of his Consulate by presenting the Chambers with the Civil Code, then he fixed the public debt at fifty millions; he also founded the system of credit, and, by the institution of indirect taxation relieved landed property, which he also freed from incumbrances in spite of the war.

Extending over a thousand details, both in the museums and the civil and military libraries, the impulsion of the same hand is manifest in the active and intelligent care which re-established order in them, collecting from all parts the highest works of art, of science, and of letters, and stores of precious manuscripts, whilst a hundred engineers, exploring the whole of the French and the allied territory, carried our topographical knowledge to a fresh degree of perfection; the marvellous and simultaneous execution of works of so varied a nature exalting to a higher pitch the enthusiasm of France.

But what each one of us, intimate witnesses of Bonaparte's private life, owes to his memory, (without denying his ambition, which from that time was evidently tending towards supreme power), is to bear testimony to the grandeur of his thoughts, wholly and incessantly directed towards the public welfare; to his active benevolence; to the gentleness, economy, and simplicity of his private life; the constancy of his attachments to those about him, and his calmness of mind in the midst of a thousand acts of treachery and the secret dangers by which his steps were surrounded.

For each moment revealed some new perfidy, or disclosed some fresh trap set for his life. The more he devoted his genius to the welfare of France and the more grateful she showed herself, the more did the rancour of his enemies find vent in atrocious designs.

It was at this time, during the autumn of 1803, at St. Cloud, that the charge of his personal safety devolved almost entirely on myself. Amongst the officers who seconded me, those of the picked gendarmerie frequently confided to me their causes for anxiety. At one time it would be the discovery of a projected ambush on the road to Malmaison, when someone was to have sprung into the carriage of the First Consul. At another that of a mine tunnelled under part of the road to St. Cloud on some selected spot on his passage where a planned obstacle should arrest his course; another time our night rounds discovered an assassin standing on a block of marble placed near the lintel of the window of Napoleon's study—the one which opened on the terrace of the Orangery—and leaning close up against the statue erected on this pedestal.

One day amongst others, one of these officers who seemed rather more anxious than usual, asked me if I had not remarked through the window of the Salon de Mars, my usual post, a man broadly and strongly built, with eyes overhung by dark brows, with a sinister expression and a massive head sunk into his shoulders. This description answered to that of Georges Cadoudal. It was even said that this chief of conspirators had come himself to reconnoitre on this side, whence an easy access could be obtained on the ground-floor to the apartments of the First Consul. I then remembered having seen a somewhat similar figure hanging about the place, but at that time the conspiracy of Cadoudal was rather a supposition than a certitude. It was not known then that on August 22nd, 1803, a vessel of the English royal navy had landed on our shores this Chouan general with some of his accomplices; that in December, 1803, and in January, 1804, MM. de Rivière and de Polignac, Pichegru, and other plotters had followed on the steps of Georges; and that all of them, to the number of about forty, had met together and were concealed in the capital.

England in her astonishment was for the first time alarmed on her own account. Her government, in its growing anxiety, after having armed her on all sides, had listened to every proposition which had been made for her safety, even to the most unworthy of all, an assassination! Neither premeditation, nor payment of agents, nor preliminary steps, nothing, in fact, was wanting to the odium of so criminal a project: and this is how little by little it unfolded itself under our own eyes in all its naked horror.

Whilst our *émigrés,* with double pay from England, were awaiting secret orders from the English Cabinet and the Prince de Condé to assemble on the banks of the Rhine, where, by an unfortunate chance, the Duc d'Enghien happened to be (January 14th, 1804), other French exiles, most of whom had come from London or Brittany, to the number of about a hundred conspirators, were to find their way to Paris. The plan was that the latter, who were to have been paid with a million of English money that was seized on the person of Georges Cadoudal, the moving spirit of the plot, should disguise themselves in the uniforms of our Guard, take up their position on the road to St. Cloud or Malmaison, attack the First Consul in the midst of his escort of about a dozen men, and kill him in this ambush.

This murder on the high road had been glorified by the name of combat, a gross subterfuge so blindly accepted by the Comte d'Artois that he sent his aides-de-camp to win their maiden spurs there, and even his second son, the Duc de Berry. The latter whom his youth rendered excusable, only escaped this crime and its consequences in the very town in which he was one day to be the victim of an equally odious crime, because, at the moment when he was landing at the foot of the cliff which his comrades had already ascended, a signal warned him that the plot had missed fire.

As for results, the mistake had been made of reckoning on the French army. This error on the part of the exiles arose from the attitude and the ever-increasing hostile observations of Moreau and his party upon the First Consul. It had even been expected that this general would have been gained over to the plot, and have espoused the cause of the Pretender through Pichegru, one of the conspirators and a former friend of Moreau, who had been summoned from London to Paris by Georges Cadoudal. In this Georges and the Comte d'Artois had been misled by a report of Lajolois, a cashiered officer who was their go-between—the report of a spy and therefore an exaggerated one. It is known, however, that Moreau's only participation in this plot was his cognizance of it, not daring to take any steps himself, but leaving the work to others and waiting till they had got rid of the First Consul; to whose position as Chief of the Republic, he even had for a brief period the ridiculous pretension to aspire.

But on the side of Napoleon, the fact of the existence of such close danger was unknown, in spite of the arrest of some Chouans whose actions had tended to arouse suspicion. It was only known that Drake, the English Minister in Bavaria, whose confidence had been gained by a secret agent of Bonaparte, was exciting our malcontents to profit by a crime which he seemed to have foreseen; and it was vainly conjectured how it had come to pass that the approaching death of the First Consul and the restoration of the ancient dynasty were proclaimed throughout the whole of Europe. Thus passed the autumn of 1803. Even towards the end of January,

1804, when the winter had brought us back to Paris, there had been no change in the usual occupations of the First Consul.

It was the beginning of February. Duroc, the governor of the palace was absent, and Caulaincourt had taken his place. I was on duty, and was fast asleep in my camp bed when about an hour after midnight I was aroused by being roughly shaken; quickly sitting up, I perceived this general near me. 'Get up,' he said: 'The parole and the countersign must be changed immediately, and the duties must be carried out as if in presence of the enemy. You understand me; there is not an instant to lose.'

I obeyed by immediately forming patrols and rounds in the château, in the garden, and the neighbourhood, arranging them in such a proportion that each sentry would have to reconnoitre at least three times in every minute. The duties were carried on in this manner for several weeks until the crisis was over. The reason of this alarm I will proceed to show. We have seen that the First Consul, although only vaguely anxious up to this moment, had suspected a plot, and that several men who had laid themselves open to suspicion had been arrested. But it was not yet known that amongst these were five of the conspirators. During the night of January 8th, Napoleon who had awoke at two o'clock in the morning according to his habit, had asked for the various reports of his ministers. His lucky star threw out a ray upon the interrogatory of these five prisoners to which little importance had been attached, and as soon as his eyes fell upon it he was seized by a sudden inspiration, and ordered that judgment should take place.

It would seem, however, that here his good fortune was dubious; the first two indeed had been acquitted, and they were really the most guilty. Two others who had been condemned merely as spies had submitted to the death penalty without betraying their cause. The fifth of them, named Querelle, also condemned to death, was on the point of carrying his secret with him into the next world, when he demanded a pardon in exchange for revelations which were made to Murat in the first instance, and which appeared most unlikely to be true. It must here be remembered that Fouché, who had become a senator, was no longer a minister;

that his suppressed office had been merged in that of the minister of justice, and that the ill-governed police had been perfectly blind in the moment of danger.

Querelle was only able to denounce the first landing, that of Georges six months before, on the cliff of Biville, which he had ascended like the smugglers by means of a rope secured to a projection in the cleft of the rocks, whence from one hiding-place to another, he had at last managed to get to Paris. But once set on the track, Napoleon did not lose it. He roused Réal, then head of the Police, he took council with Fouché, and he availed himself of the activity of Savary, the colonel of gendarmes of his guard, so that two other landings were soon disclosed. As for the names of the conspirators, the only one then revealed was that of Georges, nothing was known beyond their number, and that their aim was to assassinate the First Consul. This was the cause of the nocturnal alarm in the château of the Tuileries and the sudden precautions which I had been ordered to take.

It was then that Danouville was seized at one of the halting places used by Georges and his accomplices and in desperation he hanged himself in the Temple. This suicide confirmed the gravity of the plot without throwing any light upon it, until on February 12th, Bouvet de l'Ozier, another conspirator who had just been arrested, endeavoured to strangle himself as Danouville had done. But Bouvet was succoured in time to be restored to life and misery, in his first cries involuntarily uttering the name of Pichegru; then, making up his mind as to what course to pursue, he brought a formal accusation against the implicated Moreau of having with his irresolute republican ambition, betrayed the royal cause to his own profit.

It was thenceforth known that after Lajolois had been sent to England and had returned with Pichegru, a first interview between Georges, Pichegru, and Moreau had taken place on January 26th on the Boulevard of the Madeleine; then a second with Pichegru, at Moreau's own residence, and finally a third at Chaillot, at the abode of Georges Cadoudal. The sorry part that Moreau played in this conspiracy may be sufficiently indicated by an exclamation of

Pichegru: 'That b——' he exclaimed as he left him, 'is also ambitious; he wants to reign, a man who would not be able to govern France for twenty-four hours!'

It was in this wise also, that a second supreme cry of baffled disappointment revealed the reason why the conspiracy had not broken out at the proper time. Georges had said that day in a fit of discouragement when he no longer foresaw any favourable result to the Bourbons from the murder of the First Consul: 'Usurper for usurper, I prefer Bonaparte to this Moreau! He has neither head nor heart!' Nevertheless it is certain that even then Georges, unaware that he had been discovered, was persisting in the project to get rid of the First Consul.

At the first news of such unexpected complicity, an exclamation of astonishment broke from Napoleon. 'Moreau!' he cried. 'What! Moreau in such a plot! He, thus to destroy himself, the only one who had any chance against me! I have indeed a lucky star!' However, he would not allow himself to be led away during the days of February 13th and 14th, but refused to have him arrested. 'No,' he replied; 'he is a person of too much importance, I have too great an interest in his culpability; public opinion would fasten upon this; I must have other proofs, above all that of Pichegru's presence here.'

It was not long before these were laid before him. Pichegru had a brother in Paris, an ex-monk, who having been suddenly sent for and interrogated, confessed in his agitation that he had just seen this general. Therefore, in the night of the 14th to the 15th a council was held and emissaries were dispatched to seize Moreau in his country-house. He was arrested on the 15th, about eight o'clock in the morning on the bridge of Charenton, as he was coming back from Grosbois, and was taken to the Temple.

Here, in spite of the revolutionary horrors which surrounded the first steps of Napoleon, his relations with the immoral government of the Directorate; the Machiavellian necessities which the government of two conquered countries, the one corrupt, the other barbarous, and that of France during five years had imposed upon this conqueror; finally, in spite of the frictions of contested authority, and the disgust so often inspired by the spectacle of human nature unveiled before our eyes, one is glad to recognise in the first impulse of this great man, the pure and noble emotions of his early youth, those of the generous conqueror of Mantua and Wurmser, those of his youthful heroism at once antique and chivalrous.

Up to this time, Moreau had never shown him anything but repulsion and hostility. Oftentimes had this general met his advances with disdain. In his manner he affected not to recognise the authority of the First Consul; in his speech he described Bonaparte as a usurper, and although perhaps at first unjustly suspected of complicity with Pichegru, he was now for the second time discovered in the very act of association with this traitor. This appeared so revolting that in the Council a military commission was proposed and prompt and vigorous measures were enjoined. Either on the grounds of justice or policy, Napoleon opposed this, and no praise is due to him for doing so; but he did more: forgetting all his own grievances and compassionating so great a downfall, he, held out a generous hand to his adversary. He did his best to draw him out of the pit by sending Régnier with a proposal that before the examination came off he should divulge everything to him alone in a secret interview which would put an end to the whole matter.

But Régnier was very unfit for this delicate mission; he accomplished it coldly, was received in the same manner, and at once substituted the official interrogatory. Moreau, on his side, whether from want of heart or mediocrity of mind, did not seem to appreciate his nor the extent of his culpability, nor the uselessness of his disavowals. The depositions of his accomplices had been kept from him. He entrenched himself in haughty denial, and Napoleon finally decided on leaving him to the hands of justice.

On that day in the course of my duty, I followed the First Consul from his study to his Council of State, where acting on Régnier's report, he had made up his mind no longer to have any reservations in the matter. On leaving the Council his agitation was extreme. I remember that as we walked back through the guard room, he turned towards me and exclaimed in a loud and singularly excited voice which the grenadiers could not fail to overhear: 'Moreau! Moreau is of the plot. 'Here are the proofs.' At the same time he showed me while waving them in the air the papers with which his hands were full.

From that moment the facts were public property; Moreau, Georges, Pichegru, and their accomplices were accused of attempting the life of Napoleon, and of high treason against France. There followed a unanimous cry of indignation, and protestations of devotion from public bodies and the heads of the different arms of the service; but a part of the army, especially those staffs which had taken part in Moreau's triumphs, persisted in believing in the jealous hatred of the First Consul rather than in the complicity of the victor of Hohenlinden. This opinion found an echo in the Chambers and amongst the people.

Moreau being arrested, accused, given up to justice, and defended by public incredulity, it became more than ever necessary, in proof of the accusation, to get hold of his principal accomplices; yet neither Pichegru, nor Georges, nor Rivière and the Polignacs were seized. Thus compromised with the Revolution itself by the Counter-Revolution, Napoleon grew indignant, and decided on sparing no means to bring the truth before the eyes of the whole of France. The jury was then suspended, the harbouring of conspirators was declared to be a crime of high treason, and their denunciation was decreed under penalty of six years in fetters. The garrison and the whole of the guard were then simultaneously placed on a war footing; descriptions of suspects were given to them; all barriers by land and water rigidly closed were entrusted to their vigilant supervision, and Paris, completely surrounded by night and day with posts, bivouacs, and stationary or movable vedettes was given up to the strictest investigations of the police.

Nevertheless, for twelve days longer all these precautions were of no avail. Pichegru constantly followed and frequently tracked, yet found every night (and this even through the commiseration of Barbé-Marbois which was condoned later on by the generosity of the First Consul) some brief but safe refuge. It was only on February 28th that betrayed at last, and discovered asleep in a house of the Rue Chabannais by six picked gendarmes, he was taken. The struggle was severe, and was only ended by violent pressure on the most tender part of his body causing him to become unconscious.

As for Georges Cadoudal, tracked as he was escaping in a vehicle on March 9th about seven o'clock in the evening, pursued and captured in the square of Bussy, he killed two men before giving himself up to the populace who threw themselves upon him. He did not denounce anybody, but compromised his associates as well as himself by declaring frankly that he had come to Paris to attack and kill the First Consul.

The scene was becoming more and more tragic. The conspirators, assassins and others, when they had been arrested had been found provided with passports, armed with daggers, and with English gold upon them. Another of them had escaped from justice by committing suicide. The principal conspirators, eager to free themselves from the odious charge of an attempt at assassination by a confession of an attempt at counter revolution, declared unanimously that they had only been waiting for the presence of a prince of the Bourbon blood in Paris itself to put it into execution. Savary and his special gendarmes had been at their pains for nothing, when on the look-out for the landing of the prince on the cliff at Biville. On the other hand, double-faced spies had handed over to the First Consul the correspondence of those English residents most accessible to France. These, without exception, incited not only to revolution, but to the murder of Bonaparte. It was averred that Drake at Munich, Smith at Stuttgart, and Taylor at Hesse-Cassel were paying with the same English gold that had been given to the conspirators who were despatched from London to France, the armed exiles whom they were calling to our frontier. Lastly, in spite of his father's advice and the entreaties of his most devoted officers, the Duc d'Enghien persisted in remaining in Ettenheim. From these headquarters, two hours march from France, he replied by letter: 'There where danger was, was the post of honour for

a Bourbon. That, at this moment, when the order of the Privy
Council of His Brittanic Majesty had summoned the *émigrés* in
retreat to the banks of the Rhine, he could not, whatever might
happen, abandon these worthy and loyal defenders of the French
monarchy.'

How could it be believed that the prince was ignorant of this
plot which had been known to the public for over three weeks! He
should have recognised the significance attached to his presence
at the very gates of France, together with other exiles who were
paid, armed, and assembled by the orders of England, and to what
suspicions of complicity he thus rendered himself liable!

Each day, however, revealed to Napoleon more clearly the murderous intentions of his adversaries. He was enraged at seeing
himself thus placed by them, as it were, beyond national law,
outside the pale of European civilization and exposed to the most
atrocious and perfidious attempts upon his life; his indignation
increased with the arrest of the aides-de-camp of the Bourbons,
who were associated with Georges, and the confessions of the latter
brought it to fever heat.

Being disappointed in his expectation of seizing the chief of the
conspirators in Normandy, he turned his thoughts towards the
Rhine. The confirmation of the presence of the Duc d'Enghien
in Ettenheim was brought to him through a report of the gendarmerie which also included a General Thumery. This name pronounced German fashion (Thoumeriez) was the finishing stroke.
For it caused him to believe that the prince was accompanied by
Dumouriez. It was also said that the young Duke had already
made several appearances in France; some said in Strasburg only,
others, in Paris itself.

On hearing this the First Consul was thoroughly exasperated.
'What,' he cried; as Réal entered, 'you did not tell me that the Duc
d'Enghien was only four leagues from my frontier! Am I a dog to
be killed in the street? Are my murderers sacred beings? Why was I
not warned that they are assembling in Ettenheim? My very person
is attacked. It is time that I should give back blow for blow. The
head of the most guilty amongst them must atone for this.'

Several days previously, his indignation had found vent in similar remarks, and he had decided on his course. Cambacérès overheard this last outburst and considered it a mere sudden fit of anger, but when he endeavoured to allay it, he was met with a crushing reply. Immediately after this, following upon a sitting of the Privy Council composed of the Grand Judge, Fouché, Talleyrand, and the two Consuls, whose objections were overruled, Caulaincourt, and Ordener were sent, the one into Strasburg, the other to seize the prince at Ettenheim, which was very unfitly designated his headquarters.

On March 16th half-an-hour after mid-night, Fririon, Ordener, and thirty dragoons of the 26th, and twenty-five gendarmes, crossed the Rhine at Rheinau, which is almost opposite Ettenheim. The gendarmes were commanded by Chariot, the head of their squadron, and it was he who two months later almost on the very spot, narrated to me the following details.

They had left in reserve on the left bank three squadrons of dragoons of the 26th. During their rapid and silent march they passed through three sleeping villages without attracting any attention. Day was breaking when they arrived at the gate of Ettenheim. Ordener and his dragoons posted themselves there, Charlot entered the town with his gendarmes. Pfersdorf, one of his non-commissioned officers, who had gone down the day before to reconnoitre the place, acted as guide. They marched straight to the house which the prince was occupying, and without hesitation, according to a pre-arranged plan, the commandant and twenty gendarmes spread themselves out in the street under the windows, whilst four other gendarmes, scaling the garden wall, took up their positions in the yard on the other side of the building.

The prince was living there with two aides-de-camp and eleven servants. He had 2,000,000, and 3 to 400,000 francs in a cash-box. His firearms were all at hand ready primed, there were sixty charges in all.

Hardly was the place surrounded when, as the boots of the gen-darmes resounded on the pavement and their weapons jingled, a window was opened and someone cast a rapid glance around, then the aide-de-camp, Grunstein, rushing in to the Duc d'Enghien, said to him: 'You are surrounded.' Upon which the prince, jumping out of bed, seized a repeating rifle, and seeing through the window the French commandant pass by, he took aim at him and was on the point of firing. Twenty windows from which a volley could have been fired all looked out upon the street; there was only a step to take to fly and escape to the mountain; but at that decisive instant, Charlot drew himself up and said in a loud voice: 'Gentlemen, we are in force; no resistance, it would be useless.' But the fatal shot would have been fired, thus beginning a conflict in which all the chances, according to the commandant himself, would have been against the assailants, when the prince's evil genius caused Grunstein to put his hand on the prince's pistol and turn away his aim, saying: 'The odds were too great,' and that he saw that any resistance would be vain. The same fatality led the duke to follow this fatal advice and allow himself to be disarmed.

The door having been opened, they then took possession of the place, seizing all present with their arms. Charlot, however, when in presence of the duke demanded his name. 'You should know it,' was the answer. The demand being repeated, he added, 'Surely you have the description of me?' The bailie³ had just appeared upon the spot to whom the commandant repeated the same question, and this magistrate after a first refusal, ended by naming the prince.

At this juncture cries of alarm were heard. The instructions given attached so much importance to the taking of Dumouriez, that at this sound, Charlot, under the guidance of Pfersdorf, left his illustrious and unfortunate prisoner, to hasten to the house which this general was reported to occupy. The first person whom he met was the grand master of the hunt at Baden whom he got rid of by evasive replies. But the alarm was growing and one of the inhabitants running in haste to the church, cried out 'Fire! Fire!' and was on the point of ringing the alarm bell when the commandant perceiving him, caught him up, and striking him with his sword, made him desist from the attempt. A little further on a group of inhabitants, moved with indignation at the

sight of armed French men on their sovereign's territory, were
assembled; these he calmed by saying that 'the exiles alone were
wanted. The French Government was on friendly terms with their
prince of which they would shortly be assured; their duty was to
remain quiet.' He received no further interruption, but instead
of Dumouriez, he only seized the General Marquis de Thumery,
whose ill-pronounced name had occasioned the mistake. On his
return to the duke, he interrogated Grunstein, whom the prince,
forgetful of himself, endeavoured to defend; saying to the commandant: 'But for him, I should have killed you; you owe your
life to him.' Then no doubt regretting he had given himself up,
he fell into a condition of silent melancholy; when his papers
were being seized, he laid both hands over them saying: 'Do not
be surprised, sir; you see here the correspondence of a Bourbon,
of a prince of the blood of Henry IV.' And perceiving that the
letters of the Princesse de Rohan would not escape scrutiny, he
added: 'I hope you will be as discreet as possible in all that does
not concern the government.' When he had drunk this bitter cup
to the dregs, and the gendarmes came to report their failure in
the real object of their search; perceiving with surprise that it had
been Dumouriez, he proceeded: 'I give you my word of honour
that he is not here. It is possible he may have been taken with his
majesty's instructions for me: but I have neither seen him nor do
I know where he is.'

The unfortunate prince was then obliged to let himself be led
away as a prisoner in the midst of our men, with Generals Thumery
and Grunstein, Lieutenant Schmide, two abbés, a secretary and
three servants. Thus escorted, he passed through Ettenheim on
foot as far as the gate of the burg where he was received by Ordener
and placed in a hastily harnessed labourers cart, when the journey
back to the bank of the Rhine was proceeded with. Perceiving an
encampment of cavalry on the way the prince exclaimed: 'It looks
as if great importance is attached to my arrest. But might is right,
and you will be justified.' When crossing the river, he said in reply
to Ordener: 'Why should I have returned to France? To be a colonel there? I could have no existence but with the Austrians.' Then

addressing commandant Charlot: 'This expedition must have been conducted very secretly. It surprises me that I was not forewarned, for I was beloved at Ettenheim. To-night you would not have found me. Only yesterday the Princess of R—— begged me to depart, but I put it off, thinking that you would not have time to arrive in the night. I am sure that she will come, and will want to follow me; she is very much attached to me; treat her well.'

Charlot added that two battalions and a battery were in position before Offenburg on the right bank of the Rhine; that Caulaincourt was in command of them; that he had orders to seize a Baroness de Reich, but that was all he knew. Long afterwards Caulaincourt often declared his ignorance of what had been going on, a fact which was indeed quite in accordance with the absolute secrecy observed on similar occasions by the First Consul. We were always equally reserved amongst ourselves. We would suddenly leave our families without their having any idea as to our destination, and this was so thoroughly understood that no one ever dreamt of asking us any questions on the point.

We found other troops under arms at New-Brisach. As soon as we had landed on the left bank, the prince was placed in a carriage, taken to Strasburg, and shut up in the citadel.

He remained there two days under the charge of the head of the squadron, Charlot, without being entirely cut off from his companions in misfortune. This officer has affirmed to me that in the whole of the correspondence so unexpectedly seized, there was not a single word, or the least trace of any connivance of the prince in the Paris plot. The commandant could discover nothing further than the evident proof of a concerted meeting of exiles on the right bank of the Rhine, and of many communications with the left bank.

This unhappy prince could hear the sound of the river flowing by the prison to which he had just been taken. This stream alone separated him from the honours due to his rank, his liberty, his safety, and a young and beautiful woman whom he loved, and to whom, the report ran, he had secretly united himself in spite of his family. The thought of all he had lost, which was yet so near, led him to attempt an effort to recover it. Finding himself alone with the commandant, he said: 'Do you not feel any compunction in thus seizing one of your former princes?'—'No, Sir,' answered the officer of the gendarmerie, 'I obey legitimate authority.'— 'However,' retorted the prince, 'there is the Rhine; it rests with you to set me on the other side of it, and your fortune is made.' But the commandant answered shortly that it was not his way of thinking, and ordered him to go into the next room. The prince then, resigning himself, added: 'Shall I remain in prison for the rest of my life? I much esteem Bonaparte, and look upon him as a great man; but he is not a Bourbon, he has no right to reign over France, he ought to give back the crown to my family.'

The next day, however, he seemed to have a dark presentiment of the cruel fate which awaited him. 'I ought to have killed your husband,' he said to the wife of the commandant, 'I had a right to do so. I was defending my liberty; I shall probably repent of not having done so.' As she exclaimed at this, he continued: 'It would have been your fault; why not have sent a note to warn me?' —'And how could I,' she answered, 'when I knew nothing about the matter?' The Duc d'Enghien was not mistaken: Madame de Rohan came in tears, begging permission to see him, and to be allowed to go to Paris, no doubt to throw herself at the feet of the First Consul; but the commandant sent her back to Schee, the Prefect, who told her that she would not see the prince and that she might not go beyond Saverne. Replying to a remark that was addressed to her, she said, 'Yes, I know that there were many papers found upon him.' Nevertheless, it must be again repeated, there was not a single one that related to the conspiracy of Georges.

Amongst these documents the attention of the commandant had been attracted by a letter dated in 1792; this was from the Duke's mother, a Bourbon princess of a curious turn of mind, who was then in favour of constitutional principles; in this letter she urged the young duke to return to France. 'Why not have listened to her?' he said to the prince.—'My obedience,' he replied, 'was not due to her but to the king alone.' Then, irritated by these interrogatories, by his position and his bitter recollections, he gave way to anger for the first and only time, recalling the murder of Louis XVI, of the Queen, and Madame Elizabeth, and cursed the French Revolution. With the exception of that one moment, the commandant often told me that during these two days, in the midst of such overwhelming misfortune, the prince had shown a politeness which was entirely free from pride though replete with dignity; that his whole demeanour inspired the greatest consideration, and kept persons at a respectful distance, and that at the most trying moments, even on being awoke to receive the announcement that he must leave the citadel, he maintained the same calm and firmness. To the very last when his three officers were sobbing as they wished him farewell, he spoke regretfully of leaving them: 'My friends,' said he, 'I grieve that I can no longer do anything to help your fortunes.'

Such was, word for word, the commandant's account of the first part of this woeful catastrophe. He wound up with these words: 'I put the prince in General Ordener's carriage, and he left by post for Vincennes.'

He arrived there March 20th, at five o'clock in the afternoon; at midnight he was awoke and interrogated by d'Hautencourt, captain adjutant-major of the special gendarmerie.

Two hours after midnight he appeared before a military commission, presided over by General Hulin. The audience was composed of an aide-de-camp of Murat, some officers and some gendarmes. The prince was without counsel. He related that he had spent two years at Ettenheim, staying on there out of love of sport. He frankly declared that he was ready to make war with France in concert with England; but he protested that 'he had never had any relations with Pichegru, and was glad of it, after all the infamous reports as to the way in which he wanted to make use of him, if indeed they were true.' As in his first examination, he finished by demanding to communicate with the First Consul: both by word of mouth and by letter: 'Being persuaded,' he said, 'that Napoleon would not refuse, out of consideration for his name, his rank, his way of thinking, and the horror of his situation.'

But the aide-de-camp, who was colonel of this special gendarmerie, had just assumed the command at Vincennes on the previous evening, and did not allow this request to reach the ears of the First Consul. He had presided over and hurried on the judgment; he now hastened its execution. This was left to d'Hautencourt, and the unfortunate prince was hurriedly led to the castle moat, where he was shot, and buried in a grave that had been already dug.

Witnesses of the event assert, but I have not been able to verify the fact, that it was then about five o'clock, that the judgment had hardly been drawn up and signed, and that the judges were still deliberating whether they would send the letter of the prince to the First Consul, when Savary, breaking in upon them, transfixed them with horror by saying to Hulin: 'What are you doing here? All is over; he no longer exists, there is nothing more for you to do!' Then only were the castle gates opened and Murat's aide-de-camp returned to his general, and found him still in bed at six o'clock in the morning. He expatiated on the frank and manly replies of the prince in spite of the efforts of the judges to point out how dangerous they were, and then described the judgment and its immediate execution in spite of his request to be allowed to see the First Consul. The aide-de-camp himself told me that at this point he was interrupted by the sobs of Murat and the tearful exclamations of Caroline Bonaparte: 'Ah, this is too dreadful; leave off, say no more, you cause us too much pain!'

During this fateful night, I happened to be on duty at the Tuileries. The arrival of the prince was not then known in Paris, the report of his arrest beyond the Rhine only then being bruited about, although it was known to the Royalists. The first intimation I had had of it was by a chance expression of a woman of their party whom I met on the evening of March 20th. Feeling convinced, as I was by many previous examples, of the magnanimity of the First Consul; I had replied, that if the fact was true, it was because he wanted to create an opportunity of retaliating by an act of generosity, on the odious attempts that had been made against his life. Either doubting the truth of this fact, or preoccupied with other things, I returned to my post, with no further thought of the rumour which was quickly becoming public property. It was still unknown at the château of the Tuileries, but no one was then residing there, and in any case the greatest reserve was always maintained there.

At nine o'clock the next morning as I was on my way to General Duroc to give an account of the twenty-four hours' duty, I met on the grand stair case the adjutant-major of the special gendarmerie. As usual he was coming to join me to hand in our reports together. Astonished at his livid pallor, at the distortion of his countenance, and the disorder of his dress, I asked him the reason of it. 'Ah! …' he cried with an oath, 'there is nothing to wonder at after the fearful night I have passed!'—'Why, what has happened then?' said I, and stopping short, he retorted: 'A thunder-bolt has fallen during the night.' This exclamation alarmed without enlightening me; but when I entered the reception room, General Duroc not yet being down, I found Hulin, very red in the face and very excited, pacing up and down in the greatest agitation. This colonel of the guard was a tall and very stout man; soon he was joined by the adjutant-major, when I overheard Hulin exclaim several times: 'He did quite right, it is better to kill the devil than to let the devil kill you.' I then felt convinced that a catastrophe had happened.

Not knowing of the prince's arrival at Vincennes, I could hardly have conjectured that it concerned him. Nevertheless, in my anxiety, drawing near to Hulin, I hazarded the remark: 'They say the Duc d'Enghien is arrested!'—'Yes! and dead into the bargain!' he answered abruptly. Duroc having then come in, we drew round him, and after having given in my report, in reply to a brief and almost inaudible interrogation, d'Hautencourt answered: 'He was shot in the moat at three o'clock in the morning,' then drawing from his pocket a little parcel a few inches square, soiled and crushed up as if it had been carried about a long time, the adjutant-major added: 'When the last moment had come, he drew from his bosom this paper and begged me to give it to the princess. It is the hair of ——!' these last words were said with an affectation of carelessness which froze me with horror from head to foot. I felt myself growing pale; the ground seemed giving way beneath me. It being then time for me to go off duty, I retired in unspeakable grief.

And yet I knew this adjutant-major well for a worthy and excellent man, usually humane and gentle, but either through being taken out of his sphere, or feeling biassed by his colonel in his dependent position, what a sudden transformation was here! This is the danger which exceptional circumstances create for those whom a beginning of dearly-bought prosperity keeps in a state of subservience, lacking the superior associations whose verdict they might have stood in fear of, accustomed to obedience as a duty, and whose obscurity obviates the necessity of having to reckon with history. Even amongst men brought up in the midst of social safeguards such as these men did not possess, does not history show us many for whom under similar circumstances these safeguards were all too insufficient? Add to these considerations, which apply equally to the judges and to those who put the judgment into execution, surprise, haste, the habit of obedience, an appearance of legality, and that fatal mistake as to the complicity of the prince in Georges's odious plot, a mistake which was confirmed by the exclamation of Hulin which I have just repeated.

Unhappy prince! His warlike heroism and chivalrous youth should have rendered impossible even the bare suspicion that he could be an accomplice in the contemplated assassination of Bonaparte!—Yet innocent of this crime, he had been its victim.

On my arrival home, hardly knowing how I got there, so absorbed and dismayed was I by this tragic event, threw myself into a chair at the foot of my father's bed, saying: 'The Duc d'Enghien has been shot during the night. We have returned to the horrors of '93. The hand which drew us out of them now thrusts us back. Is it possible to remain any longer associated with such deeds?' My father said nothing; he was completely dumbfounded and could not believe me. I related to him the events which I have just narrated, and in his horror, he, like myself, made no allowance for the causes that had provoked this vengeance. He was also of opinion that after this sanguinary beginning, no supreme ruler would be sufficiently master of himself to stop short in such a baneful course, and that one ought indubitably to dissever oneself from it.

It was, however, too important a step to decide on without knowing thoroughly all that could have led to the cruel deed. My father, who was then a councillor of State could better than any other, obtain such information. During the three following days which he devoted to this object, shut up in my room, deploring that fatal night, and perpetually haunted by the horrible spectacle which was ever before my eyes, I remained completely crushed! Justly proud up to that moment, of the great man whom I served, I had made a complete hero of him; I felt convinced that no reason, whether of policy, of personal security, or of vengeance, would prevail against the generosity of his character, and the details which I shall proceed to give—the fruits of careful research on my part—will show that I was not entirely mistaken, and that the generosity which had been obscured by a first movement of anger, would regain its sway when too late, and when a fatal chance had rendered it powerless to be of any avail.

Nevertheless, the first news which my father was able to bring us, extenuated but slightly the impression which the too premeditated violence of this cruel *coup d'état* had produced upon us. After the instructions given to Ordener, Napoleon had been afraid of himself; having withdrawn to Malmaison during the whole of the following week, he had turned a deaf ear to the intercessions of Josephine; and although he knew that there was nothing in the papers seized upon the prince in any way implicating him in the murderous attempt, he none the less persevered in his own angry conviction. In vain had Murat, then commandant of Paris, declined to obey his orders of March 20th and refused to take any part in this act of vengeance; with unmoved inflexibility he had taken all upon himself, he had even dictated every detail and signed it himself—the names of the military judges, the order to pronounce judgment at a single sitting, and to execute it at once, whatever it might be. Finally, he had elected, to ensure the following out of his instructions, the only one amongst his aides-de-camp whom he knew to be capable of unhesitatingly obeying such orders.

It was said, it is true, that he had thought better of it that evening, and had despatched orders to Réal to submit the unfortu-

nate prince to an examination which would doubtless have saved
him; and that this councillor of State, shut up in his own room,
had only received the order at five o'clock in the morning, when
the execution had already taken place. This extenuating act was
not only true but altogether probable; indeed I had myself one
evening, just a little before this sad time, been the bearer from
St. Cloud to Paris of urgent orders for General Berthier, which I
was only able to deliver into the minister's own hand after a night
journey of eight leagues, having to drag him out from an almost
inaccessible retreat. Réal, during that unhappy night had apparently shut himself up in the same manner. Our days and even
our nights were so overwhelmed with work that it was sometimes
necessary, for the sake of breathing time, to steal a few hours rest
from the service of the First Consul.

Thus it was quite true that a blessed feeling of remorse had
moved the soul of Napoleon at the last moment. We must therefore trust, for the honour of him who was entrusted with this
message of succour, that he was unaware of its full importance;
otherwise be would surely have religiously fulfilled his mission to
Réal, as I did mine to Berthier, in a case when promptitude was
not so indispensable.

Another fact attests the truth of this. When Savary arrived at
Malmaison about seven o'clock in the morning with his terrible
story, the First Consul, interrupting him as soon as he had begun
to speak, asked: 'Had he not seen Réal?' On his reply that he had
just met him at the barrier, going to Vincennes, the First Consul
fell into a sombre and silent reverie broken by such evident agitation, that for a long time neither his secretary nor his aide-de-camp
dared to interrupt it. Doubtless in his eyes this was a decision
of fate, which he resolved upon accepting, and afterwards with
Caulaincourt, Fontanes and others, both his words and his silence
were in conformity with this belief.

I can also give the substance of another narrative of this disastrous event which I held from King Joseph, whom, as will be seen,
I attended eighteen months later as aide-de-camp at the time of
the conquest of the kingdom of Naples. Réal's narrative is included

in it; it too positively confirms all that I myself knew, heard, and saw, it is attested to by too many witnesses, most of whom I knew, for the possibility of any doubt as to its truth.

On the eve of the fatal deed which had been but too truly commanded by him in the first instance, the First Consul fell back into a state of indecision. He was hesitating between many urgent entreaties, and the advice of a minister who was the only one believed to have been opposed to them, when Joseph, intervening, tried to recall him to his role of moderator, of centre of attraction, 'of key-stone of the arch' between all parties; then reminding him that it was entirely due to the encouragement of his victim's father that he had chosen the artillery and refused the navy, (a choice of such influence upon his destiny) he did not leave him till he felt sure of having won him over to clemency. The result of this was the counter-order which was that very evening dispatched to Réal, as Réal himself declared, but an unhappy fatality had ordained that this councillor of State, having been twice awoke during that cruel night to receive missives of no importance, had impatiently locked himself up in his room, and only opened the letter of the First Consul several hours after it had been received, towards five o'clock in the morning at the very moment when the murder was being committed; so that, as we all knew later, when his carriage crossed that of Savary at the barrier of Vincennes, he returned horror-struck at the irreparable consequences of his unfortunate slumber. That was why, when Josephine cried out in horror: 'Alas, my friend what have you done!' Napoleon replied, 'The wretches were too quick!' and on the other hand, when alone with Joseph, he allowed himself to indulge in a furious burst of anger against Réal, whom he unjustly accused, on account of his revolutionary antecedents, of having purposely delayed to obey his counter-instructions. Then, recovering himself, he said to his brother: 'After all, one must make the best of things. That very likely if he had been assassinated by the agents of the prince's family, the prince would have been the first to show himself in France, sword in hand, to profit by it. That it was for him henceforth to bear the responsibility of the event; that to throw it upon others, even

justly, would too much resemble an act of cowardice for him ever
to allow himself to be suspected of the weakness.'

In the course of the first Council of State which soon followed
this catastrophe, my father heard the First Consul after a violent
tirade against rumours, and the modern violations of sanctu-
ary, say: 'That he knew how to make France respected. That he
respected public opinion only so long as it was not founded upon
error. That he despised its caprices and that when it swerved from
the right way, all governing men like himself, instead of following
it, should enlighten it, that he would have commanded the judgment and public execution of the Duc d'Enghien, who was guilty
of conniving with the agents of England, of taking arms against
France, of secret understandings with our frontier departments,
with the object of inciting revolt, and lastly of complicity in the
plot which had been laid against his life, if he had not feared
giving the partisans of this prince the opportunity of compassing
their own destruction; that Rivière and the Polignacs had not been
seized amongst these, but in obscure hiding-places; that besides,
the Royalists were quiet; that he asked nothing more from them;
that anyone was at liberty to cherish regret; that those who pretended to fear general proscriptions did not believe in them; but
that as for himself, he would not spare any guilty persons.'

All these counts of accusation which he heaped up upon his
victim were true, except the last, that of complicity with Georges
Cadoudal, the only fact which could have explained, without justifying, so cruel a vengeance. Bonaparte may have believed in this
complicity, but it never really existed. The prince probably was
cognizant of the plot through public rumour, but at that time it
had missed fire, and the prolongation of his stay within reach of
the Rhine was thus devoid of any motive to justify the suspicion
to which he fell a victim.

It was evident therefore that, irritated by the succession of
attempts against his life, the First Consul had resolved to put
an end to them by a decisive blow. If any excuse could be found
for such a barbarous act, it was in his real conviction, through
a fatal concurrence of circumstances, that he was obeying

political necessity, the right of personal defence, and that he was only punishing a conspirator; a fatal error, proving more than ever, that one should never constitute oneself judge of one's own cause, and that protectionary measures should be respected, so as not to run the risk of defending oneself against an attempted crime by the commission of another crime.

Let us trust that the feeling of remorse which caused him to send Réal to delay the execution of his first decision may have extenuated its horror in the eyes of God, as well as in the eyes of man.

Thus also should history judge it. As for us, in our ignorance at the time, the accusation brought against this unhappy prince seemed likely to be only too true. Looked at in this light, however fearful may have been the blow struck at Vincennes, was our much provoked chief the only, or the most guilty, one? It was, nevertheless another circumstance which influenced our decision.

On one side we knew that Caulaincourt was a butt for royalist animosity. They accused him of, and held him responsible for, the arrest, the judgment, and the execution, although he not only did not know of it, but was away from Paris at the time. The denials of his friends, his own despair, his fainting fit at the First Consul's when he learnt the murder, and the bitter violence of the reproaches which he addressed to Bonaparte when restored to consciousness by Bonaparte's own efforts, were not enough for them. They demanded his resignation and exacted it in proof of denial of his participation in this sanguinary action.

On the other hand, my father noticed that several ex-Jacobins who had united together were triumphantly applauding this first retrograde step that Napoleon had taken in their own atrocious path. What were we to do in the midst of these two inimical parties? To satisfy the one, must we give up to the other, the ground which had been so fortunately taken back from the Terrorists? It was in Bonaparte alone that we had trusted to draw France and ourselves out of the revolutionary abyss. Up to that moment this hope had been magnificently realized. Four years of benefits, and of an admirably generous and restorative administration, had attached us to his fortunes; should we then, at his first step in a contrary direction, however deplorable it may have been, abandon everything? Should we, by being the first to draw back from him, give him up to, and even push him into the hands of the most dangerous of these parties, whose influence had been combated by our co-operation?

Why should we pre-suppose a sanguinary future? Fear alone could have drawn the First Consul into such a course; and we know that after the explosion of the infernal machine of the Royalists on the 3rd Nivôse, interrupting one of his councillors, who had asked: 'Are you not afraid, Citizen-Consul?'—he had answered: 'I, afraid! Ah! If I were afraid, it would be a bad day for France.'

This political crime might therefore remain a solitary one, and as our future and that of the whole of the healthy-minded party in France depended on the First Consul, why should we give way to despondency? His hitherto unsullied rectitude of conduct had, it is true, suffered a lapse; he had slipped away from us, but that was all the more reason why we should strengthen our grip and endeavour to regain the ground that had been lost. If he played us false again, we could then take counsel together as to our future course.

Such was the exact direction to which our thoughts tended during many days of anxiety, sadness, and discouragement, but having once decided on a line of action, I urged my father to make an attempt to restore Caulaincourt's courage and that of our friends which had no doubt been shaken like our own. On the following Sunday (I think it was March 25th), we were all to meet at the Tuileries, and we promised each other that, while not attempting to hide our sorrowful reprobation, we would endeavour to conform our words and action to the resolution which we had taken.

There was a considerable gathering of all the authorities that day at the palace. We had only been able to communicate our own feelings to a few friends, and yet without any pre-arrangement we were all in complete accord. Caulaincourt maintained a firm and steadfast demeanour, but, with his drawn mouth, his jaundiced complexion, and his contracted features, he seemed to have aged by ten years, and was indeed hardly recognisable. He became even paler when I pressed his hand, but remained motionless as a statue.

A little further on, I met the same d'Hautencourt whose remarks to Duroc had offered so cruel a contrast to his agitated manner. In reply to my questions he said that the last words of the unhappy prince had been: 'I must die then at the hand of Frenchmen!' Having asked him one last question which I could hardly enunciate: 'He died as a hero,' was the reply.

At this juncture Bonaparte re-appeared amongst us, passing through the silent crowd who made way for him on his road to the chapel. There was no change in the expression of his countenance. During the prayers of the mass, I watched him with redoubled attention; and there, before God, while I seemed to see the bleeding victim of a hurried death finding a refuge before the supreme tribunal, in the anguish of my heart, I waited for some sign of remorse, or at least of regret, to manifest itself on the features of the author of the cruel deed; whatever, however, may have been his inward feeling, not a trace of it was visible; he remained perfectly calm, and, through my own tears, his countenance appeared to me as that of a severe and impassive judge.

After thus seeing him before God, I wanted to see him before men, and to this end I attached myself to his steps during the audience which followed. His manner was at times calm though constrained, at others gloomy, but rather more accessible than was his wont. He walked slowly up and down and from side to side of the large rooms with a more measured step than usual, appearing desirous of observing in his turn, stopping every few steps, and allowing persons to gather around while he addressed a few words to each. All he said had reference directly or indirectly to the night of the 20th to the 21st of March. He was evidently sounding opinions, expecting or even provoking replies which he hoped would be of a satisfactory nature. He only got one meant to be flattering, but so clumsily expressed that he cut it short by turning his back on the speaker. It was a kind of involuntary accusation of having repaid an attempt at murder by a murder. The various groups which formed around him from time to time, listened to him with watch-ful curiosity, in a dejected and embarrassed attitude, and for the most part in a silence of evident disapproval.

His haughty and severe demeanour, though at first inclined to expand, became more and more sombre and reserved. Withdrawing into himself, he tried to convince himself that political necessity had absolved him; that excepting the manner of the deed, in all the rest he had right on his side; which was false. However, he had attained his aim, as from that moment there was an end to all royalist conspiracies.

He retired abruptly from this audience greatly dissatisfied, but inflexible; without appearing or being any more disturbed by the unanimous disapproval than he was on other occasions hereafter when the subject was introduced, and in his last moments at Saint Helena.

But the horrors of this terrible drama had not yet reached their termination. Between eleven o'clock and midnight on April 5th, Pichegru added a fourth suicide to them. It was that of one of Napoleon's former professors at the College of Brienne; and whether on account of this connection, or because at that time he was less irritated against those of his enemies to whom the Revolution had given birth than to those of the old order, the First Consul had promised him not only an unconditional pardon, but complete rehabilitation and the governorship of Cayenne. The unfortunate man however, either in weariness or utter disgust of a life which treachery had disgraced, after some hesitation, preferred to make an end of it. He freed himself from the shame of living or the fear of yet meeting with his just deserts, by slowly strangling himself in his bed, by means of a stick which he had twisted into his silk necktie. He was thus found the next morning with a volume of Seneca lying by him, open at the page describing the suicide of Cato.

Six weeks later, Fate, which was then all in Bonaparte's favour, for the second time led one of Napoleon's bitterest enemies to this very prison in the person of Captain Wright, the Englishman who had landed Pichegru and his accomplices on our shores.

At last the preliminary inquiry of the great trial was concluded. Moreau had persisted in protesting his innocence during forty-four days till he was confronted with three of his accomplices, and the confession of his interview with Georges and Pichegru was dragged from him.

Forty-six accused appeared before justice on June 10th. They were tried under every condition that could be favourable to them, before a numerous public, and in the midst of eager and even seditious manifestions on the part of military men of all grades who were ardent partisans of Moreau. In spite of his flagrant culpability the judges hesitated, and, at last, some other influence being brought to bear, or with a show of equity they adopted half measures. Moreau was found guilty, but excusable, and condemned only to two years' imprisonment. Four of the others, whether justly or through pity, were awarded the same sentence. Twenty-one were acquitted, and twenty condemned to death.

We were then at St. Cloud. On learning the sentence, the generals about the First Consul gave vent to their rage in furious exclamations that it was a denial of justice, an act of revolt. There was even talk of proceeding to some extraordinary measures against the condemned, the judges, and even against Paris itself, which was declared unworthy to be a capital and the residence of the head of the government. They would have desired Moreau's condemnation to death, knowing very well, it is true, that Napoleon would have commuted it, but indignant that the prevaricating tribunal should have robbed him of the opportunity of doing so.

As for Napoleon, however angry he may have felt, he managed to contain himself. He agreed with Moreau to purchase his estates which were considerable, and insisted on his exile to America.

He pardoned eight out of the twenty who had been condemned to death. We even noticed that when granting the life of Armand de Polignac to the prayers of Madame d'Andlau and this conspirator's wife, he was much moved, and mingled his tears with theirs.

One of the consequences of this plot was, together with the prorogation of special tribunals, the re-establishment of Fouché as Minister of Police. Napoleon distrusted him: he set a watch on him and increased the counter police. One of these offices was entrusted to his aide-de-camp, Lavalette, who was also to make himself acquainted with the contents of letters. He told my father that he learnt more through these agencies, and especially through the cure's than by any other medium, and added with regard to Fouché that he had reinstated him not so much to know everything that was going on, as to have the appearance of knowing everything.

I meant to pursue this tragic event to the bitter end. But it had already brought in its train another of the highest importance. For the space of four months, that is to say from the commencement of February 1804, and on the first outbreak of this conspiracy, many addresses had openly demanded the re-establishment of the throne and the foundation of a new dynasty. On March 27, the entire Senate in acknowledging reports of the criminal correspondence with the English agents of the Lower Rhine, replied to Bonaparte: 'It was you who drew us out of the chaos of the past; you cause us to bless the benefits of the present; protect us against the future. Great man, finish your work, make it as immortal as your own glory.'

The reply of the First Consul to this official advance, was measured: 'He would consider it,' he said. Consequently the State Council was consulted on the establishment of a hereditary government. Twenty out of twenty-seven councillors approved of it. But as they had not agreed about the guarantees, my father proposed that each should send in a separate vote with its grounds duly set forth. His was for the Empire with a constitution resembling the English Charta as much as possible.

On May 18th 1804, the Second Consul brought forward the project of *Senatus-Consultus*, which created the Empire and the almost absolute power of Bonaparte; this project was at once adopted, and by unanimous consent, minus two votes that were null and void, and three against it. The latter met with the same treatment as the others at the Emperor's hands, and it is worthy of note that when the names of the candidates to senatorial office were laid before him, he was indignant not to see any of those who had voted against the Empire.

This was a unique epoch in our history. We were living, as it were, in a rarefied atmosphere of miracles; on that 18th of May, especially, a day of intoxicating splendour and triumph. The senate had hardly passed its vote for the Empire, before all the members, tumultuously following on the steps of the Second Consul, came in a body to St. Cloud in a burst of enthusiasm. Napoleon being proclaimed Emperor, then sent them back to closet himself with Cambacérès, settling then and there the transformation of the Italian Republic into a kingdom; the inauguration of the Order of Honour; negotiations with the Pope to come over and consecrate him himself; and pending his arrival, the invasion of England.

France, being consulted, declared that she desired the Empire, and Napoleon for Emperor, in one loud response of 3,524,254 voices! Truguet was the sole admiral of the fleet who refused to accept it; if there were any dissentients in the army they kept silence: when the accession of the First Consul to the Empire was proclaimed in its ranks, it was received with unanimous acclamations. One colonel of infantry alone, a man of splendid stature and of well-known merit turned round and in bold accents exclaimed: 'Silence in the ranks!' This was Mouton, afterwards a marshal and Count de Lobau. Napoleon's reply to this republican manifestation did not tarry. It was worthy of each of these brave spirits; for shortly after, the colonel received with his general's brevet that of aide-de-camp to the Emperor.

It is known that the principal motive alleged for the creation of the Empire was to discourage attacks on the life and temporary power of Bonaparte by making this power hereditary in his family. So that to restore the Republic or the old monarchy, there would not be one man alone to strike down but an entire dynasty. Thus, as always happens with abortive plots, like that of the 3rd Nivôse which, having doubled the power of Napoleon, had the effect of soon after causing him to be made Consul for life, this one made him Emperor, even before sentence on the conspirators had been pronounced, and in spite of the murder of Vincennes!

XI

THE CAMP AT BOULOGNE

THE ARMY AT THAT TIME better organized, clothed, disciplined and trained than it has ever been since, had been placed on the most formidable footing: 150,000 men, 58 French ships of the line, 12 Batavian vessels, and 1800 armed transports were to be kept in readiness to invade England. On July 18th Napoleon suddenly re-appeared at Boulogne-sur-Mer, in the midst of his camps and his flotilla. His first words to Marshal Soult on arrival were: 'How much time do you require to be ready to embark?'—'Three days, Sire.'—'I can only give you one,' retorted the Emperor.—'That is an impossibility,' answered the Marshal.—'Impossible, Sir!' exclaimed the Emperor, 'I am not acquainted with the word; it is not in the French language, erase it from your dictionary.' He at once indeed prescribed such measures as would ensure the possibility of embarking within twenty-four hours.

But on the morrow, whether from his usual success in overcoming great difficulties, or from the knowledge that he had so often proved himself right, even when the wisest were opposed to him, he was carried away by too great confidence. Thus good fortune and even experience itself may lead us astray. That very day, his mind being entirely on his fleet, he insisted that all sails should be set, and on exercising it under the eyes of the English squadron, in spite of menacing skies and against the advice of a rear-admiral. As the one persisted in his opinion, the other got into a fury, and his violence was such that the sailor, with a hand on the hilt of his sword, thought it necessary to hold himself upon the defensive. The Emperor, however, who was incapable of personally laying hands upon him, caused him to be disarmed, and paying no attention to his advice insisted that the vessels should put out to sea. What the rear-admiral had foreseen, took place. Napoleon, it is true, gained a victory over the English by driving away their squadron and taking one of their vessels, but was conquered by the storm in which he had refused to believe. He himself very narrowly escaped, and four of his vessels perished. Then recognising his two-fold error, he did his best to retrieve it; in the first instance by spending the whole night in the tower of Heurt in efforts to succour his ship-wrecked mariners, and secondly, tacitly acknowledging his own error by forgiving the admiral's, and causing him to forget his first hasty movement of violence.

During the following twenty-five days he gave up his attention to his gigantic plan of invasion, which we shall soon see in its entirety, and to his various camps before which he paraded for the first time as the Emperor. He inspected the broad road-ways and the drainage canals which had been executed by his orders, a work which not only preserved the sanitary condition of the camps, but facilitated the means of communication between them and the surrounding country. His active and ingenious soldiers had beautified their huts by laying out numerous gardens adorned with flowers, with inscriptions in his honour, obelisks and pyramids which were generally surmounted by the laurel-crowned bust of their Emperor. He would mix with them freely, entering into every little detail of their comfort and bestowing with discrimination his praise, his favours, and any well-merited advancement, thus provoking their utmost enthusiasm.

But the climax was on August 15th, his fête day. This anniversary marked one of the most solemn functions of his reign, that of the distribution of the Order of Honour to the army. It was announced by the guns of Boulogne, and those of Antwerp and Cherbourg, proclaiming at the same time the inauguration of these two new ports, answered the salute. The victorious entry into Boulogne that same evening of a strong picked detachment of the flotilla brought to a close this memorable day which has been celebrated by the erection of a monument.

The day of his departure, August 26th, was signalized by a fresh success of the flotilla, which the Emperor, aided by Bruix, obtained against the enemy's squadron, a vessel of which was sunk, and which was on the point of being boarded. Under our fire it drew back within half range, in sight of Napoleon, who was himself in command and most dangerously exposed to the English broadside. The Emperor's first victorious attempt brought to a conclusion this martial journey which had caused the whole of England to shudder with terror. Having exhausted her money and her resources, she had been so much alarmed that every man, including her ministers, had volunteered and was bearing arms; and even before London itself, the passage of the Thames had been barred. At that time Pitt once more cherished the hope of buying a new coalition, and his lucky star ordained that just then Latouche-Tréville should die of an illness which he had contracted in the Antilles. He was the best of our admirals; he alone was in the secret of the whole enterprise; in conjunction with the fleet at Toulon he was to have hoodwinked Nelson, raised the blockade of our ocean ports, rallied our squadrons there, and protected our descent which had to be put off to a later date, and whose fate, by an unhappy choice of the minister Decrès, was entrusted to the incapable hands of Villeneuve.

It would seem, however, as if the Emperor's mind were halting between several diversions, one of these, which he afterwards gave up to concentrate all his strength in the Straits, was a plan of landing in Ireland.

From Boulogne Napoleon proceeded to Aix-la-Chapelle, where Josephine was awaiting him. There the two Cobentzels, one of whom was a minister, and the other the Viennese Ambassador,

were obliged by threats to cause their master at last to acknowledge
the Emperor. Aix-la-Chapelle had been the town of Charlemagne.
He revived the annual celebration of the honours which had
been formerly paid to the memory of this great ruler, and for
the first time for a thousand years, the delighted people thought
that in Napoleon their hero was reincarnated. The remembrance
will doubtless always endure of the thousand benefits which he
heaped upon these hitherto neglected countries, and of all the
advantages which he bestowed upon their towns, opening up new
communications between them by land and by sea, and further
on, towards Coblentz, constructing the road along the bank of
the Rhine, 45 feet in width, which was cut out of the rock for the
space of ten leagues.

We may add to all this his solicitude for the poor; the asylums
which he secured for them in a country eaten up by mendicity,
and the touching remembrance of the peaceful retreat on an island
of the Rhine which he granted to the unfortunate religious whose
convents had been suppressed.

We may also cite in proof of that tender-heartedness which his
blinded enemies would never recognise in Napoleon, an instance
of his beneficent goodness which took place on another island
on this stream; it will recall that of the St. Bernard in 1800. This
time a poor widow was the object of it. He had been touched
by the sad sight of this woman's poverty and by her grief at the
enlistment of her only son. Without revealing his identity, he had
gained her confidence. 'Console yourself,' he said, mentioning a
fictitious name, 'come to my house to-morrow and ask for me;
I have some influence with the ministers and will recommend
your cause.' Thus reassured and encouraged, the poor woman took
heart and ventured to present herself the next day. She was at once
received, and when, in the midst of her wonder at the imperial
luxury around her, she recognised the Emperor in the charita-
ble unknown of the previous evening, her confusion was at first
extreme; it was speedily, however, succeeded by boundless joy on
hearing the order given that her house which had been destroyed
by the war should be rebuilt, that a small flock of sheep and a few

acres of ground should be added to it, and that her only son then serving under our banners should be restored to her.

A few days later, the name of Guttenburg received flattering recognition in Mayence which had been at the same time fortified and improved. I happened to be there at the time, for Napoleon who was much more considerate for those around him than was generally supposed, knowing that I was in great trouble in Paris, had paternally called me to Mayence by way of diverting my mind. It was there, in the midst of a numerous assemblage of German princes, that we heard the young Hereditary Duke of Baden, when questioned by Napoleon at a levee as to what he had been doing the previous evening, answer with some hesitation that he had been walking about the streets; on which the Emperor reproved him in this wise: 'That was very foolish of you. You should have gone round the fortifications and examined them carefully. How do you know but what you may be one day attacking the place yourself? For instance when I was a young artillery officer walking about Toulon, how could I have foreseen that one day it would be my fate to retake that town?'

During his stay there the Emperor had temporarily entrusted me to look after the Empress whom he had been obliged to leave behind. She related to me that at Aix-la-Chapelle she had been shown a piece of our Saviour's cross which Charlemagne had long carried about with him as a talisman, adding that almost a whole arm of the hero remained in good preservation and had been offered to her, but that she only accepted a splinter of bone which she showed me, saying: 'That she would not deprive Aix of such a precious relic, more especially as she had the support of an arm belonging to one almost as great as Charlemagne.'

It had been through no fault of the English Government of the day that the course of his journey had not been interrupted by the carrying-out of a fresh crime on the part of its minister to the court of Hesse. Two assassins in the pay of this diplomatist had been discovered in Mayence by Bonaparte and their correspondence seized. Rumbolt, another English agent who had been taken away from Hamburg with the proofs of a similar attempt, was incarcerated in the Temple and then released on the complaint of Prussia. These were the last dying embers of the great conspiracy of Pichegru and Georges Cadoudal. The publicity given to these infernal machinations and the severity with which they were suppressed put an end to it.

The accumulation of so many criminal attempts will explain why the Pope during that very year consented to consecrate the new Emperor. These infamies were no excuse for the murder which they provoked; but the indignation caused by them may have had a share in the motives which induced the Holy Father to decide on this solemn act.

XII

THE CONSECRATION

EVERYTHING IN THIS SOLEMN FUNCTION, its perfect order, the serene skies, the full concurrence of the Holy Father, the public acclamations outside as well as inside Nôtre Dame, combined to gratify Napoleon's expectations to the full. I can answer for this, I was a witness of it; I was in command that day in the cathedral, I had taken military possession of it from the previous evening; this was a matter of right and custom, and the safety of the Emperor demanded it. The imperial insignia had been entrusted to me and amongst them the sword of Charlemagne. I even remember that during the night which we passed standing in the church, one of the officers under me who had the charge of this sword, was foolish enough to draw it against one of his comrades, who having vainly parried with his own sabre, congratulated himself on having been overcome and slightly wounded by the sword of so great a man.

The Pope had desired that the Emperor should communicate publicly on the day of the consecration, and Napoleon had taken counsel on the point; my father raising the objection that previous confession would be necessary, that he might not care to accede to this, and that there was also the chance of absolution being refused to him.

'That is not the difficulty,' replied Napoleon; 'the 'Holy Father can distinguish between the sins of Caesar and those of the man.' Then continuing: 'I know,' he said, 'that I should give the example of respect for religion and for its ministers: wherefore you see me treat the priests with consideration, go regularly to mass, and assist at it with a solemn and devotional demeanour. But men know me for what I am; and with me as with others if I were to go further—what think you? would it not be giving at the same time an example of hypocrisy and committing a sacrilege?' The case thus set forth was a foregone conclusion; my father was obliged to confess this, and the Pope also.

This family souvenir recalls another; it is that on the very day this conversation took place, I was put under arrest by the Emperor. I had been obliged to refuse the indiscreet request of a person, politically only too well known, for extra seats in Nôtre Dame. This individual came to my father's house to complain to him, personally in very unmeasured terms. I was present, and although he had been better received than he deserved, I heard him, when he was leaving, make use of threatening language. It should be said that this enraged ex-Jacobin was reputed to have caused the imprisonment of my grandfather, the Marshal de Ségur, and of having singled him out for the scaffold, the 9th Thermidor alone having saved him from the ferocity of this wretch. With this cruel memory revived by the impudent presence of this Montagnard amongst us, my anger may be imagined, and there was certainly every excuse for it. He even experienced the effects of it on the way from the drawing-room to the street door, and that perhaps ought to have been enough; but with vengeance in my heart I went further; I desired at once to bring the matter to an issue, and as he alleged the darkness of the night, I forced him to agree to a meeting for the next day.

During this interchange of blows my father, much taken up with the approaching consecration, had returned to the Emperor, who noticing that he appeared anxious, asked him the reason of it. Having been informed on the point he forbade this duel and ordered me to remain indoors, and an hour afterwards, the ex-

Terrorist, battered as he was, came back by his orders to close the incident by making my father a humble apology.

To return to a less personal subject. The then entirely respectful and affectionate regard of Napoleon for the Holy Father has been denied, but such aspersions were calumnious as I should and do affirm. From the moment of the arrival of this pontiff, in every way worthy of universal veneration, up to his return to Italy, it was I who had the charge of looking after him and his guard. He was occupying at the Tuileries by the side of the Emperor that wing of the palace which looked out on the Pont-Royal and over the Seine. Nothing was spared to please the members of his suite, who had been rather curiously selected, and their somewhat remarkable tastes. The same care and respect was shown His Holiness as to the Emperor himself. In the furnishing and arrangement of his rooms, everything had been done to try and remind him as much as possible of Rome, and in the style to which he was accustomed.

As for Napoleon, we all remarked his sweet and grateful cheerfulness, and the filial and caressing deference which he showed to his guest. It is known that he fully satisfied the spiritual and temporal demands of the Pontiff either by certain concessions, or by such convincing and well-turned explanations that it would have been impossible not to accept them.

When the Holy Father used to bestow his blessing from his window, and especially during the frequent audiences which he gave in the gallery of the Louvre to a numerous public attracted by his presence there, an active supervision held in check or repressed French indiscretion and lightness. We saw the atheist Lalande himself fall at the feet of the Pontiff and kiss his slipper. The Pope was received as a sovereign in all the public places he honoured with his presence; he was not allowed to distinguish between mere curiosity or piety, and I have often seen this really holy successor of the apostles, whose venerable countenance bore the imprint of the most peaceful benevolence, frugal, simple and austere as he was for himself, and so amiably and paternally indulgent to others, profoundly moved by the lively and pious impression which he produced.

The Pope remained four months in Paris, after the consecration, and then departed on April 4th, 1805. I was ordered to reconduct him as far as Voghère, the last town to which imperial jurisdiction then extended. The French Cardinal de Bayanne, during this journey, used to enliven all our meals by his witticisms. It was at table above all that his Italian colleagues consoled themselves for being still in France. He, dainty rather than gluttonous, used to show the most amusing distaste for everything that was not exquisitely delicious. 'Leave that, eat this,' he used to say to me, 'and believe me, an old priest is always the best judge of what is good.'

The conversation turning upon war, the cardinal gave an account of an awful wound which had been miraculously and radically cured. A general who was present took advantage of the opportunity to speak of an equally serious wound which he had received in Egypt, and which still troubled him: 'Oh!' retorted the cardinal, 'that is because your bullet was Turkish, an infidel bullet; whilst the one I am telling you about was Christian and apostolic, that is very different. It only just missed being Roman!'

That day Marquis Sachetti chose to introduce the confessor of the Holy Father to us as a saint who had obtained a miracle from the Holy Virgin. But the Pope smiled as he listened to him, to which the Cardinal de Bayanne drew our attention; leading us to have more faith in the Pope's smile than in the hearty and sincere testimony of the major domo.

We were then at Châlons where the Holy Father was received beyond our every expectation. Macon was cold. Since the terrible siege of Lyons in 1793, the Montagnards, who had taken refuge there, had left their evil spirit behind them. Quite recently, when it had been attempted to re-establish the barriers, the bust of the Emperor and the barriers themselves were all thrown pell-mell into the Seine.

Lyons on the contrary, pious and imperial, received us with open arms and hearts. When on the day after our arrival, the Holy Father allowed the people in the Cathedral to come and kiss his slipper and receive his blessing, the crowd was so considerable and their eagerness so excessive, the last comers pushing up against the earlier ones to such a degree, that he was nearly crushed up against the altar and at one moment really seemed to be in some danger. Fortunately I had ordered a battalion of Hanoverians to be placed at my disposition, who, good honest Germans as they were, implicitly following orders, had no hesitation in answering to my call. It was high time. An absolute charge was necessary to rescue the Pope, who had been at first moved, and then seriously alarmed by the extreme ardour of his devotees. The need of repulsing the crowd was absolute, but was not effected without many cries of distress, followed by fainting fits and even by childbirth, so it was said; several men and women having been carried out more dead than alive. I had no cause to blame myself, for had I not had recourse to extreme measures, the Holy Father, whose glance had implored help, would certainly not have left the church alive.

To leave nothing untold, I may as well add that I had preceded his arrival in this former city by a few hours. Cardinal Fesch was its first pastor, an excellent priest as to generosity, and it was his rough and unskilled negotiations, seconded by the solicitations of Bishop Bernier and Caprara, which had decided the Pope to undertake this great expedition. The sojourn of His Holiness at Lyons was to be its last remarkable episode. This sojourn necessitated a certain amount of expense; and whether from a spirit of mischief, or economy, on the part of the Emperor who looked into everything, he had planned that his uncle, the Cardinal, should bear all expenses, and that I should arrange it with His Excellency. But at the first word of this unpalatable proposal, the Cardinal's indignation was so great that, half choked with rage, he could only reply by inarticulate cries. I persisted, less from any hope of succeeding, than because I felt quite disposed to prolong a scene whose comic side caused me much amusement. But as the Cardinal's anger was making him grow redder than his hat, I thought it prudent to take my departure, and seek other ways and means of providing funds for the reception of the Holy Father.

It was here, I think, if not at Turin, that the Emperor on his way to be crowned at Milan, and the Pope on his return to Rome, met once more, and took leave of each other. The farewells of these two great Powers, temporally and spiritually the greatest then existing in the world, were touching. Each perfectly satisfied with the other, could no more than ourselves foresee how different would be their second interview, eight years later, at Fontainebleau.

XIII

PREPARATIONS AGAINST ENGLAND

NAPOLEON HAVING BEEN CROWNED KING of Italy, took two days and a half to return from Turin to St. Cloud, and at once apparently busied himself solely with home affairs, being desirous of prolonging by a few hours the feeling of security which reigned in England; but when the time had come and his last orders had been given, he hastened to Boulogne on August 3rd. There, as on the high seas, all had been propitious. The uniformly victorious Verhuel had joined the flotilla lying between Ostend and Ambleteuse. Exposed to the attacks of Sir Sydney Smith, he had had to double two capes, and in this perilous journey, without any losses on his side, he had destroyed three of the enemy's corvettes. Other manœuvres from Texel to Brest were attempted, and Napoleon by these means assured himself as to the embarkation in a few hours of 10,000 horses and 160,000 men.

Never was seen in any army such glowing ardour as in ours. Officers and men were alike buoyed up with the expectancy of conquering and pursuing the English, even into London itself. On our arrival in Boulogne on August 2nd, when Rapp and I informed Soult that the Emperor was to arrive the next day, and that soon after the invasion would be attempted, the marshal in a transport of delight clapped both hands to his head, and bounded from one end of the room to the other. The Emperor was still more impatient. The moment he alighted from his carriage the next day, he announced that instead of twenty-four hours as he had said the previous year, only four hours would be allowed for the embarkation of the troops. Everything was immediately put on board and they were to hold themselves in readiness for the first signal.

However, in his anxiety concerning the arrival of Villeneuve, he said the next day: 'This invasion is by no means a certainty. After Campo-Formio I would have asked the Directorate for 26 millions of money, 36 vessels, and 36,000 men, and the conquest of England would have been a certainty; I should not have hesitated a moment. But it is quite another thing now, I cannot risk matters in that way; I have become too important a person!' Then in a more sanguine mood, he added: 'The knell of England has sounded, we have to avenge the defeats of Poitiers, of Cressy and of Agincourt. For five hundred years the English have been paramount even in Paris itself. The English are masters of the universe. We can in a night put them back into their places. They conquered France under an idiot king; we shall conquer England under a demented one!'

According to his usual custom, Napoleon was aiming straight at the heart; all was to be over in a fortnight. The shores of Kent and of Sussex were the goal of the flotilla whence the army should spring upon London; whilst the expedition of the Texel, with the same end in view should have sailed up the Thames.

Everything really concurred to warrant these high expectations. On our shores, in our ports, and in our roadsteads, all was in readiness; and as the Emperor said himself: 'The nature of his plan was so good that in spite of all kinds of obstacles every chance was in his favour.' But to our eternal regret, so unique an occasion never again to be met with, such a formidable host, such an enormous outlay backed up by every effort and care, the most vast and best combined plan ever conceived by the genius of our Emperor, in short, the fate of France was to be jeopardized by one man!

To govern, it is said, is to choose; and the choice of the minister Decrès was a very bad one. Villeneuve, who was modest and disinterested, was also timid and irresolute. The courage of the soldier sank under the sense of the overpowering responsibility of the general. More crushed than honoured by the Emperor's choice, he would indeed have prepared to relinquish the post. With the candour which distinguished him, Villeneuve exclaimed: 'That it was too much; that he could see his way to command a squadron, but not so considerable a fleet.' Like all minds so unfortunately constituted, he only looked at things from the dark side, imagining that the very thing he had decided not to do, was always better than the course he had taken, and always thinking the enemy all powerful. Decrès had paid no heed to this; he had not understood his character. Villeneuve was the friend of his childhood, and the minister persisted in believing in the temporary and factitious ardour of his early impulses. Thus the fate of England, and of France, of our sailors and our Emperor, depended on a chief who had not any greater trust in others than he had in himself.

Early in June after receiving the first dispatch of this admiral, Napoleon, with his eagle glance, had perceived the minister's mistake and tried to bring about his recall. His instructions from Milan were as follows: 'I consider that Villeneuve has not sufficient force of character; that he has had no experience of war; and as soon as he returns to Brest, Gantheaume must be sent to replace him.' He concluded by saying that he would sign and despatch the order on the spot. I am ignorant if Gantheaume did possess more strength of character, but it was impossible to put the order into execution, and our fate remained in the hands of Villeneuve.

As long as it was only a question of avoiding Nelson, the admiral conformed to the spirit of his instructions. But in spite of excellent seamanship, whether wearied out by his continual fears, or by some days of contrary weather, when he appeared on July 22nd with twenty of his vessels off Cape Finisterre, and at mid-day met Calder and fifteen English vessels, he lost two whole hours hesitating what to do. At last they engaged in combat. Calder presented a close front, while Villeneuve was too scattered; the result being that a thick fog having spread over the two fleets and rendered signals useless, two Spanish vessels which had become dismasted after a blind and violent struggle were left without succour. Help could have been afforded them, for the fog having lifted, it could be seen that they were in danger; but our admiral refused to come to their aid, and they were taken, having been forced by the wind into the very midst of the English fleet.

Calder, however, who had suffered more than ourselves, withdrew on the following day, and Villeneuve remained master of his movements; but with his usual indecision, he missed his opportunity, tried to seize it again when too late, and allowed his adversary to escape, went on to Vigo, thence to Corogne to refresh and lighten his fleet, and unite it with that of Ferrol.

I have it from Lauriston, afterwards a marshal and peer of France, then aide-de-camp to Napoleon, who was on Villeneuve's fleet, that the day after this battle, Rear-admiral Magon was a prey to such violent indignation when the first signal was given by the admiral to let the English fleet go, that he stamped and foamed at the mouth; and that whilst he was furiously pacing his own ship, as that of the admiral passed by in its retreat, he gave vent to furious exclamations and flung at him in his rage whatever happened to be to hand, including his field-glass and even his wig, both of which fell into the sea, but Villeneuve was not only too far off for these missiles to reach him, but was entirely out of hearing.

From my own knowledge of Magon, with whom I had been brought into relation in various missions, I believe with Lauriston, that had he been in Villeneuve's place, the orders of the Emperor would have been obeyed, the invasion probably effected, and the face of the world altered; but where too many secondary interests have, to be considered, such characters give too much ground for jealousy: they are made use of in subordinate positions. Thus, he who would have suited Napoleon, from that very fact was distasteful to his minister.

The unfortunate Villeneuve remained three weeks in Vigo and Corogne to revictual and refit his fleet. He really could not rouse himself owing to his extreme dejection through this reverse which might have been avoided. The reproaches which came to his ears, as well as those which he heaped upon himself (for he was his own worst enemy), threw him into the most deplorable state of dejection. He left this anchorage about August 12th, when he had 34 vessels, counting those of Lallemande. Left master of the sea he could perfectly well have obeyed the express commands of the Emperor, and those of his minister who had repeatedly instructed him, with his 34 sail against only 18 of Cornwallis, at all hazards to raise the blockade at Brest of 21 vessels; and thus with a strength of fifty-five sail to take possession of the Channel where our army was embarked, where Napoleon was awaiting him, and where he could have ensured our landing. But he was haunted by the spectre of Nelson! His fright gave him courage to disobey. After a state of hesitation which lasted for four days on the open seas, Villeneuve, who was personally brave as a man, though cowed by his responsibilities as a commander, took fright at a slight gale which on that day unfortunately was blowing up from the north east. If it had happened to blow from the south, as was told me by another witness[4] he would probably have taken advantage of it, and would not thus have failed to fulfil the expectations of the Emperor and of our army, and might have made the fortune of the empire.

With this fatal irresolution of Villeneuve, a slight incident, a breath of wind swayed the balance. On so little hinges the fate of the world—on a mere breath of wind, not even a storm. It pleased fate to overthrow by this faint breath the entire work of Napoleon, and the grandest hope ever conceived by France. So little weight have the greatest of men, their largest conceptions and the most powerful empires, in the scales of fortune!

On August 21st, at the very moment when the advent of this unhappy Villeneuve was more than ever hoped for and expected before Brest and in the Channel, the admiral was turning his back upon us. He was entering into Cadiz where he allowed himself to be blocked up by six of the enemy's sail, thus, rendering completely useless his fleet, our flotilla, the Emperor himself, and the whole expedition, which was vainly expecting him at Brest, at Boulogne, and at the Texel.

Thus it was that England was saved! Let it not again be said that the diversion which Pitt had prepared on the continent could possibly have kept our Emperor there. This danger had been foreseen and guarded against. Our forces were already assembling beyond the Rhine, on this river and in Italy: they held Austria in check. Duroc had been immediately despatched to Frederic to give up Hanover to him in exchange for an offensive alliance which for the second time he seemed ready to accept. Besides which, the treaty of London with Russia only dated from April 11th. The idea of a war in her territory was distasteful to Germany; Bavaria was devoted to us; Vienna in spite of threatening preparations, hesitated. Her formal accession to a third coalition could only have been obtained on August 11th, and she had not dared to avow it. On September 3rd she still appeared as a mediatrix; and at that very time the fate of London might have been settled a fortnight previously. Had that been the case, this capital, the very brain and centre of all coalitions, being taken, and Pitt in all probability forced to capitulate, Napoleon would have imperiously dictated to Austria the conditions which would have suited his policy.

XIV

THE PLAN OF THE CAMPAIGN OF AUSTERLITZ

WHILST VILLENEUVE AT CAROGNE AND in Cadiz was thus disappointing our cherished hopes, at Boulogne everything had been organized and completed. Reviews, manœuvres, embarkations and disembarkations, a thousand eager and anxious glances incessantly fixed on the sea, a thousand conjectures addressed by day and night to his minister, had occupied Napoleon in the midst of the extreme agitation of his weary waiting. With his mind thus on the stretch, he had in his impatience made Lacrosse, with seventy-five of the flotilla, attack the English cruising-station, and victory had remained with them. On that day half the channel belonged to us during some hours; England thought she was on the point of being invaded; in her distress Calder was put on his trial, but on receiving the news of Villeneuve's inconceivable inaction and of his flight to Cadiz, she was triumphant, and her joyful outcry reached the ears of Napoleon who was kept better informed by our spies and the English press than by his own messengers and the telegraph wires. His displeasure was first manifest on August 7th at the news of the battle of Finisterre, and his disappointment on the following days on hearing that Villeneuve had entered Ferrol, believing him to be blocked there. At this first

instance of disobedience to his orders, although the mischief at
that time was not irreparable, the Emperor, who knew better than
anyone the value of time, perceived that his admiral was by no
means aware of its importance, that he had not understood the
vastness of his mission, and that in this great drama, which had up
to then so satisfactorily unfolded itself, Villeneuve, not being equal
to his part, would fail them at the most important crisis.

It was about four o'clock in the morning of August 13th that
the news was brought to the Emperor at the imperial quarters
at Pont-de-Briques. Daru was summoned, and on entering he
gazed on his chief in utter astonishment. He told me afterwards
that he looked perfectly wild, that his hat was thrust down to his
eyes, and his whole aspect was terrible. As soon as he saw Daru,
he rushed up and thus apostrophized him: 'Do you know where
that—fool of a Villeneuve is now? He is at Ferrol. Do you know
what that means—at Ferrol? Ah, you do not know? He has been
beaten; he has gone to hide himself at 'Ferrol. That is the end of
it, he will be blocked up there. What a navy! What an admiral!
What useless sacrifices!'

And becoming more and more excited, he walked up and down
the room with great strides for about an hour, giving vent to his
justifiable anger in a torrent of bitter reproaches and sorrowful
reflections. Then stopping suddenly and pointing to a desk which
was covered with papers: 'Sit down there,' he said to Daru. 'Write!'
and then and there, without any transition, without any apparent
meditation, and in his brief, concise, and imperious tones, he
dictated to him without a moment's hesitation the whole plan
of the campaign of Ulm as far as Vienna. The army of the coast,
ranged in a line of more than two hundred leagues long, fronting
the Ocean, were, at the first signal, to face about, to break up,
and march to the Danube in several columns. The order of the
various marches, their durations; the spots where the columns
should converge or re-unite; surprises; attacks in full force; divers
movements; mistakes of the enemy; all had been foreseen during
this hurried dictation. Two months, three hundred leagues, and
more than two hundred thousand of the enemy separated thought

from results, and yet, time and space and various obstacles were all overcome, and the whole future illumined by the genius of our Emperor. His foresight which was as much to be depended upon as his memory, could already predict, starting from Boulogne, the principal events of this projected war, their dates and their decisive results; and he dictated these to Darn with such certainty that a month after they had been fulfilled, he was able to remember them. The various fields of battle, the victories to be gained, even the very days in which we were to enter Munich and Vienna, all was foreseen and written down as it really happened later, two months in advance, at this identical hour of August 13th, and from these head quarters on the coast!

Although accustomed to the sudden inspirations of his chief, Daru was perfectly amazed, and still more so when he found that these oracular predictions came true on the very days named up to the time of our arrival in Munich. If there were some little variations as to time, though not as to results, between Munich and Vienna, they were to our advantage. Long afterwards and frequently did this minister, still under the same spell of astonishment, tell me over and over again, that he had not less admired the clear and prompt determination of Napoleon to give up such enormous preparations without hesitation, than the correctness of his previsions when he suddenly changed all his plans to concentrate them against other adversaries.

These dictated directions to Daru remained unknown. A new hope had taken possession of the Emperor. His spirited and last instructions on August 11th, 13th, and 22nd prove this. They were: 'That it would be too ridiculous that a skirmish of three hours should cause such vast projects to fail; that one should on the contrary persist in them. Gravina is all energy and force of character. Why does not Villeneuve resemble him? Why should Villeneuve, at the head of so many brave sailors, let everything go to destruction through sloth and despondency, when the English, threatened on every side, are altogether wearied out and dispersed? Will eighteen vessels allow themselves to be blocked up by fourteen!'

On August 22nd he again vainly wrote to Villeneuve and to Gantheaume: 'Make a start! come into the Channel, and England is ours, and six centuries of shame and insult will be avenged!' On the following days, in spite of more and more alarming accounts from Austria of the flight of Villeneuve and the discouragement of Decrès, he had not yet given up hopes of taking England, but towards the, end of August, when the irreparable defection of his admiral was at last only too certain, at table one day, he dashed down the glass which he was holding and exclaimed: 'Well if we must give that up, we will at any rate hear the midnight mass in Vienna.'

Having secretly arranged everything since the 23rd, for this sudden return to the Danube, and on the 26th for a fresh levy of 60,000 men, he cast a last glance of regret and sorrow towards England; giving vent to his anger by dictating seven heads of accusation which should annihilate the culpable Villeneuve. Still master of everything, even of himself, he recovered his equanimity; and, in a memorandum free from any bitterness, he set forth the grandeur of the plan which he was constrained to abandon; resuming all its details as if to preserve or record its conception, justify its possibility, and prove how nearly he had been on the point of succeeding. He pointed out, how with certain modifications it might some day be resumed, and in the meanwhile what ought to be done with the flotilla.

In subsequent instructions he ordered that Rossilly should replace Villeneuve at Cadiz and that with a strength of forty sail, he should dominate the Mediterranean. We shall see later that disaster resulted from the execution of this order by Villeneuve himself. For the fatal battle of Trafalgar was the outcome of this, and if Nelson perished in it, so also did our navy. We no longer had a fleet, we had only a few squadrons. Then began the fortunate cruise of Lallemand whom Villeneuve had abandoned in the sea of Ferrol, thus increasing his own despair by making Lallemand famous.

As for the other squadrons, one of them was to be sent into American waters. A vague prescience of the future would seem for the second time specially to have fixed Napoleon's thoughts on St. Helena. He ordered that it should be taken possession of and several times reiterated this command. The importance which he at that time attached to the possession of this rock, in the light of subsequent events, became remarkable.

At last on September 1st Napoleon left Boulogne, and six days later began the counter-march of the great Imperial army. The coasts were deserted and given up to our navy. Thus miscarried the greatest and most important, the most skilfully conceived and laboriously prepared design that ever emanated from the grand mind of the Emperor.

XV

THE GRAND ARMY ENTERS GERMANY

I N ORDER TO ACCELERATE THE progress of his army on the march, the Emperor conceived the idea of conveying them by post-stages. Having sent for the Mayor of Lille, he said to him: 'Go now, receive and congratulate my divisions on their way through, and organize means of conveyance to facilitate their march. You may expect 25,000 men, for whom waggons must be ready: you will thus initiate this movement and set the first great and useful example!' This magistrate having declared that it went very much against him to welcome General V—— whose Jacobinism he commented upon: 'Do not dare to say anything of the kind, he exclaimed; do you not see that now we are all equally serving France? I would have you know, Sir, that between the 17th and the 18th Brumaire I have erected a wall of brass which no glance may penetrate, and against which all recollections must be dashed to pieces!'

On the day that had been settled, and at the hour that had been decided upon, all the marshals having reached their destination, amongst them Bernadotte (the only one who by speaking out relieved himself of the annoyance that obedience always caused him), I received the order to be at the Luxembourg on September 23rd, where, with a detachment of the Imperial Guard, I was to take over the command of this Palace of the Senate so as to receive Napoleon, who came there at once to declare the war. My father and Regnauld de Saint-Jean d'Angely, both councillors of State, were the bearers of the projects of *senatus-consultus* for the new levies of 80,000 men and of the national guard. Napoleon wound up with these words: 'Frenchmen, your Emperor will do his duty, my soldiers will do theirs, you will do yours!' After which he returned to St. Cloud whilst I departed for Strasburg, preceding him only by twenty-four hours.

He arrived there with the Empress on September 26th. Whilst listening to the reports of the position of the enemy he roused the enthusiasm of his people by an eloquent proclamation; he also collected 20,000 Alsatian waggons and caused them to be loaded with stores, and whilst from the first moment he was pushing forward all the various bodies of his army, he was reassuring Germany by a notification that there would be no encroachment of France beyond the Rhine, and ended by enlisting in his cause the greater part of the reigning princes on the right bank of this river.

Placed between two fires, they had not yet quite made up their minds. The Elector of Bavaria, who had retired to Wurtzburg with his army, and who was pressed in contrary directions, on the one side by Bernadotte, and the other by an Austrian minister, hesitated to declare himself on the offensive. As soon as Napoleon saw in the distance the officer whom he was sending to him, he cried out: 'What news do you bring me at last? is it for us or against us?'—'For us,' answered Lagrange. 'That is better!' responded the Emperor, who could not, however, have had any doubts in the matter.

General Mouton, afterwards Count de Lobau, was despatched to the Elector of Wurtemburg through whose States we had to make our way. Ney, at the same time was marching upon the capital of this Electorate; he had even forced open the gates, when an aide-de-camp of Napoleon arrived at our minister's. 'Your mission is a difficult one,' said the latter, 'the Elector is raving, and what is very rare, he is at the same time irascible and firm; he will make a fine noise about it!' 'Not so much as a cannon,' answered the aide-de-camp, 'and I am accustomed to that.' He then had himself presented to the prince, who having been prepared for his coming received him in the midst of his Council.

The minister had predicted rightly; the scene was a violent one. The Elector broke in at the very beginning, scarlet with rage: 'What you do you want?' he exclaimed; 'your troops are invading my States, they are violating my neutrality, it is a piece of treachery! What business has your Bonaparte here? Shall a prince of yesterday, a parvenu sovereign, offer violence to me? to me, a prince of old time and of the race of princes! But I am master here. I shall soon prove it, I will send off these brigands.' But the aide-de-camp, who was standing, preserved the impassible immobility of his martial countenance and remained motionless. He allowed the torrent of invective to break against his imperturbable composure. When the prince, who was out of breath with rage, and who through his extreme obesity had exhausted all his energy, was obliged to stop to take breath, the general answered coldly: 'That he had not come to listen to personalities, nor to reply to them, but to treat; and that all these wild words made no impression on him and were quite futile, as he should not even repeat them to the Emperor; that he had much better listen to his propositions, all the more so because Marshal Ney, with 30,000 men, was at the gates of his capital!' The Elector was still fuming, but the contrast of this firm composure with his own unmeasured rage surprised himself. He felt that he had found his master, and realized that the blood of such men was as good as his own. Then changing his tone, he discussed the matter, and in an aside he let fall: 'That such and such neighbouring possessions were in his way, that if he had them and his electorate was made a kingdom, matters might still be arranged.'

When the aide-de-camp, from whom I heard all this, reported the result to Napoleon, the latter began to laugh, saying: 'Well, that suits me very well; let him be a king, if that is all he wants!'

All the bodies of our army on September 25th, fronting the east, were bordering the Rhine from Strasburg to Mayence; that of Bernadotte would soon arrive at Wurtzburg, where the Bavarian

army was awaiting it. Not a conscript was wanting: all were con-
sumed with eagerness; the signal was given! The marches of each
chief were predetermined; the days and the hours calculated
according to the diversity of arms, of distances, of the difficulties
of the ground and its various irregularities. These instructions,
of such infinite detail, had been traced out by so firm and sure a
hand, that all these masses of men, arms, horses and artillery, store
and baggage waggons were ready to be set in motion, and would
simultaneously reach the goal indicated with the most unheard-of
quickness and in the most admirable order. On September 26th
each body of the army was to cross the Rhine; and by a wheel to
the right, the left wing being in advance by Wurtzburg, the whole
army, executing the greatest change of front ever known, would
on October 6th suddenly find itself in line, facing the south, from
Ulm up to Ingolstadt on the Danube, the imperial stream being
at once crossed at Ingolstadt, Neuburg and Donawerth, then at
Gaulhburg. Suabia and Bavaria, Munich and Augsburg would
be simultaneously reconquered, and Mack and the Archduke
Ferdinand, being separated from the Russians and Austria, would
be forced to let themselves be killed on the spot, or give themselves
up prisoners.

This plan is the prophetic account of the campaign. It will suffice for the future, when, owing to the accumulation of centuries,
history will be forced to shorten all details, to allow of time to read
it. This is the same manœuvre as that of Marengo, but at closer
quarters and much bolder; sure, instead of being rash; without the
Alps to cross or recross, with an army three times the strength of
Mack's instead of an army weaker by half than that of Mélas, and
against a very different general.

Notwithstanding this, on September 26th, the day of Napoleon's
arrival, as important and complete a result still depended upon the
blindness and inaction of the Austrian army in its venturesome
position, which was neither offensive nor defensive, with its front
towards the Black Forest, its advance-guards thrown out into the
defiles of these mountains, and only looking straight ahead. It was
requisite to concentrate and fix its attention there, and divert it

from the great movement which was in readiness to turn its right. That is why on the eve of the Emperor's arrival, September 25th and that of this general movement, Murat with his cavalry and Lanne's grenadiers, passed the Rhine at Strasburg. There, contrary to the rest of the army, they turned to the right, again proceeded up the right bank of the stream towards Friburg, filling the valley with tumult, and displaying the advance-guards of their menacing columns at every opening of the Black Mountains.

But on the morrow, whilst Mack, believing himself attacked on his front, was concentrating all his means of defence on that point, the grand army, crossing the Rhine from Strasburg to Mayence, was hastening onwards to surround him; and Napoleon, at the pivot of this manœvre, was completing his negotiations at Strasburg, having misled the enemy by his sojourn there, and having waited there till October 1st, till the movement of his marching wing was accomplished.

From Murat's reports that day, he believed that his previsions were realized, that Mack had been deceived by his first strata-gem, and that success was indubitable. And here is the proof: I had just received orders to precede him, first at Ettlingen, then at Ludwigsburg and at the Elector of Wurtemburg's, when the Empress said, on taking leave of me: 'Depart, and carry with you my best wishes. May you be as fortunate as the army and France.' Noticing my astonishment at such a positive assertion, she continued: 'Do not doubt it for a moment; the Emperor has just informed me that in eight days the whole of the enemy's army will infallibly be taken prisoner.' This was on October 1st, and on the 8th, Mack was completely turned; and a few days later it had become my lot in Ulm to force him to decide on the very capitulation which had been announced to me by the Empress.

The Elector of Wurtemburg, who had been conciliated, as we have seen, received the Emperor magnificently at Ludwigsburg, when Napoleon completely gained him over to his cause. The Electress herself, though a princess of English blood, was won over by the care which Napoleon took of her private interests, and by the charming manners, recalling those of his early youth, which he displayed to fascinate her. He succeeded so completely that by way of excusing herself, she wrote: 'His smile is positively delightful and enchanting,' in a letter to her mother, the Queen of England.

Napoleon knew that Mack could no longer face him in the Black Mountains; Murat had therefore been called back from their openings on the Rhine, at the same time that Ney was, in his turn, pushed on from Stuttgart to Ulm, around which he took up a position with his left towards the Danube. He thus covered and concealed the rapid march of the other bodies upon Donawerth, Neuburg and Ingolstadt; a second time misleading and detaining upon the Iller the enemy's unfortunate general, whose feeble sight could not pierce through this screen, and who was awaiting Napoleon in Ulm firmly, whilst, outstripping him at Ludwigsburg, the Emperor was marching from October 5th by Gmund and Nordlingen upon Donawerth.

If Mack had any suspicions of this they were very vague; for, like all weak minds, satisfied with half measures, he contented himself by making Kienmayer and 10,000 men keep watch over the Danube and the bridge of Donawerth below him.

Suddenly he learnt that on October 6th this division was overthrown; then he learnt successively; that on the 7th, the Danube was crossed, not only at Donawerth but also at Neuburg and Ingolstadt; that behind him, Suabia and even Bavaria were invaded and the Lech seized: that the next day October 8th, twelve battalions of grenadiers whom he had summoned to his help from the Tyrol, having been encountered by Murat at Vertingen, were either taken, killed, or dispersed, and that Augsburg must have fallen into our hands. On the 9th he was overwhelmed by another blow, the attack directed against the three bridges situated between Ulm and Donawerth; and what was even worse, the news that Ney had just forced the Danube, behind him, by a fourth passage! The bandage over his eyes being thus torn away, Mack fell thunderstruck off his stilts. He recognised that without knowledge of the locality, without any conjecture a to the direction from which our forces had hastened, or as to what he had most to fear, our numbers, and the character of his adversary, he had just allowed 200,000 men to pass by him unrecognised; and that he had not perceived this until, surrounded by them, they were masters of his retreat, and had interposed themselves between him and the Russian army which he was expecting; that they had separated him from Austria which it was his duty to have defended, and had driven him up on Ulm, with his back against the Black Mountains and that very Rhine from which his foolish pride had braved Napoleon and dared to threaten France?

It was supposed that this general adopting a desperate course then faced us in the rear, from Ulm to Meningen; but the facts, which alone testify on his side, and our own impressions of the moment are, that he did not take any course at all, but that from October the 6th to the 11th, five whole days, the unfortunate Field-Marshal remained in a state of stupefaction, crushed under the triple weight of his conscience, fear of the fate which awaited him, and of universal reprobation. In fact, till October 11th, he remained at Ulm in the same state of stagnation in which we had found him when we crossed the Danube, on the 6th. The body which he had opposed to us at Donawerth, under Kienmayer, more fortunate than himself, had taken flight towards Austria; the one he had summoned from the Tyrol was destroyed at Vertigen; that which he had left at Meningen, having neither received orders to rejoin him, nor to take flight to the mountains, retrenched itself isolated in that town. On the other hand his advance-guard, which was resisting Ney on the left bank of the Danube, crippled by the loss of 4000 men at Guntzburg, was on October 9th thrown back upon Ulm, upon which point Mack had also been driven with his 60,000 men. It may be remembered that, in 1800, Aray, having been in the same way turned and broken up by Moreau on both banks of the Danube, turned round upon our right wing at Nordlingen, and, escaping without striking a blow, was able to take up a position again between our army and, Austria; why not imitate him to-day? Mack is near Prince Ferdinand, and is responsible for him; will he allow an Archduke to be taken in Ulm, with himself and his army?

XVI

ULM

HAD MACK WITH HIS 60,000 men passed through Ulm, leaving a detachment there, and thrown himself on the left bank which the Grand Army had quitted, he could have dispersed by way of that bank, demolishing the bridges which he would leave on the right of his passage. During this retreat he might have picked up or destroyed our camp-followers, our great parks of artillery, our baggage, and might possibly have triumphantly returned to Bohemia, where he could have rejoined the Russians.

But the distracted and feeble mind of such a general was not in accord with so sudden and thorough a course, so that instead of coming to a decision, he lost four whole days.

On the night of the 14th to the 15th the Austrian chiefs met at a council where they could not come to an agreement, and Mack was only able to make himself listened to by the help of a power of authority, signed by his Emperor which had hitherto been held in reserve. But this general, who could neither flee nor defend himself, continued to hang on from day to day, the sport of the enemy and of circumstances. Verneck, however, and 12,000 men separated from him, were on the road to Nordlingen; it was only then that the Archduke, escaping by night from Ulm with some thousand horse, hastened to join him. Mack was in hopes that they would thus be able to get as far as Bohemia. As for himself, with the rest of his soldiers, of whose very number he was ignorant, left without provisions or means of retreat in Ulm itself, and on the entrenched heights which look down upon it, he was heard to exclaim: that he should defend himself there and divert attention from the flight of the Archduke; that the Russians would have hastened up within a week, and that Napoleon, in his turn caught between two fires, would be obliged either to flee or surrender. Such was the gist of Mack's speeches, for harassed as he was, words in default of deeds had not yet failed him.

But on the next day, the 15th, attacked on both banks of the river, from the heights which surround Ulm he descended into the town, where, having been in danger of being burnt out on the 16th, he received a flag of truce during the night, and agreed to give himself up on the 25th if the blockade had not been raised by the Russian army. Vainly, and on three different occasions, first this offer of truce, secondly Berthier, and lastly the Emperor himself in an interview with Lichtenstein, allowed Mack six days only, but he held out obstinately for eight. These two days respite, which in no wise really altered his position, seemed to his fevered imagination to be the only means of saving his responsibility, his honour (which was already lost), and even Austria itself. Finally, on the evening of the 1st, he obtained this vain concession. Having signed his capitulation it was to be consummated on the 25th, and up to the next day, the 19th, the unhappy man, apparently consoled, seemed to triumph in this delay which he had obtained, as if it had been a victory.

But on the morning of October 19th, thirty-six hours later, being summoned to the Imperial quarters, he there learnt: that on the 16th, a day out from Ulm, the Archduke had already been attacked by Murat with a loss of 3,000 men, and that a little further on before Neresheim, attacked for the second time on the 17th, the prince had abandoned his main body and taken flight with a few squadrons towards Bohemia; that on October 18th and 19th near Nordlingen, only two good days' march from Ulm, Verneck and the rest of his 20,000 men who had left Ulm eight days earlier, with 600 carriages and guns with which they had been burdened, had laid down their arms; that on the other hand Bernadotte, Davout and the Bavarians, in short 60,000 men were occupying Bavaria where the Russians had not yet shown up. Then, crushed under the weight of so many misfortunes, the unhappy man, losing all hope, also lost the little presence of mind which still remained to him, and his distress was so great that he was on the point of swooning away. Perfectly distracted he gave up every effort, even to the last service which he could have rendered his country by keeping our army before Ulm to the 25th, and, completely subjugated by Napoleon's ascendency, he not only renounced the two days concession which had been so much contested, but agreed on the next day, the 20th of October, to give up Ulm with his arms, his horses, the 33,000 men that were left to him, and the time which was so valuable to his adversary; thus hastening by five days his own loss and that of Austria.

Now that by this summary we have been able to view this important event in its entirety and that I am more at liberty to descant on its details; passing from history to memoirs, I shall proceed from my notes of each evening to reproduce in detail the narrative of these fourteen days of manœuvres, engagements, and of a capitulation which will ever remain famous. Without that, especially as far as concerns us, I should only have presented the outside of things and too little the men themselves.

I have already said that on October 6th the Emperor having outstripped and turned Mack, had slept at Nordlingen. He had already during that evening pushed on to Donawerth in his impatience to see the Danube for the first time, and to assure and hasten the success of his manoeuvre. On October 7th, about one o'clock in the day, having returned to the bank of the Danube, he encouraged the workers to repair the broken bridge; the rain which never ceased during that month, and which caused the first part of this campaign to be so trying, had then just begun; wrapped up in our cloaks, Mortier, Duroc, Caulaincourt, Rapp, and I, surrounded Napoleon, receiving and executing the orders which he kept on multiplying. At one moment I would be despatched to Rain to push on Marshal Soult, and the next to hurry Vandamme's passage beyond the mouth of the Leck. On coming back I always found him stationed in front of this burnt-down bridge of Donawerth, and in his haste to see it reconstructed on both banks, he ordered me to cross the stream too soon. This was the first danger to be braved and the most perilous. A single log of wood which was long and narrow and badly secured, had only just been thrown across from one pile to another. But under the eyes of Bonaparte I sped off with such an impetus, that in spite of the insecurity of this beam which was quivering under my feet, and the hindrance of my cloak which impeded my movements as it flapped in the wind, I reached the middle of the second arch without wavering. Once there, however, the oscillations of the frail and shaky foothold caused me to stagger. I was losing my equilibrium; beneath me the charred and half-burnt joists of the bridge, which had fallen into the stream the night before, were whirling round its foundations with a tumult in which I seemed about to be ingulfed and crushed; neither able to advance nor retreat. I was suspended over this abyss and already swaying towards it, feeling myself a lost man, when an exclamation from Napoleon: 'Good God, he will be killed!' gave me fresh courage; this cry from his heart seemed to strengthen mine, and with a supreme effort I pulled myself together and managed to reach the right bank.

An order which I received the next day, October 8th, is all the more deeply impressed on my memory because ten years later, a hesitation exactly resembling the one of which I was a witness occasioned the loss of the Grand Army and Waterloo, and the destruction of Napoleon himself! The Emperor, who was still at Donawerth, had sent me that day towards Augsburg, bearing an order to Saint Hilaire's division to take prompt possession of that town. I joined him not far from the latter, abreast of Mark a village on the edge of the road. Saint Hilaire, hearing the roar of the guns on his right, had just halted there, uncertain if he should not turn to that side; but acting on the order which I had brought him, he was again setting forward, when one of Murat's officers, hastening from Vertingen came, in the name of that prince who was engaged in the action whose firing we had heard, to summon him to the rescue.

Saint Hilaire, a man full of heart and intelligence, immediately made up his mind. 'You hear,' he said to me, 'I must make as much haste as possible, the cannonading compels me; notwithstanding contrary orders, in such an unforeseen case it is a matter of principle to respond to the call.' And he immediately turned the head of his column to the right, upon Vertingen.

But as generally happens, he had not taken a hundred steps in that direction, than harassed by the responsibility which he was assuming, he asked my opinion. Frankly I knew nothing about it, but at all hazards, thinking it my duty to impress the object of my mission upon him, I insisted on the importance which the Emperor attached to it. The general's anxiety increasing, he stopped short and exclaimed that I was in the right, then turning back his column, he resumed the road to Augsburg. Then came the turn of Murat's envoy, this officer in desperation so vividly describing the prince's peril that Saint Hilaire, much moved, was not able to resist him, and for a second time started off towards Vertingen.

But while on the march, apostrophizing me: 'You are attached to the person of the Emperor,' he said. 'You should know his motives.'—'He did not confide them to me,' I answered, 'but it is evident that we are turning the Austrian army, and Augsburg being on the line of operations or of retreat, it is of the most urgent importance to seize it. As for Prince Murat, he can just as well be supported from Donawerth, which I left full of troops.' This reflection seeming to strike him, he made another halt in his perplexity, and, changing his mind, once more set his column on the road towards the capital of Suabia.

But that cursed west wind which was drenching us with rain, also bore us the sound of the cannonading with greater distinctness, and restored his former scruples. Once more he halted. 'Good God,' he said, 'what a position! The guns are coming nearer, how can I draw back? The Emperor did not know of this battle

when you left Donawerth.' I was obliged to own the truth of
this. 'His own brother-in-law,' 'he exclaimed, 'how can I abandon
him when he is calling upon me, when he is perhaps completely
overwhelmed. It is impossible.' And for the third time the worthy
general turned his column again and dashed across country, abandoning Augsburg for Vertingen.

I was marching on with him, myself in a state of uncertainty,
and had almost given up the idea of persuading him, when the
head of his staff pointed out to me that night was drawing on,
and that we could not possibly arrive on the scene till after the
issue of the conflict was decided. This being to my advantage, I
again returned to the charge, representing to the general that if
he persisted in this direction when it was too late to respond to
the prince's appeal, he would be disobeying the Emperor's order
which could still be executed. This new point of view seemed to
decide Saint Hilaire, who changed his mind for the fourth time,
after having spent two hours in wandering from one direction to
another, finally resuming that of Augsburg. Feeling sure this time
that he would continue on his way, and believing that my mission
was fulfilled, I turned back to give an account of it.

But it was my turn to be in fault: as the bearer of so important
an order which should have been executed at once, I ought to
have remained to see to it. Had I done so, my report would have
been more interesting and useful, and Napoleon would have been
better satisfied. Not that when he saw me, he made any observation about it; he was still standing before Donawerth, dressed
as I had left him the night before, and it was then two hours
after midnight. Out of consideration for Saint Hilaire I did not
descant on his long hesitation, I only mentioned the place and
the hour when I had succeeded in bringing him to a decision.
'All the better,' said the Emperor, 'as the enemy was well beaten at
Vertingen.' Then leading me up to a side table, he added: 'Come,
where did you leave Saint Hilaire? show me on this map.' Having
consulted my own to some purpose, I was able to do this without
hesitation, and I had taken note of the distances on the spot, so
that I could draw conclusions as to the hour when Augsburg must

have been occupied. 'Very well,' said Napoleon, 'now let us go and rest.' He did nothing of the kind himself, as can be proved by his dispatches to his marshals which were dated that very night, and I remember myself that three hours after I had left him, when I was again summoned to him at daybreak on October 9th, I found him on horse back on the right bank of the Danube.

Almost as soon as we were on the march, Duroc said to me: 'Tell me what happened yesterday with Saint Hilaire.' I did so. 'Thus,' he said, 'you really believed and told the Emperor that Augsburg must have been last night in the occupation of that general?'—'Most certainly,' I answered.—'Well,' continued Duroc, 'it is just the contrary. Would you believe that directly you had left him, another spell of hesitation on his part made him return to Vertingen, this time for good. It was past midnight when he arrived on the battle-field, and as you may well imagine, he found neither friends nor foes; so that wanting to be everywhere, he was nowhere, neither where he thought he was going, nor where he was wanted to go. His hesitation caused him to fall into the very disasters which he was trying to avoid, so that he has been worse than useless.'

I was dismayed by this error which had become inexcusable; it would, however, be difficult to say what Saint Hilaire really ought to have done in such an alternative. But henceforth and after the fatal example of Waterloo, what Frenchman in such a case would hesitate to repeat the first words of the general to me: 'I must go at once, the cannonading compels me, and in spite of contrary orders, the case being unforeseen, it is a matter of principle to obey the call'?

That day, October 9th, the Emperor pushed on as far as Vertingen, to examine, according to his custom, the spot where the battle had taken place, to judge of the moves, to review and reward the conquerors, and thus in the glow of success, to fertilize the field of this first victory. His words, especially those addressed to Klein's division, excited them to the highest pitch, not only as a mass but individually. To quote one example amongst others, a non-commissioned officer of dragoons who had been cashiered the night before by his colonel, saved his life the next day at the risk of his own. Napoleon accosted him. 'I was wrong the day before yesterday,' answered the soldier, 'yesterday I only did my duty.' Upon which the Emperor decorated him midst the acclamations of his comrades.

A certain major had been cited; he was immediately admitted into the Imperial Guard.

Exelmans, who had already attracted attention by his rapid insight and intrepid firmness, and who dared at once to put into execution the thing he advised, had been the first to stop the march of the enemy's flank by charging home upon the head of his column; then making his dragoons dismount, he had with this improvised infantry carried the village of Vertingen. 'I know it is impossible to be braver than you are,' said the Emperor, 'and I create you an officer of the Legion of Honour!' This was a double promotion for the officer, and the emulation which it caused can be imagined.

On the 10th the Emperor continued as far as Bergau, whence he went on to reconnoitre the enemy up to Pfaffenhoffen. He had just written to Josephine: 'That the Russians were still beyond the Inn; that he was keeping the Austrian army blocked on the Iller, that the enemy being already beaten had lost their heads; that everything predicted the shortest and most brilliant campaign, though carried on in a deluge, the weather being such that he was forced to change his clothes twice a day.'

At the end of the day his headquarters were established at Augsburg where he only arrived at ten o'clock at night and remained two days. We have seen by the preceding summary what detained him there; but our subject now concerning Napoleon and ourselves specially, other details are necessary.

At this time and after the passage of the Danube, the Grand Army, divided in two, was at the same time facing Austria and France: Austria, with 60,000 men, masters of Bavaria, under Davout and Bernadotte; Mack and France, with 140,000 men scattered in Suabia from Albeck up to Langsberg; the greater part of whom it was now important to unite on the point of attack. Napoleon, who had arrived in Augsburg on October 10th, thus found himself placed between these two masses. There he remained till October 13th with one eye fixed on Austria where he was counting the footsteps of the Russians, the other on the Tyrol and the army of the Archduke John, whose various corps, detached to relieve Mack, were coming up to be beaten separately; lastly watching Mack himself whom he had broken through the two previous days at Vertingen and at Guntzberg, and was now pressing back on Ulm and on the Iller.

However little he held this field-marshal in esteem, judging the present by the past, he could not believe that Mack with his 80,000 men as he thought, should not at Ulm follow the example of Mélas at Marengo; and that in his hopeless position he would not endeavour to seek death or salvation by a battle.

Two other courses remained open to him; either to throw himself into the Alps by Upper Suabia, or to fall back upon Bohemia by the left bank of the Danube. Napoleon rendered the first of these impossible, by pushing Soult from Landsberg and Augsberg upon Meningen and Biberach. As for the second, whether the Emperor had been misled by the reports of Murat, or that he had reckoned too much on Dupont seconded by d'Billiers who had failed him, (both of these still occupying the left bank of the Danube towards Albeck), he neglected this bank under the impression that Mack was waiting for him on the Tiler, where his magazines were. It was there that he commanded Murat to draw all around him: Lannes, Ney himself, Marmont, Soult, 100,000 men, in short. Thence resulted Ney's desperate passage of the right bank by the bridges below Ulm, on October 9th, followed by the too complete abandonment of the left bank of the Danube.

Napoleon had at the outset misled Mack by the rapid execution of his first and great manœuvre, and in his turn was himself misled by the inconceivable and stagnant irresolution of his adversary. On the 9th, and even more so on the 10th, he was so convinced that this field-marshal would make some great attempt either upon Augsberg or towards the Tyrol, and above all that he would assemble his army upon the Iller, that supposing Ulm to be almost abandoned, he ordered Ney, and then Dupont even by himself, to take possession of it. Indeed, on the evening of the 10th, he so entirely believed in a battle on the Tiler that he announced it to his marshals with the day and the hour. 'Mack,' he wrote from Bavaria to Davout and to Bernadotte, 'will succumb on the Iller on the 14th; and all being over on that side, they would see the Emperor come to their aid with 40,000 men.'

But during the night of the 12th to the 13th all had changed. A letter from Lannes full of the warlike instinct which that marshal possessed to so high a degree, disclosed to Napoleon the fact that Murat was misleading him by his reports, that looking only straight ahead, he was attracting all to himself and that in spite of Ney he had given up to the enemy Dupont and the left bank of the Danube. On the other hand the news had just arrived at the Imperial quarters of the engagement at Albeck, where Dupont, one against four, and abandoned by d'Hilliers, was surrounded; and although left conqueror on the battle-field, had been obliged to retire leaving his stores behind him. This letter of Lannes and the news from Dupont which Napoleon had been so far from expecting, at last drew his attention to the left bank; he began to be doubtful of a battle on the Iller, and the fear of Mack's retreat towards Bohemia by Nordlingen could no longer be regarded by him as groundless, for he had just demonstrated its possibility. The most lively anxiety took instant possession of the mind of Bonaparte. His great park of artillery, his reinforcements, his line of advance, indeed his line of operation were not sufficiently protected on the left bank of the Danube. Mack in Ulm is on both banks: it would even seem as if he would profit by this advantage to take flight. It was therefore necessary, if indeed there were still time, on the one hand suddenly to re-possess himself of the left bank; on the other, thoroughly to reconnoitre the enemy along the right bank as far as Ulm itself, to obtain a certainty as to his intentions on both banks and to keep him there.

October 13th the issue of a hundred instructions, the most important of which was an order to Marshal Ney, which he was not able to execute till the next day, to recross the Danube at Elchingen that very day at all hazards. In his restless anxiety Napoleon had already sent me the previous evening to Murat as the bearer of orders and to bring back news; and the prince, at last discovering his error, had informed me that the enemy was no longer before him but had crossed to the opposite bank. My instructions were to return that night to Guntzberg where the Emperor arrived on the 13th at day-break. There, warned by me that part of the enemy had been perceived on his way, in his astonishment he sent me to reconnoitre up stream the bridge of Leiphen which he thought was held. This was admitting the very possible supposition that the enemy had already been able to advance so far from Ulm by going down the stream on its left bank to escape us.

It was not till the afternoon that I found the Emperor at Pfaffenhoffen with Murat. On my report that Leiphen was full of our troops, but that they did not seem to contemplate holding the bridge, he said to his brother-in-law with a shrug of the shoulders: 'It is always the same. You see how our orders are executed.' It is difficult to say if a reproach thus worded, was intended for Ney or for Murat; but the Emperor evidently perceived that during his stay at Augsberg everything had got behindhand; that the enemy had been neglected and badly reconnoitred; that it would be necessary in the future for him to be present everywhere himself, and that he could rely only on his own discernment.

He immediately sent order upon order to Lannes and Marmont to press Ulm closely, and recalled Soult there from Meningen; the night reports having arrived, he reproached Ney who had only too well obeyed orders, for having left Dupont alone on the other bank, and reprimanded him for having feebly attacked the bridge of Elchingen that evening and having met with a repulse. 'He thought it quite right,' he wrote, 'to draw the enemy into partial engagements which could only be favourable to us, but that it was necessary above all to avoid risking those slight reverses which raised the courage of the enemy and restored the spirit of an army which had lost it.'

It must be admitted that from Guntzberg to Pfaffenhoffen, the army presented an aspect of the greatest disorder; the roads which were full of ruts, were strewn with our Alsatian waggons stuck fast in the mire, with their drivers at their wits' end, and with fallen horses dying of hunger and fatigue. Our soldiers were rushing right and left, helter-skelter across the fields; some looking for food, others using up their cartridges shooting the game with which these plains abounded. Hearing all this firing, and the whistle of the bullets, one might have fancied oneself at the advance-posts, and one ran quite as great risk.

It was difficult to check this licence, for the soldiers without rations could only live by pillage, and were foraging for their officers. The Emperor passed by without appearing to take any notice of this disorder; an inevitable consequence of the myriad rapid movements which are requisite to attain the most glorious results. Indeed these enormous armies, like giants, require to be seen at a distance when defects pass unnoticed, which is the case of the world itself, whose whole strikes us with admiration, but in which so many details appear sacrificed to this admirable whole.

I must confess for my part that I might have made my recognizance of the bridge of Leiphen more useful to the Emperor. I ought to have made him acquainted with its approaches, the configuration of the two banks, and above all the fact that the right commanded the left one. I neglected insisting on this point, although its importance was very great.

My immediate regrets were at first only a question of *amour-propre*, but became more serious later on. Had I, in fact, drawn the attention of the Emperor to the facility of this passage which was then free, whilst on the contrary that of Elchingen, strongly occupied and at two hours distance, was very dangerous of access, he would probably have chosen it, or, at any rate, he would, by a double attack, have divided the enemy's forces, and thus diminished his resistance. The brilliant but bloody action of Elchingen on the next day, when Ney, taking the bull by the horns, might have met with a repulse, would have been the more assured and less costly; thus the smallest details are never unimportant and there is no such thing as a trifling error in critical moments. My only excuse was in my excessive fatigue; however, worn out as I was by a consecutive journey of thirty-six hours, on my own horses at first, and then on those of orderlies and country people, the Emperor, who was preoccupied with what was going on the other bank, sent me several leagues further, with orders to his heavy cavalry to reconnoitre along the Danube. It was then that Marshal Ney, obeying his orders with too great precipitation, had caused the approach of the bridge of Elchingen to be vainly attacked by an insufficient advance-guard. While pursuing my way, the sound of the firing attracted me to this engagement where I should have found myself without a mission, acting the useless and unbecoming part of a mere spectator. A curious meeting, however, stopped me. I was walking across the fields at nightfall when suddenly a sentinel from behind a bush, opposing me with his bayonet, cried out: 'Who goes there!' in such good German, that, taking him for one of the enemy, I thought I had better rid myself of him before he had time to alarm his guard. I therefore answered in the same language, and drew my sword which I was going to make use of, when, surprised by his confidence, I asked him in German: 'What part of the world do you come from?' 'From Strasburg,' he answered. Then, discovering my mistake, with some relief, I must admit, and cured by this adventure of my ill-timed martial curiosity, I bethought myself of executing Napoleon's orders, after which I went on to sleep at Guntzberg where the headquarters remained, though without the Emperor, who had gone to pass the night at Pfaffenhoffen.

On the next day, October 14th, no longer trusting anybody, Napoleon left at daybreak for the castle of Hildenhausen, himself to begin the engagement which on this side was to drive back the enemy into Ulm. Immediately afterwards, going down the bank full gallop, he reached the passage of Elchingen where I found him at the moment when the 69th regiment, overthrowing the enemy on the bridge, had just taken possession of it, and when supported beyond it by the 76th infantry and the 18th, 10th and 3rd dragoons, the Rifles, and Hussars, Ney in three assaults took possession of the elevated and formidable height on which is situated the thenceforth celebrated abbey of Elchingen. Whilst the marshal was thus driving onwards up to the foot of Michaelsberg, the true rampart of Ulm, Laudon, who was flying with a loss of 6,000 men, Napoleon had pushed on through the midst of reinforcements of all branches who had thrown themselves upon the bridge, and the dead and wounded who encumbered it. He was making his way with difficulty through this narrow passage, covered with blood and wreckage, when noticing that the wounded left off moaning to salute him with their customary greeting, he stopped short. Amongst these was an artillery man whose thigh had been carried away by a cannon ball; remarking him specially, he drew near him and taking off his own star, placed it in his hand, saying: 'Take this, it is yours, so is the Hotel of the Invalides where you may still have the consolation of living on happily.'—'No, no,' replied the brave soldier, 'there has been too much letting of blood this time! But no matter, long live the Emperor!'

On the other side of the bridge a grenadier of the former army of Egypt lay on his back with his face exposed to the pelting rain. In the excitement of action he was still crying: 'Forwards!' to his comrades. The Emperor recognised him as he was passing by, and taking off his own cloak, he threw it over him, saying: 'Try to bring this back to me, and in exchange I will give you the decoration and the pension that you have so well deserved.'

Then from the top of the steep height of Elchingen, giving his whole attention to the engagement, and seeing that victory was decided, and the left bank at last retaken, he sent General Mouton on to Albeck, where the hazardous position of Dupont disquieted him; and crossing the bridge, rapidly rode up the right bank beyond Hildenhausen, desiring to assure himself of the success of this other attack which had been engaged by him at daybreak. Decided for the future only to believe his own eyes, he drew near, remaining so long on a hillock near the enemy, that we were obliged to turn ourselves into sharp shooters, and even to open a pistol fire upon the Austrian dragoons to drive them away from his person. Night was falling before he retired satisfied, and he returned again to the right bank to sleep at Ober-Falheim, near Elchingen, at the house of a village priest where Thiard made his bed, and one of his aides-de-camp made him an omelette; but as everything had been pillaged, he had to do without all he required; neither dry clothing nor anything else could be had, not even his Chambertin wine, causing him to remark gaily, 'That he had never gone without that, not even in the midst of the Egyptian desert.'

On October 15th, at three o'clock in the morning, which was his habit, because the reports of the day before were then to hand, he dictated his orders, to the effect that during the day, Mack was to be completely thrown back and hemmed in between the two banks within the walls of Ulm. He already suspected that a troop of the enemy might evade them by Nordlingen, but he did not then foresee a sudden attack on his rear towards Donawerth. He took the precautions which were then necessary.

As soon as it was light he took up his position in the abbey of Elchingen where he drew up the order of attack on Mount St. Michael, towering over Ulm, and the key to that town. Mid-day was the hour decided upon for this last blow which was to be struck by Ney, supported on the left by Lannes, with a reserve of the guard and our heavy cavalry.

Towards eleven o'clock, Napoleon in his impatience mounted his horse again, and proceeded on the road to Ulm, even passing Ney's advance posts and pushing on as far as the foot of Mount St. Michael. Twenty-five mounted riflemen of his guard and a few of us alone were following him. He was getting impatient of the delays in the arrival of his columns which was the inevitable result of the passage of the bridge of Elchingen behind us, and was anxious that it should be over. At last when some of the enemy's balls fell near us, not being able to take another step without grave imprudence, he stopped and called me to him: 'Take my rifle-men,' he said, 'go to the front and bring me back some prisoners.' Thus began the battle of Ulm. It was the Emperor in person who engaged it with his escort.

The enemy had perceived him;—it occupied the top of the hill, and a squadron of Uhlans barred the road. My own squad which was badly officered by its lieutenant, missed its charge, stopped and nearly caused me to be taken as well as a brigadier who alone had followed me, and had been wounded at my side by the thrust

of a lance. Getting back dissatisfied, as may be imagined, I reprimanded the riflemen, their officer especially, and dispersed them
as sharpshooters. Then the firing began.

Why I remember this circumstance, in itself not very remarkable, is on account of a strange meeting which I had just made
unconsciously, and that of the temporary disgrace which the whole
body of riflemen of our guard contrived to draw upon itself that
day. Before my departure from Paris for the army, a female relative
of the young Prince of Windischgraetz had recommended him to
me in case he were taken prisoner; and on the contrary, it was this
self-same brilliant young officer who at the head of his platoon of
Uhlans had very nearly taken me. As for the mounted riflemen
of the guard, some spirit of false pride had taken possession of
this picked corps. They had become so haughty that they not
only looked upon the advance post duty with disdain, but on the
night of this action, on their return to Elchingen, they treated the
Imperial livery with disrespect, taking possession of the best places
for their horses, by hook or by crook, and leaving the others outside. They were soon, however, set down, for Napoleon, in a rage,
sent them off at once to his brother-in-law, and two days after,
being drafted into his cavalry without any distinction of person,
the entire corps made amends for the error of a few amongst them
by contributing to make 20,000 men lay down their arms.

The firing that I had just initiated soon extended over the whole
line commanded by Ney. We had thought that we were covering
the Emperor, but he had grown tired of these skirmishes and the
never ceasing rain, and had sought shelter at Hasslach whilst waiting for his guard and the corps of Marshal Lannes. I found him in
a farm house of this hamlet, dozing by the side of a stove, whilst
a young drummer was dozing also on the other side. Somewhat
surprised at this spectacle, I was told that they had wanted to send
the child elsewhere; but the drummer boy would not hear of it,
saying, 'That there was plenty of room for everybody, that he was
wounded and cold, that he was very comfortable, and that he
meant to stop there.' On hearing this Napoleon began to laugh,
saying: 'That he must be allowed to remain as he made such a

point of it.' So that the Emperor and the drummer slept side by side, surrounded by a circle of generals and high dignitaries, who were standing whilst waiting for orders.

The cannonading, however, was drawing nearer, and Napoleon aroused himself about every ten minutes to send off messengers to hasten Lannes' arrival, when that marshal entered abruptly with the exclamation: 'Sire! what are you thinking of? You are sleeping, while Ney, single-handed, is fighting against the whole of the Austrian army!'—'Why has he engaged them?' answered the Emperor. 'I told him to wait; but it is just like him; he cannot see the enemy without falling upon him!'—'That is all very well,' retorted Lannes, 'but one of his brigades has been repulsed. My grenadiers are here; we must hurry up; there is no time to be lost!' And he carried off Napoleon with him, who in his turn becoming excited, pushed on so far ahead that Lannes, not being able to persuade him to stop, at last roughly seized his horse's bridle, and forced him back into a less dangerous position.

Ney had indeed refused to defer his attack; his left wing had just been shaken by a sally of 10,000 men, notwithstanding which he had ordered Dumas to tell the Emperor, 'that he would see to all, and that he answered for everything, and had no need of Marshal Lannes; glory was not a thing to be shared!'

The imminence of the danger was of short duration. In a very few moments, with three battalions carried the retrenchment of Michael's Berg; and Suchet, on the other side, detached by Lannes, soon crowned the heights of the Frauenberg. Thus master of the outskirts, the Emperor from the summit of the first of these hills, was able to contemplate at his feet within half-range of his shells, the town of Ulm completely surrounded, and full of the enemy packed closely together, without provisions, without forage, unable to move within its walls.

From that moment, knowing that his prey could not escape him, Napoleon began to set his lines in order, to unite and strengthen his positions, to threaten the town with a few shells, and when night came on he left to pass it at Elchingen, where I joined him too late to fulfil my duty of establishing his headquarters, and seeing after his guard. The fact was that at the hottest moment of the day, led away by curiosity and a desire to be one of the first to enter Ulm, I had left Napoleon to follow the attack of the 17th light infantry on the gate called 'Stuttgart.' It was at the very moment when Colonel Vedel, entering pell-mell with the enemy, had lost the half of his first battalion in Ulm, and had been taken with the remainder. Having got away from the scrimmage, I went off to seek my fortune elsewhere, with such recklessness that I was on the point of falling into an ambuscade when Marshal Ney, who was behind me on the slope of the Michael's Berg, saved me from this misfortune.

I was somewhat roughly admonished about this the next day by Rapp and Caulaincourt, who asked me if I thought I was in the army entirely on my own account and for my own pleasure. They added that as an officer of the Emperor's staff, my duty was to remain within hail, to be at hand to convey his orders, and that while waiting to receive them, I could take observations, if I wanted to do so, within my range of vision. This well-merited lesson was all the more useful to me in that while recalling me to my duties as one of the staff, it caused me to reflect on the means by which I could best fulfil them.

I indulged in this examination of conscience while reposing on the straw at our halting place, Elchingen; and it was probably of a very different kind to that of the monk to whose pallet I had succeeded. Imagining that our part of the campaign was over, I only got up in time to aid the Emperor to mount his horse, and to repair my inadvertence of the previous day by taking possession of the abbey. Its inspection was a sad and painful business, for the horrors of war asserted themselves with only too much prominence. To begin with, the ambulance was installed there, as I soon knew from the cries of the wounded who were undergoing amputation, and whom it would be my duty to see and encourage. But a still more terrible sight awaited me.

I was going over every part of this immense gothic edifice, visiting the guards and rectifying the orders when, passing by a dark cellar, I thought I heard stifled moans mingled with noisy singing and bursts of laughter. I stopped to question a sentinel who told me that the same groans of pain broken by out-bursts of mirth, had excited his astonishment. We listened together, and then hearing nothing but the chink of glasses I was going to pass on when another feeble, plaintive cry reached our ears.

Much troubled, after having vainly sounded all the surrounding walls, I went into a low-pitched room whence proceeded the convivial sounds. A party of couriers and valets were at table making merry with the wines which they had just laid hands upon. I told them to be silent, enquiring if they had not heard moans and groans from some point quite near to them. They replied that they had, but not knowing what it meant, they did not trouble themselves about it. 'But several of you slept here last night,' I said, 'and in the stillness, you must have heard even more plainly.' They gave the same answer, 'that the moaning had disturbed them, and that they had also been annoyed by a foul, corpse-like smell, but that they had been able to fall asleep again.' This was too much for me: 'Get up at once,' I exclaimed, 'and follow me.'

Our researches took some time, but at last in this very cellar which they were occupying, behind a heap of planks, we discovered a massive door which seemed to have been carefully hidden from view. For some time it resisted our attempts to open it, but when open, such a fetid smell issued forth that I drew back; I had, however, seen enough to force myself to overcome my disgust.

This cellar of small size, though fairly well lighted, had disclosed to me in a glance every torture of suffering, every manifestation of agony and misery. I have witnessed many horrible scenes but the details of this one will ever remain graven on my memory.

The door had been barricaded by the bodies of Austrian soldiers who had died of hunger or of their wounds, and who having pulled the door upon themselves, had not had the strength to open it again. One of their officers was lying there in a dying condition though still breathing, but almost suffocated by the unfortunates who had expired while they were lying on him. Further on many bodies were stretched out here and there, some of which had their arms gnawed off; of these some bore an expression of rage, others were in an attitude of prayer. In the middle of the cellar, a second officer, all bloodstained, tried to raise himself on his knees when he heard us enter; he extended his hands to us, but fell forward in his weakness, first on his hands, then on his forehead, frothing at the mouth, and gave up his last breath with the death rattle in his throat. A third officer was crouched on a table which he had probably mounted to reach the air hole and cry for help; his head wagged from one side to another, and his hands moved about as if seeking a hold on something to cling to, the light of day, the outer world, the life that was ebbing away! … But enough—perhaps too much; courage fails me to continue. In short, these unfortunates, dead or dying of their wounds, of hunger, and above all of thirst, numbered about fourteen or fifteen, amongst whom hardly three could possibly be saved. Unfortunately I had only discovered them on the third day of their agony; it was during the night before last, in an endeavour to save themselves from the excesses of victory, that they had inflicted this torture upon themselves.

Whilst I was engaged in this sad inspection, the Emperor who had been falsely informed of the flight of the Archduke, believed him to be on his way towards Biberach and the Alps. He counted on his retreat being cut off by Marshal Soult. Again on the positions of the Michael's Berg which had been conquered the previous night he was cannonading Ulm, piling up fascines, and threatening an assault on this town and army which were already surrounded and dominated on all sides.

Mack, on his side, a prey to the animadversions of his generals, was telling them that the Russians would soon arrive, being on their way to succour them; and he forbade them on their honour, even to pronounce the word surrender. But he contradicted himself by asking Marshal Ney on that very day, Oct. 16th, for a suspension of arms, who, however, made short work of his appeal, vouchsafing no other reply than the eloquence of his pieces of ordnance.

The Emperor had just returned to Elchingen; and the night of the 16th to the 17th of October had commenced. As soon as he heard of these parleyings, which indeed he had expected, he sent word by letter to France and elsewhere that he held the Austrian army prisoner; that it would capitulate within an hour, and, sending for me, he gave me verbal orders with brief and concise instructions, to go and negotiate the conditions of the capitulation with the Field-marshal.

I shall now proceed to reproduce the narrative of this event in the same terms in which I drew it up a little later, from notes taken on the spot, for General Dumas. This general was then engaged in writing a summary of the campaign in which my report figures as *pièce justificative*. The very few modifications which may be remarked in this document render it more conformable to the original notes.

IMPERIAL HEADQUARTERS OF ELCHINGEN.

OCTOBER 17TH

Last night, 24th Vendémiaire (October 16th), the Emperor called me into his study, and ordered me to enter Ulm, and make Mack agree to surrender in five days, or to grant him six if he absolutely required them. Such were my instructions. The night was pitch dark, and a furious gale had risen; I was very nearly blown over several times during the storm. It was pouring with rain, and I had to travel by cross country roads, avoiding the bogs where man, horse and mission might come to an untimely end. I arrived nearly to the gates of the town without meeting our advance posts: there were not any to be seen; sentinels, vedettes, guards, had gone under shelter, the parks of artillery even were abandoned, there were no fires and no stars. I wandered about for three hours striving to find the general, and I passed through several villages where I vainly interrogated those of our troops who were occupying the various houses. At last I discovered a trumpeter of the artillery, half drowned in the mud under an artillery waggon, where he had taken shelter. He was stiff with cold. Together we approached the ramparts of Ulm where we were probably expected, for at our first call, M. de la Tour, an officer who spoke very good French, presented himself to conduct me to the field-marshal. He bandaged my eyes and made me ascend by the fortifications. I ventured on remarking to my conductor that there was no need of a bandage on such a very dark night, but he said it was customary. It seemed to me rather a long way, and I took advantage of this to make my guide talk, with a view of finding out what eminent chiefs were in the town. To this end I complained of fatigue, asking if Marshal Mack's quarters were far from those of the Archduke. 'They are contiguous,' answered M. de la Tour, from which I concluded that we held in Ulm, with the prince, all the remainder of the Austrian army. In course of conversation I felt confirmed in this conjecture, which the departure of the Archduke at that very moment had rendered an erroneous one.

We at last arrived in an inn where the general-in-chief was lodging; it might then be about three hours after midnight. This general seemed to me to be tall, old and pale, the expression of his countenance denoted a keen imagination, and his features were drawn by an anxiety which he vainly endeavoured to conceal.

I announced my name and after the exchange of a few compli-ments, I entered on my subject by telling him that I came from the Emperor to call upon him to surrender, and to settle with him the conditions of the capitulation. He seemed to find these expressions unpalatable, and he would not at first agree that it was a necessity for him to listen to them. On this, however, I insisted, dwelling on the fact that having received me after his demand for a suspension of arms, I should naturally conclude, as the Emperor had done, that he fully realized his position; but he replied impa-tiently, that it would soon be completely altered, that the Russian army was approaching, that it would extricate him and place us between two fires, and that perhaps it would be we who would capitulate. I retorted that in his position it was not surprising he was ignorant of what was going on in Austria, because we had entirely cut him off from it; that in consequence it devolved upon me to inform him that Marshals Davout and Bernadotte, and the Bavarian army, were occupying Ingolstadt and Munich, and that their advance posts were on the Inn where no one had yet heard anything of the Russians. 'May I be the greatest jack-ass,' exclaimed Marshal Mack in a rage, 'if I do not know on positive authority that the Russians are at Dachau! Do they think they can humbug me like this? Am I to be treated like a child? No! M. de Ségur, if I am not succoured in a week, I agree to surrender my position, and that my soldiers should be prisoners of war, and their officers prisoners on parole. By then there would have been time for succour to reach me, and I should have fulfilled my duty. That succour will come, I am certain.'—'I have the honour again to tell you, sir,' I retorted, 'that we are not only masters of Dachau, but of Munich and Bavaria, up to the Inn. Besides, allowing your assertion were true, and that the Russians are at Dachau, five days would be sufficient for them to come and attack us, and His Majesty has granted them.'—'No, sir,' resumed the marshal, 'I demand eight days. I will not listen to any other proposition. I must have eight days, they are indispensable to vindicate my responsibility.'—'Thus,' I continued, 'the difficulty lies in the difference between five and eight days. I confess that I cannot understand the importance which Your Excellency attaches to this, when His Majesty is before you at the head of more than 100,000 men, and when the corps of the Marshals Davout and Bernadotte, and the Bavarian army would quite suffice to delay the march of the Russians by these three days, even supposing them to be where they are very far from being at present.'—'They are at Dachau,' repeated the marshal. 'So be it, Baron,' I exclaimed, 'Let us even say at Augsburg, all the more reason that we should wish to finish with you as soon as possible. Do not force us to take Ulm by storm, for instead of five days' delay, the Emperor would be here in a few hours.'—'My dear sir,' replied the general-in-chief; 'do not suppose that 15,000 men will let themselves be taken so easily. It would cost you dear.'—'A few hundred men,' I replied, 'while for you it would mean the loss of your whole army, and the destruction of Ulm, which Germany would consider your doing; in short, all the horrors of a siege which His Majesty desires to avoid by the proposition he authorized me to make to you.'—'You had better say,' exclaimed the marshal, 'that it would cost you 10,000 men, the strength of Ulm is sufficiently well known.'—'It consists,' I resumed, 'in the surrounding heights which we are occupying.'—'It is impossible, Sir,' he answered, 'that you should not be aware of the strength of Ulm.'—'Without a doubt,' I answered, 'all the more that we can see down into it.'—'Very well, Sir,' then said the unfortunate general, 'you see men who are ready to defend it to the last extremity, if your Emperor will not give them eight days. I can hold on some time. There are three thousand horses in Ulm, and sooner than surrender, we would eat them up with a great deal more pleasure than you would if you were in our place.'—'Your horses!' I exclaimed, 'ah! Marshal, you must indeed be in sad straits already if you are thinking of such a sorry resource!'

The marshal hastened to affirm that he had ten days' stores, but I did not believe it. The day was beginning to break, and we had made no progress; I might grant six days, but the baron so obstinately held out for eight, that, considering the concession of a day quite useless, I would not mention it. I therefore took my leave, telling him that my instructions commanded me to be back before day, and that in the event of a refusal I was to convey to Marshal Ney as I passed by, orders to begin the attack. On this General Mack complained of the marshal's rudeness towards the bearer of a flag of truce to whom he would not listen. I took advantage of this to say that this marshal was indeed of a most hot-headed and impetuous disposition and incapable of self-restraint; that the body of men which he commanded was not only the most numerous but the nearest to them; that he was impatiently awaiting orders to storm the place, which I should deliver to him on my departure from Ulm.

The old field-marshal would not be intimidated; he insisted on his eight days, and that I should convey the proposition to the Emperor.

This unhappy general was ready to sign the loss of Austria and his own, and yet in this hopeless position, when he must have suffered cruelly in every way, he would not give in; his mind retained its faculties and his arguments were lively and tenacious. He defended the only thing that remained to him, time; either because he really thought the Russian army near enough to come to his succour, or that he sought to retard the downfall of Austria of which he was the cause, and to give her a few days longer to prepare for it. Lost himself, he still struggled for her. He was a man of conversation rather than of action. Bewildering himself by vain conjectures, he tried to play a game of diamond cut diamond. It is also possible that he may have desired to turn our attention from the flight of the 50,000 men of whose escape by Nordlingen we had just been informed.

This morning before nine o'clock, I returned to the Emperor at the abbey of Elchingen, giving him an account of this negotiation, whose details appeared to please him. His glance denoted the liveliest satisfaction when misinformed by me as to the presence of the Archduke in Ulm. After twenty minutes' conversation, seeing that I was worn out with so many days and nights of fighting and fatigue, he gave me permission to take off my clothes and retire to rest. But before I was half undressed, I was ordered back to him in hot haste, and as I kept him waiting a couple of minutes, he sent Marshal Berthier in person to seek me in my cell where I was wearily struggling into my clothes again. This major brought me at the same time the new propositions written on half margin, and the order to go back at once and make the marshal accept them.

The Emperor granted eight days, to date from October 15th, the first day of the blockade, which really reduced it to the six days which I could have conceded but had not chosen to do. However, in case of a persistent refusal, I was authorized to date these eight days from October 16th, and the Emperor would still be the gainer of a day by this concession. He was anxious to enter Ulm quickly so as to increase the glory of his victory by its rapidity, to be able to turn back and throw himself upon Vienna before that capital had recovered from its consternation, so as not to leave the Russian army time to take measures for its defence; and also because our own provisions were beginning to run short.

Marshal Berthier caused me to be informed that he would approach the gate of Ulm, and that when the conditions were settled, I was to procure his admission. I returned to Ulm towards noon. This time I found Mack a few paces from the gate of the town on the ground-floor of a small, dirty, and miserable pot-house. I handed to him the ultimatum of the Emperor, and he immediately went up to the first story to discuss it with some generals, amongst whom were MM. de Lichtenstein, Klénau and Giulaï. Twenty minutes later he came down again alone, once more to argue with me upon the date of the respite which had been granted to him. His obstinate tenacity made me relinquish all hope of overcoming it, so that I judged it right to concede the only day which I was authorized to yield. A misunderstanding, due no doubt to the difference of the two calendars which we were each using, led him to imagine that, dating from 25th Vendémiaire (October 17th) he was thus obtaining the eight days for which he held out. Then in a singular transport of joy he exclaimed: 'M. de Ségur, my dear M. de Ségur, I was not mistaken in relying on the generosity of the Emperor … tell Marshal Berthier that I thoroughly respect him … tell the Emperor that I have only a few slight remarks to make …, that I will sign anything you bring me … but also tell His Majesty that Marshal Ney has used me with great severity …, that that is not the way to treat … Be sure to tell the Emperor that I relied on his generosity …' Then he added in an effusion of increasing delight: 'M. de Ségur, I value your esteem … I think a great deal of the opinion that you may form of me. And I will show you the paper that I had already signed, bearing my unalterable resolution.' Thus saying, he unfolded a sheet of paper upon which I read these words: 'Eight days or death! *signed* 'MACK.'

I was transfixed with astonishment when I noted the expression of happiness which irradiated his countenance. I was astonished and almost taken aback by this puerile joy over such a futile concession. In so entire a shipwreck of his hopes, what a miserable branch was this for the unhappy general-in-chief to hang his lost honour upon, in the belief that it might also be strong enough to bear that of his army, and the safety of Austria. He took my hands and pressed them in his own, allowing me to leave Ulm with unbandaged eyes, and even permitting the introduction of Marshal Berthier into the place without any formality; he was, in short, happy at last!

There ensued, however, a lively discussion with General Berthier still concerning these dates. I had explained the misunderstanding, and the matter was laid before the Emperor. Marshal Mack had assured me on my night visit that ten days' provisions were left, but as a matter of fact, so little remained, as indeed I had remarked to His Majesty, that he had asked permission in my presence for some to be sent in that very day. This consideration alone would leave the Emperor free to take back the twenty-four hours which he would give up. He therefore yielded as to the date; and that very night, October 17th, this capitulation, whose negotiation he had entrusted to me, approved by him, was signed by Marshals Berthier and Mack.

Mack finding himself turned and driven back upon Ulm, thought that by throwing himself into it, he would attract and keep the Emperor before the ramparts of the town which would thus favour the escape of his other corps in different directions. He believed that he had sacrificed himself and this was what kept up his courage. At the time of my negotiations with him, he seemed to think that our whole army was motionless and, as it were, stationary before Ulm. He arranged the furtive evasion of the Archduke who went to join Verneck and Hohenzollern. Another division that had remained at Meningen was also to attempt to escape, and yet another under Jellachich took flight towards the mountains of the Tyrol. But it was hoped that all would be taken prisoners.

It is known now (night of 17th to 18th October), by a report of Prince Murat and the capture of 3 to 4,000 men that the body of 20,000 men encountered by Dupont towards Albeck on October 14th was on that very day, and still more on the 15th, cut off from Ulm and thrown back upon Heidenheim; that the Archduke Ferdinand who, it was believed, had only left on the previous day (the 16th), about an hour after midnight on the very night I had been sent there, had rejoined this detached corps which had been attacked by Prince Murat, and that he was flying with the remains of it to Nordlingen. To-day, (October 18th) the Emperor's attention which was now easy on the score of Ulm whose capitulation was signed the previous night, and whose gate designated

'Stuttgart' had been given up to us, was eagerly concentrated on the Archduke. He sent order upon order to his foot dragoons, to Marshal Lannes, Oudinot, Nansouty, even to the cavalry of his guard. Some were to defend our reserve parks which were left without protection on the passage of the Archduke's flight; the others in divers directions, were sent forth to help Murat to seize the Austrian prince, and at all hazards, to possess themselves of his person; others were to clear our line of operations whence the Emperor was expecting the stores which we were in need of, and which the overflow of the Danube prevented us from transporting from the right bank. In the anxiety of his suspense he lets nothing escape him. He has just given me the order to question in the following sequence the couriers who arrive from Stuttgart by way of Nordlingen, and to write him their answers. 'What have they learnt? What have they seen? What enemies have they had to avoid? How numerous were they? Who were the generals? How many guns? In what direction were their columns marching?'

This morning (October 19th), the Emperor having learnt through Prince Murat that the 20,000 men cut off from Ulm, had been all taken, together with their guns and the whole of their baggage, he sent word to Mack to come and see him at Elchingen. The unhappy general reached it about one o'clock and then all his last delusions were destroyed. His Majesty, in order to persuade him no longer to keep him uselessly waiting before Ulm, forced him to contemplate the full horror of his position and that of Austria. He informed him of our success on all points; that Verneck's corps with all his artillery and ten generals had capitulated; that no doubt the Archduke himself had been taken, and that nothing more had been heard about the Russians. The unfortunate general was overwhelmed by all these blows; his strength failed him and we saw him turn pale; in fact he would have fallen down if he had not leant up against the wall for support. Then only, breaking down under the weight of all his misfortunes, did he own his distress: that he had no more stores in Ulm; that instead of 15,000 men, there were 24,000 combatants and 3,000 wounded, and that the confusion was such that every moment more were discovered; that he was fully aware that no hope remained, and that he consented to surrender Ulm and his army from the following day, (October 20th) at three o'clock in the afternoon.

He, however, exacted a declaration, signed by Marshal Berthier, as to the position of the Russians, and that Marshal Ney and his corps should remain before Ulm till the 25th. This last demand was puerile to a degree, because in any case it would be necessary to leave forces there to guard the captured army and to escort it into France.

On leaving the Emperor and perceiving me he exclaimed: 'That it was cruel to be dishonoured in the mind of so many brave officers! and yet in his pocket there was his own opinion written and signed to the effect that he had refused to allow his army to be broken up, but that he was not in command of it, for the Archduke was there.'

It is possible that there was a disinclination to obey Mack, and it is certain that after my last conference with him in Ulm, when the capitulation had evidently been agreed upon, the attitude of several of the Austrian generals around him quite revolted me: I could easily see that their envious jealousy, gratified by the ruin of the chief who had been imposed upon them, was paramount to all feelings of propriety, and made them for the time quite oblivious of patriotism. It is true that several others amongst whom were MM. de Lichtenstein and Klénau, made no attempt to hide their bitter mortification.

To-night (October 19th) it is known that Jellachich's six thousand men who had evaded Marshal Soult beyond Biberach, were in flight towards Feldkirch, while on the opposite side, the Archduke was fleeing towards Bohemia with a few squadrons. It thus followed that after several partial combats beginning at Donawerth on October 6th, in the space of fourteen days and without a single battle, this army which numbered about 48,000 men inclusive of the reinforcement sent by the Archduke John, and not including the 18,000 men who had escaped with Kienmayer, Jellachich, and Prince Ferdinand in three separate directions, was either decimated or taken prisoner.

To-day (October 20th), 33,000 Austrians and eighteen generals with forty flags and sixty mounted guns have surrendered as prisoners of war. This captive army defiled past the Emperor at the foot of a rock between Ney's and Marmont's corps ranged in order of battle to right and left with loaded arms. As they passed by, the prisoners, seized with admiration, arrested their march past to contemplate their conquerors, and many cried out: '*Long live the Emperor!*' With very different emotions, some with evident mortification, and others eagerly without waiting for the order, laid down their arms. The infantry threw down their muskets on either side of the roadway, and the cavalry, dismounting, gave up their horses to our cavalry, and the artillery their guns, of which our artillery took possession. The officers, sent home on parole, alone retained their arms.

An outburst of enthusiasm which was with difficulty repressed, broke out in our ranks at the sight of this triumph. During the long defile, which in succession brought back to Ulm this mass of prisoners, the Emperor kept the Austrian officers by his side. His manners and his words were gentle, kind, and even affectionate. He endeavoured to console them for their reverses, saying:—'That war had its chances, that being frequently conquerors, they ought to console themselves for being sometimes conquered; that this war in which they had been engaged by their master was unjust and motiveless; frankly, he did not know himself what they were fighting for, nor what was expected from him.'

There was a moment when one of these generals, noticing that Napoleon's uniform was much splashed, remarked how fatiguing the campaign must have been for him during such very wet weather. 'Your master,' he answered with a smile, wanted to remind me that I was a soldier; I hope he will own that the Imperial purple has not caused me to forget my first trade.'

In the course of the conversation some threatening words, it is said, were let fall concerning the Emperor of Austria. Mack was present during the whole painful scene; and one of us who did not know him by sight, and was anxious to contemplate the unfortunate general, asked him to point him out. 'You see before you the miserable Mack!' was the answer of the field-marshal.

Miserable indeed, unfortunate man! What a sad example, what a lamentable downfall, what a cruelly different fame to that which he had sought! (*End of the copy of my notes.*)

The Emperor who had returned for the sixth and last time to Elchingen, after this triumph, lost no time in dividing its trophies between his allies and France. Paris received those of Vertingen: the Senate, the flags taken at Ulm; France, 60,000 prisoners, 'destined,' he said 'to take the place of our soldiers in field labour.' But all did not achieve this destiny, a good number of them having escaped before reaching our frontiers. The Russian recruiters were blamed for this, but it was partly owing to the carelessness of our own soldiers who did not like acting as escort to them. Their careless negligence when not fighting, and their gentleness after victory is, besides, well-known. During the same night of October 20 to 21, a proclamation of Napoleon to his army, dated from the abbey of Elchingen now for ever famous, testified his gratitude to his soldiers. He showed them their glory in the results of the victory which they owed to him. Suabia and Bavaria conquered in a fortnight, with all the parks and magazines of the enemy, 200 cannon, 90 flags, 72,000 men killed or taken! He went on to laud their devotion and praise, their intrepidity, taking credit to himself for having spared bloodshed by conquering by manoeuvres without a battle, and winding up with these words: 'My soldiers are my children.'

He added deeds to words, and decree upon decree proved the extent of his gratitude. By one of these they were to benefit by all the taxes levied on the enemy, and by the proceeds of the sale of the magazines that had fallen into our hands. The most magnificent of all, selecting the preceding fortnight from the rest of the year, declared that this month of October alone should be reckoned to them as a campaign in their record of service.

In the midst of these grateful acts of recognition and his usual work, he had not neglected what had remained to be done. Our army of Ulm with the exception of Ney, was already on the march to rejoin that of Bavaria. And as in his proclamation, when announcing the arrival of the Russian army to his soldiery, he had told them proudly: 'That, as for himself, there was no general there with whom he could find any glory to be obtained, but as far as they were concerned, they would be able to prove for a second time that they were the first or the second infantry in the world,' it was not difficult to see that he had been so lavish of thanks with a view to incite them to further deeds; or at any rate, that there was as much thought of the future as remembrance of the past in this remarkable outpouring of gratitude.

Thus ended, before Ulm and in Elchingen, the first part of this campaign.

XVII

VIENNA

Up to that time it was our adversaries who had changed, but not our luck. It was not long, however, before we recognised that we were going to have to do with very different men. These were 10,000 Russians under Kutusow and his lieutenants, Bagration and Miloradowitch, names which have been rendered famous by our misfortunes in 1812. They are a self-contained nation, selfish through isolation, ignorance and superstition; keenly sensitive as to their still superficial civilization, strongly constituted as to their component parts of the pride of masters and the devotion of slaves. Their chiefs possess the instinct of war, and are eager, prompt, and resolute, and the blind, obstinate tenacity of the soldier is never wanting in their generals.

Our advance-guards on the 31st, under Kellerman on the right, Murat and Davout in the centre, and Lannes on the left, carried away by eagerness to conquer, overtook and harassed the enemy; these marshals and generals had left the Emperor behind, and were in a state of anger and indignation at any show of resistance from the enemy, as if it were an act of insubordination or revolt. Nothing stopped them, neither abrupt defiles, broken bridges, pathless roads, affluents of the Danube, or fatiguing marches of ten or fifteen leagues. Napoleon's expectations had been so far exceeded that on November 5th, our advance guards had taken from the Austro-Russians 6,000 killed and wounded, also the Traun and Upper Austria from Enns to Steyer, and the Enns itself.

At Steyer, which was the end of Moreau's glory, the bridge having been burnt, Davout's soldiers passed the Enns one by one on a beam, under a hail of bullets and grape shot. They had reformed on the other bank, under the Austrian retrenchments, and then springing forwards, had dislodged the enemy by taking more prisoners than they numbered assailants. On the eve of this action, the Emperor had arrived at Lintz from Lembach and remained there five days. This sojourn proved fertile in excitement and movement. To begin with, about a quarter of a league from the gate of this town, a terrible incident, of a rare character in our army, where discipline is rendered easier through the intelligent emulation, and the fraternity of arms and origin of the soldier and the officer, had struck him with horror, which found its manifestation in impetuous speech. He was galloping past the left flank of a column of light artillery, when twenty paces before him, he noticed an artilleryman throw back his head with a threatening air, and at the same moment saw his captain by a back-handed blow of the sabre sever it almost completely, so that it inclined towards the shoulder of the unfortunate man who fell to the ground in a torrent of blood. Napoleon turned pale at this horrible sight and making his horse bound forwards, exclaimed: 'What have you done, Captain?' 'My duty!' answered the officer abruptly; 'and until I am killed by one of my soldiers,' he added in a loud tone as he looked straight at them, 'I would kill anyone of them who dared to fail in respect to their captain.' The Emperor, struck by his energy, was speechless for the moment, but controlling his emotion, he resumed in a firm voice: 'If this be the case, you have done well, you are a good officer and understand your duty. This is how I wish to be served.' He then continued his course in the midst of a mournful silence inspired by his words, and entered Lintz at a walking pace with a troubled expression of countenance.

Other emotions and preoccupations were, however, awaiting him in the town. On the one hand the Elector of Bavaria had hastened to give vent to his assurances of earnest gratitude; the deputies of the Senate had also come to express the admiration of France; Giulaï and Lichtenstein were the bearers of an insidious offer of an armistice; whilst Duroc had arrived bringing back from Berlin nothing beyond a hope, which was that Frederic would await the issue of arms to decide whether he should remain neutral or join our enemies.

As for the armistice which the Emperor of Austria, terrified at our approach, and already disgusted with Russian exaction and arrogance, had sent to demand, Napoleon answered that peace was only possible on conditions that he would dictate, which he did by letter, but that as for a suspension of arms, the request seemed untimely, as he could nowhere perceive any Austrian army with which he, at the head of 200,000 men, could desire to arrange an armistice.

That is at any rate what we of Napoleon's *entourage* learnt concerning this conference. Whilst it was taking place Giulaï's aide-de-camp complained to us with extreme bitterness of the excesses of the Russians. At the same time, M. de Thiard, who was one of us, had been drawn into a secret interview by the Prince de Lichtenstein. Whether this personage was entrusted with a mission, or whether of his own accord he favoured the customs of his Court by trying to bring matrimonial alliances to the aid of the resources of war, his insinuations were of such a nature, that on leaving him, Thiard thought it his duty immediately to seek out the Emperor, saying that: 'Lichtenstein had just been questioning him as to the rumour that the Prince Eugène had asked a princess of Bavaria in marriage,' and that on his reply the Austrian prince had added: 'Why should you stop there? Vienna has other marriageable princesses, and could not peace be sealed by another marriage?' Upon which Napoleon exclaimed impulsively: 'An Austrian princess! Ah! no, never—France would be revolted at such an idea, it would recall Marie Antoinette.' And surprised by a communication of this importance made through such a channel, he asked Thiard what had been the cause of this outpouring of Lichtenstein, and why he had selected him for such a confidence?

Thiard was well acquainted with Austria and the Austrians, in whose ranks he had served; he could speak their language and was aware that he was useful to Napoleon. He, therefore, answered without confusion or even any reticence: 'That having belonged to Condé's corps, he had often fought under the eyes of Lichtenstein, and that speaking both languages, he had frequently served as an intermediary between the Austrians and the Duc d'Enghien.'

At this name which few others would have dared to pronounce, whatever may have been the present preoccupations of the Emperor, the subject of conversation completely changed and bore entirely upon the past. During nearly an hour, Napoleon, apparently oblivious of everything else, did not cease to question Thiard upon the character, the mind, the martial talent of the unfortunate prince; and all this with a curious air of calm and natural interest, not at all as if he had been speaking of his victim to one who had long served as an aide-de-camp by his side, and whose friend he had been. Thiard's replies were uttered with such sincerity, and were so eulogistic that Napoleon exclaimed: 'He was really a man then, that prince!' And with the same calm and kindly manner, he dismissed his interlocutor.

Thiard told me besides, that very day, that this was the second time he had held converse with the Emperor on this sad subject. Their first conversation was at the time of the murder. It was Thiard himself who had enlightened the First Consul as to his mistake about the name of Dumouriez; and he told me that then, as at Lintz, he had remarked the same calm impassiveness in the attitude, the expression, and the voice of Napoleon.

Astonished as we were at this singular inflexibility, above all when we recalled so many proofs of kindness, of generosity, even of sensibility, on his part, we asked ourselves if this impassibility were the result of a misguided conscience or of political calculation. Was it a reflex effect of the habits of his natal isle? Did he believe that he had the right to avenge one crime by another crime? Or rather, under this apparent calm, was he persevering in his determination to prevent any further plots, and did he look upon the cruel act of Vincennes as a just punishment of former outrages, and a useful warning against future ones?

I find here in my notes that Napoleon during his sojourn at Lintz was seriously taken up with the care of restoring order to his army. It is very true that the rapid marches and counter-marches of the campaign of Ulm, and the breakdown of the roads through the rains, which kept back the store and ammunition waggons, rendered regular distributions impossible. It is a certain fact that had not our soldiers snatched from the peasantry their victuals and their cattle to subsist upon, had they been obliged to wait till provisions arrived by the waggons which were lagging far in the rear of their columns, the principal aim of the enterprise would have failed. Necessity was an excuse then; but the evil which had begun in Franconia, even amongst the Prussians, and in Suabia, had continued in Bavaria; it was being renewed on the Inn, and this marauding was destructive of discipline.

This came under the Emperor's observation near Lembach where he had rejoined the corps of Marshal Soult. There, in front of the ranks, he had inquired in a loud voice as to the regularity of the distributions; and whether the marshal had thought that the question was put merely as a matter of form, or that he wanted to appear satisfied so as to give satisfaction, (a piece of braggadocio which is sometimes useful before troops and is always agreeable to the chief) he had answered that the soldiers wanted for nothing; but twenty voices had been immediately rudely uplifted from the ranks to contradict him.

The same kind of thing was repeated the next day in a still more positive fashion. Napoleon was issuing from his quarters on horseback when he met Macon, whom he was always glad to see since Marengo, and whom he had attached to his person. This general was in command of the Imperial quarters and had been so moved by a scene of pillage which he had not been able to prevent, that he had just given his own purse to the unfortunate countryman who had been its victim. Macon was an old soldier of the army of Italy, whose entrance into Court circles had not altered his republican frankness. 'Well, Macon,' gaily cried out the Emperor, as he saw him, 'what have you got to tell me to-day?'—'Faith, sire,' answered he, 'I can tell you that you are followed by a crowd of plunderers who will dishonour your army and yourself if you do not promptly put things on a proper footing.' Macon would have gone on, if Napoleon had not cut short this ebullition by turning his head aside and making his horse go faster.

The reproach was only too well deserved, but it had caused displeasure by being made too publicly. The subject, however, had been again renewed by reports which were made with a little more discretion, notably by one of Napoleon's house stewards, and the Emperor had answered: 'That this dirty train of cripples and camp-followers and plunderers was an inevitable evil, a necessary result of forced and sudden marches, by means of which the enemy, hindered and disconcerted at all points, was half vanquished before fighting: and that thus heads were saved by legs!'

Without owning to it, there is no doubt that he temporarily countenanced these irregularities, because they to a certain extent made up to the soldier for his fatigues: he was in the habit of thus utilizing all springs of action. However, when it was represented to him at Lintz that this contagious evil had degenerated into the most infamous plunder, that it was becoming intolerable, and that our ranks were thinned, he suddenly stopped it in characteristic fashion. The most stringent orders were published on November 7th. The wretched creatures were tracked, gathered together and driven forwards. In Braunau alone, a fortress that had to be traversed, over 10,000 of them, it is said, were assembled, and the word having been passed round on their return to their companies, they had to undergo the indignity of a visitation, when each of them, deprived of his spoil, was given over to the rough and ready floggings of his comrades.

Murat, however, had continued his way, and had met with no serious obstacle until November 5th at Amstetten, where a skirmish had taken place, in which our cavalry, imprudently sent on into a wood, had been repulsed with a loss of 300 killed or taken prisoners. This was a new experience for Murat, who recognised that he had no longer to do with the Austrians but with very different kind of men. Oudinot hastened to the spot with his grenadiers, and from that moment commenced the determined struggle between Russian honour against French honour, or rather, so far as the soldiers were concerned, the shock of intelligent and civilized experience against primitive and barbarous courage.

In this first encounter 2,000 Russians were killed or taken; not one of them surrendered; wounded, disarmed, and biting the dust, they not only defended themselves but even continued to attack us. After the fighting was over, in order to carry away a few hundreds of them, we were obliged to prick them up with our bayonets, like a badly broken-in flock of sheep, or to knock them down with the butt ends of our muskets.

The obstinacy of this resistance confirmed Napoleon's hopes of a battle at Saint-Poelten. On receipt of this news and as soon as he had learnt the occupation of Moelkt, he left Lintz on November 9th for this enormous abbey; a magnificent residence that could vie with the most sumptuous palaces, whose cellars were able to supply all our columns with wine without being exhausted; here our Imperial headquarters took the place of those of the Austrian Emperor, who, it was said, had withdrawn to Vienna.

At the same time, Napoleon learnt that his hope of a decisive action at Saint-Poelten so ably planned by him, was dashed to the ground; that Kutusow had just slipped away by the right bank of the Danube towards the left bank, over the bridge of Krems, which he had destroyed; that the first Russian army had thus escaped him, and was on its way to join the second which would delay the war, lead it further on, and still further towards the east, thus probably giving time to Prince Charles to join it, and allow Frederic to rally his forces, to redouble his threats, and to put them into execution.

To this disappointment was added a grave anxiety which increased in the evening of November 11th with the smothered distant echo of heavy firing, which was not even interrupted by night. What unforeseen danger could suddenly have attacked Mortier? For it was doubtless he, who going forwards alone with an advance guard of 5,000 men, had unexpectedly come across Kutusow with 40,000 men; it was impossible to do otherwise than believe in the destruction of this marshal and his unhappy

division. What an effect would be produced on Austria's discouragement and Frederic's indecision by the news of the defeat of a
French corps with one of our marshals, who might at this very
moment be killed or fallen alive into the hands of the Russians!

One could only offer up prayers and await the decision of fate.
The wide and deep Danube, which was still free at this height,
separated us from the marshal. This stream had just delivered over
to the Russians one of Mortier's generals, who, in despair, was
making his escape in a barque. All announced a catastrophe: the
Emperor no longer doubted it. In his anxiety, as he drew nearer
to the sound of the combat, he had advanced from Moelkt to
Saint-Poelten where the fear of a reverse usurped the place of his
former hope of victory. Here his agitation increasing with the noise
of the firing, he despatched everybody for news; officers, aides-
de-camp, and everyone who happened to be near him. With his
mind entirely set on Mortier's peril, he suspended the progress of
the invasion; behind him at Moelkt, that of Bernadotte and the
flotilla; in front of him that of Murat whom he rebuked 'for his
precipitation in going onwards like a child up to the very gates of
Vienna,' and he even ordered Marshal Soult who was following
this prince, to retrace his steps. Finally about two o'clock in the
afternoon of the next day, (November 12th) the return of Thiard
and of Lemarois had just allayed his anxiety, when an aide-de-
camp of Mortier arrived.

The night before, towards morning, he said, Marshal Mortier
and General Gazan had driven the enemy on from Diernstein till
within sight of Krems and had carried away 1,500 of his men;
they were continuing their way when by a sudden repulse, they
perceived that they had encountered the whole of the Russian army.
It was then necessary to retreat, one against four, for the space of
two leagues which they did fighting, in good order, in the hope
of finding a shelter in Diernstein. Mortier, hotly pressed, had just
caught sight of the walls of the town, rejoicing, when suddenly he
saw another Russian army issue from it against him and found himself between two fires. His soldiers immediately dispersed through
a defile, formed on the right by the Bohemian mountains and on

the left by the Danube. There they were, pressed closely one upon the other; 20,000 Russians pushing them back, and 15,000 other Russians driving them forwards. The marshal without showing any surprise, faced them on both sides; endeavouring on the one hand to keep Kutusow in check, and on the other to open up a passage to Diernstein; but the two corps of the enemy who had caught sight of each other, through and beyond us, rushed onwards with shouts of joy, and drawing nearer enclosed and crushed our feeble troop closer and closer between their double masses.

Finally, after four hours of desperate resistance, our cavalry gave way, our firing slackened, our bayonets through constant use were bent and blunted; the gathering night instead of separating the combatants augmented the confusion which became terrible; several times Mortier himself, whose high stature made him conspicuous above all others, and a mark to be aimed at even in the darkness, was forced to kick aside or strike down with his sabre some of the most desperate. At last all hope was given up, and everyone pressed round him, urging him to take advantage of the night and escape on board a vessel, so that they might snatch from Russian pride the trophy of a French marshal taken prisoner, but he on the contrary answered: 'That he would share the fate of the brave men around him, whatever that might be; that Dupont and his division must be close at hand, and that they must make one last supreme effort.' Then, rallying and closing up the remaining troops, he pointed the only two guns that were left to him, one towards Krems against Kutusow; the other, directed by Fabvier, he turned against Diernstein, placing it at the head of the column; and as all the drums were broken, he caused the charge to be sounded on iron cans.

At this moment the Austrian Colonel Schmidt who was leading the Russian corps which was master of Diernstein, dashed forward to strike a last blow which should complete the destruction of our column. But Fabvier had heard him; hidden in the darkness he let him come near, when suddenly discharging his piece at short distance on the head of this attacking party, he overthrew it, killing its chief, and in this bloody opening, Mortier and Gazan precipitated themselves, overthrowing everything before them. Diernstein was re-taken by this impetuous dash, Schmidt's Russians fell back into the valley of Krems by which way they had secretly arrived, and took flight, whilst the delighted Mortier was hardly able to believe in his own success.

But from the other side of Diernstein came a sound of arms and numerous footsteps; and with despair in their hearts they were preparing for a fresh encounter, when, '*France*!' was the answer to our cry of 'Qui vive?' It was Dupont and his division coming to the help of the marshal. Then joyous transports and cries of '*Long live our saviours*!' succeeded to their fears.

Thus Diernstein, the famous prison of the English king Richard Coeur de Lion, became doubly celebrated by French hearts, which were as worthy of this surname and more fortunate than its owner.

On the return of daylight the roll-call was read: out of 5,000, 3,000 had perished, but by an inexplicable chance our 1,500 Russian prisoners were still to be found in Diernstein; so that the loss of the enemy, greater than our own, was estimated at 4,000 men.

We have seen that Murat had been strongly reprimanded for allowing his eagerness to carry him on to Vienna, drawing with him the corps of Marshals Lannes and Soult. The event proved, however, that this time he was not at fault; it may even be that as the urgency of the end in view increased, as we shall see, the counter-orders of the Emperor to these three corps caused them to lose twenty-four hours by which the Russians profited.

In effect his anticipation of crushing on the right bank the first Russian corps in advance of Vienna being frustrated, and Vienna and this bank having been abandoned, he cherished a fresh hope as soon as he knew Mortier was saved; it was that by hastening to Vienna by the right bank to get ahead of the enemy who was escaping from him by the left bank, he would surprise their passage of the Danube at this point, whence, precipitating himself in force on the other bank, he would interpose himself between Kutusow and Buxwoden, cutting off from the first Russian army its retreat upon the second, and taking it prisoner in Bohemia, as he had taken Mack in Suabia.

It is true that two very unlikely things were necessary for such a hope to be realized: firstly, that Vienna, strong enough to delay us for forty-eight hours, without danger for herself, should open her gates to us; then that she should give up to us intact her bridges across the Danube. This is, however, what did happen. Either from discouragement on the part of the Emperor of Austria, or a hatred for the allies, loudly proclaimed by his officers against the Russians, Vienna made no resistance; and as for her bridges, a stratagem of war delivered them into our hands.

Whilst Giulaï, who had returned as the bearer of a flag of truce, had been detained on the 12th at Saint-Poelten, Lannes and Murat and Sebastiani at their head, received orders, the one to enter Vienna, the others to spread along the bank of the Danube and take possession of the bridges of that town. On November 13th, Vienna having surrendered without striking a blow, they hastened to this passage, broke through the barrier, and at once entered into the winding defile formed by the little bridges. These were intersected by wooded islands which concealed our march from the artillery and the Austrian general posted on the last and largest bridge of the stream. Lannes and Murat had dismounted, and followed by their grenadiers, shouldering arms, they drove before them a squadron of the enemy, waving their handkerchiefs in the air to announce an armistice, and parleying with the officer in command.

This officer in his surprise drew back, not quite knowing what he ought to do, and his indecision spread to those in his rear. Thus our chiefs made their way up to the large bridge at the most critical moment; this last passage was full of inflammable material, with a battery in readiness to annihilate our column. But this sight instead of checking our marshals caused them to hurry on and when, unmasked by the enemy's retreating squadron, they saw the Austrian artillery officer seize hold of the match, they sprang forward. Dodde, then one of our engineer colonels, was the first to seize the officer's torch. A *mélée* ensued and still parleying, whilst our grenadiers cleared the bridge, and Bertrand presented himself before the Prince of Auersberg, Lannes, Murat and Sebastiani had reached the other bank and taken possession of it.

They were masters of the situation before the unfortunate prince, taken aback by this sudden stroke, had understood what was going on. The two marshals, satisfied with so important a conquest which must decide the fate of the Russians, then desisted from mystifying this general, allowing him to escape, to be lost sight of in the open, and to carry his confusion to his Emperor. Napoleon learnt the good news from Bertrand on this very day, November 13th, at Bruckersdorf, and beside himself with delight, he pushed on almost alone to Schoenbrunn. I had just preceded him there with a battalion, and was arranging the quarters when he sent for me. 'Leave at once for Gratz,' he said, 'and hand this dispatch to Marmont. 'You will find Gudin at Neustadt; you will tell him to push his posts on to the Spitalberg but not beyond. Inform yourself as to the resources to be found in Neustadt, and write to me from that town. You should come across the enemy between Neukirch and Brugg, go through them, and if you choose, invent some subterfuge; say that you are bearing news of an armistice... Get out of it as well as you can; but above all, do not allow the instructions which I entrust to you to be taken.' He was beginning to discuss the means I should employ, when I interrupted him by saying that I would get through some way or another, and that in any case I answered for his dispatches.

I must own that I did this at haphazard, in my wish to appear always ready and willing, for this doubtful and distant mission came at a very inopportune moment. I was so worn out by fatigue that a night or two previously while passing through a cantonment, I had fallen down insensible. My surprise may be imagined when on returning to my senses I found myself seated at the centre of a large, well-served and well-lighted table, in a warm room, in the midst of the officers of the mounted grenadiers of our guard. This happened quite by chance: fortunately for me, one of them had recognised me when he struck his foot against me in the dark, and extricating me from the midst of the guns and artillery waggons which would have gone over me, he carried me in his arms to this place of honour, where the cares which were lavished upon me soon brought me to myself.

There was nothing surprising in this collapse. Since we had left Munich I had been marching by day and night, especially the latter, cursing many times the necessity which obliged me to go past the fires of our infantry, who were lying on the snow, without being able to stop, envying as I did what appeared to me their comfort. Thus I would go on against time, with pressing instructions of all kinds, as long as my horses could carry me, then using those belonging to the peasants whom I met. I remember amongst other adventures that during one of these trying nights, as I was endeavouring to reach Moelkt before daylight, I encountered a river which I had to ford, and lost my guide and my horses, which were carried away by the current. Luckier than my poor beast which drifted away to the Danube, I succeeded in touching ground, continuing my way on foot, and only thankful that I had been able to arrive at the abbey at the appointed time.

As for my mission to Gratz, I spent a day and night executing it, without accident, but with greater fatigue than ever, being disappointed on my return to find that the Emperor had left Vienna. I only rejoined him at Brunn, where I learnt that Marmont was congratulating himself, that by his presence in Styria and at the defiles of Carinthia, he had turned back upon Hungary the retreat of the Archduke Charles.

At that time the Emperor was, not without reason, dissatisfied with the events which had happened since my departure from Schoenbrunn. During the night of the 13th to the 14th, which was that of my departure from this residence, he himself had passed through Vienna, unknown to the inhabitants, and had crossed the bridges to rejoice over his conquest, to convey his satisfaction to Lannes and Murat, and above all, to take advantage of it! He was in haste to make an end of the Russians all the more because he had just learnt from Giulaï that Frederic had joined the coalition. He had immediately pushed on Lannes, with the divisions of Suchet and Oudinot, Murat's cavalry, and the corps of Marshal Soult, towards Znaïm on the road to Bavaria, to cut off all retreat from Kutusow who was coming from Krems.

The combat of Diernstein against Mortier, the presence of Bernadotte who had been sent from Moelkt on the left bank with orders to urge on Kutusow, and the bad condition of the roads, must have caused some delay in the retrograde movements of this field-marshal. Thus the Emperor had expected that the first army of 36,000 Russians, harassed in the rear by 20,000 men, and cut off at the front by 50,000, would be either taken or destroyed. This result should have decided the fate of the campaign and Frederic's indecision; it had seemed to him infallible, and it had just slipped through his hands. Murat, who had been so successful, with his stratagem with the Austrians on the bridge at Vienna, was caught by the Russians by a similar stratagem at the very moment when he should have been enjoying the fruits of his own; and this is how it happened.

Kutusow, while hurrying his retreat from Krems upon Brunn, with the view of protecting it against Murat, had sent Bagration and 7,000 Russians at his right into Hollabrunn on the road to Bohemia which he would have to cross at Znaïm. Murat was coming up the same road at the head of 50,000 men; and would only have had to attack, to drive on and overthrow everything before him up to Znaïm, where he would have preceded, taken or destroyed the Russian Marshal. But he had met Bagration at Hollabrunn; and instead of passing over his body he had lost time in listening to his parleyings. A feigned capitulation of the Russian general lulled him for twenty-four hours, during which Kutusow dispersed behind Hollabrunn and towards Brunn in the utmost haste.

It was on November 15th, on the word of Wintzigerode, Alexander's aide-de-camp, that this absurd convention entrapped our Emperor's brother-in-law.

But what is still less conceivable is that Napoleon, contrary to his usual custom, should have abandoned this great stroke to his lieutenant, and that on November 14th, trusting in him, he should have returned to Schoenbrunn. Did he mistrust Vienna? Had it given him pleasure to show himself that day to its inhabitants, completely taken aback to see him return within their walls by the gate of the Danube? Was he in a hurry to proclaim loudly, as he did, the immensity of the trophies, which this capital of the enemy had surrendered to his victorious arms? Or rather, judging by my mission to Marmont and by the distribution of Davout's divisions thrown out upon Neustadt, Presburg and Brunn, on the three avenues of Vienna, had he feared a fresh attack and judged his presence on this central point still indispensable to make sure of its possession? I know not, but what is certain, is, that on the news of this insidious convention, bitterly repenting his confidence in Murat, he sent him word to break off everything at once and to attack. He himself had hastened there in a fit of anger, but he only arrived on the 17th after the tardy and bloody meeting at Hollabrunn, where on the evening of the 16th, Bagration, sacrificing two-thirds of the 7,000 Russians he commanded, had during six consecutive hours arrested the efforts of 20,000 men.

During the dark night that followed, several stratagems of war favoured the flight of the remainder of this division. Some of them on realizing their danger, cried out in French that they were of ours, and were allowed to scatter themselves, others repeating the same words let us approach until we were close to their fire, and thus added to our losses. Oudinot, whose place Duroc had taken with his division of grenadiers, fell wounded with the greater part of the officers around him. The carnage had been frightful. We had conquered, it is true, but the next day on arrival at Znaïm, Kutusow had passed by. During the following day, no one had been picked up except his laggards, who were so exhausted that they were unable to defend themselves. Two thousand fell into the hands of Sebastiani. And this retreat in which Kutusow should have perished altogether, only cost him six thousand men. At Brunn he had rejoined his Emperor, who had arrived there from Berlin; he brought back to him 30,000 men whom he was going to unite near Wischau, beyond Brunn, to the second Russian army of Buxwoden, to the remainder of the Austrian army, and soon probably to the Archduke Charles.

Thus following on the campaign of Ulm which had come to such a complete issue, that of Vienna remained undecided. It devolved on us to unite, to revictual, to prepare for the possibility of having to give a great battle in the depths of Moravia, at the end of a long line of operations, by which Prussia was threatening the whole of the left flank, from Strasburg to Vienna. Such was the danger of our position, which had just been augmented by the mistake of Hollabrunn.

XVIII

AUSTERLITZ

From znaïm the emperor proceeded towards Brunn, pursuing Kutusow and causing him to be out flanked on the right by Soult at Nikolsberg. On November 20th he pushed on this right wing from Nikolsberg to Austerlitz, and our advance guard under Murat towards Wischau on the road to Olmutz, himself arriving that day at Brunn. Surprised and delighted at the inconceivable abandonment of this stronghold which was full of arms and provisions, he made it his base of operations against the Russian army. Whilst occupied in this manner he learnt of the junction of the enemy's forces in Wischau, and that, at Posorsitz, their cavalry, after having forced back our own, had been repulsed by our cuirassiers and by the mounted grenadiers of our guard. On the 21st, he betook himself to the field of battle, studying the moves which he considered less brilliant than had been reported to him; and, learning that the enemy had retired to his reinforcements as far as Olmutz, he returned to Brunn.

On going back to Wischau he stopped on the highway about two leagues and a half from Brunn, near the Santon, a small mound by the side of the road, a kind of rather abruptly truncated cone, and gave orders that the foot of it should be dug out towards the enemy's side so as to increase its escarpment. Then turning off towards the south he entered a high plain contained between two embanked streams running from the north to the south-west. The width of this plateau is about two leagues; its length, three leagues; beyond which, turning to the west it trends downwards and falls into a basin defined by two lakes. The Emperor slowly and silently went over this newly-discovered ground, stopping several times on its most elevated points, principally towards Pratzen. He carefully examined all its characteristics, and during this survey turned towards us saying: 'Gentlemen, examine this ground carefully, it is going to be a battle-field, you will have a part to play upon it!' This plain was indeed to be a few days later the field of the battle of Austerlitz!

The following days until the 27th he remained at Brunn. His army for three months had never ceased to be on the march or in combat; he allowed it to reunite, and restore its strength, its arms, repair its foot-gear and take breath. It was thus distributed: Marmont to Gratz; Mortier to Vienna; Davout in part to Presburg, watching Hungary, which had declared itself neutral, and in part to Nikolsberg, between Brunn and Vienna; Lannes, Murat, and Soult were encamped around and in front of the Emperor on the ground defined by Brunn, Wischau and Austerlitz; finally Bernadotte at his rear but within reach occupied Iglau, watching Bohemia where the Archduke Ferdinand was holding his ground against d'Hilliers and that general's foot dragoons.

We had been in Brunn for six days when the Emperor, agitated by the news of the disaster at Trafalgar, and the increasing hostile dispositions of Prussia, and already weary of his own inaction, was disquieting himself concerning the temporizing policy favoured by the Russian army. This was indeed the most dangerous system which Alexander could oppose to his good luck. Each day increased the peril of our isolated and distant position. Napoleon having ventured into the very depths of Moravia with 65,000 combatants within reach, whilst 150,000 Prussians threatened the whole of the left flank of his retreat, found himself brought to a stand in front by Alexander and 90,000 Russians and Germans: whilst the Archduke Ferdinand and 20,000 Austrians were advancing on his rear in Bohemia, and simultaneously the Archduke Charles and 40,000 other Imperials, already in Hungary, were hurrying up against his right!

This is the reason that on November 26th with his patience exhausted after a whole night of work, he wrote to the Emperor Alexander, and sent his aide-de-camp Savary to compliment him, and to sound his war-like or pacific inclinations. Whilst awaiting his aide-de-camp's return, two Austrian envoys followed by the Prussian minister Haugwitz, the former from Olmutz, and the latter from Berlin, arrived at the Imperial quarters. On November 27th he was trying to prevent the one from entering into any explanations, and avoiding giving a reply to the two others, when he suddenly learnt that his advance guard had been surprised and overthrown at Wischau. At the same time a Bavarian officer, who had enlisted in the army of the enemy, deserted their side and came to warn us that it was Kutusow and Alexander himself who were attacking us. This at first appeared to Berthier so unlikely that he caused the fugitive to be arrested; but his report received swift confirmation by advices from Marshal Soult who was assailed in Austerlitz.

The return of Savary that very evening left no longer any doubt as to this news. This aide-de-camp came to tell us that the whole of the allied army without waiting for a reinforcement of 14,000 Russians were marching upon us; notwithstanding which, the letter he brought back seemed less hostile. From that moment Napoleon, no longer expecting anything except from Alexander or a victory, sent back to Vienna and to Talleyrand the Austrian and Prussian negotiators; again despatching Savary to the Russian Emperor to propose an interview, and very early on November 28th himself advanced to Posorsitz in the hope of a favourable reply.

But Alexander, badly surrounded and wrongly advised by a set of presumptuous youths, decided that an interview was useless, and only despatched his favourite. On his side Napoleon more and more impatient pushed on at a galop beyond our last vedettes.

Dolgorouki and our Emperor encountered each other on the high road of Olmutz in front of Posorsitz and, to our great astonishment, beyond the range of the guns of our advance posts. We did not know whether the Emperor was running this risk out of real impatience or curiosity, or with a view of increasing the enemy's presumption by a feigned anxiety not to allow any chance of investigation of our ranks by the Russians.

On first sight of each other both dismounted; we were not able to overhear all that passed in this interview; the Emperor's attitude was at first calm and restrained, that of Dolgorouki on the contrary was so vainglorious and haughty that when not irritated by it, it inspired us with pity as being utterly ridiculous and out of place.

In the midst of this colloquy which lasted about a quarter of an hour, the Emperor remarked that the Cossacks of the Russian's escort were edging up to our flanks; Dolgorouki smilingly answered for them, but either from real or simulated anxiety Napoleon ordered several of us to keep them at a respectful distance, and this was at once done by Exelmans, with his naked sabre hanging from his sword knot, and his pistol in his fist.

But as the arrogance of Alexander's favourite was becoming unbearable, the Emperor's voice rose louder. The young Russian would not hear of peace on other conditions than the abandonment of Italy, of the left bank of the Rhine, and of Belgium! 'What! Brussels also?' answered Napoleon; 'But we are in Moravia, and even if you were on the heights of Montmartre you should not obtain Brussels.' At last he lost patience. Dolgorouki had offered to let him draw back safe and sound beyond the Danube if he would promise at once to evacuate Vienna and the Hereditary States. Napoleon, no longer able to contain himself at this insult, exclaimed: 'Withdraw; go, Sir, and tell your master that it is not my custom to allow insolence; withdraw this very moment!' When he had got back to our advance guard, the Emperor, still in a state of irritation, dismounted and held converse with Savary. During the aide-de-camp's double mission, the young Russian noblemen had insulted the latter by their arrogant expressions which he repeated and Napoleon struck the ground with his riding whip while listening (a habit of his when excited) exclaiming: 'Italy! what would they have done with France if I had been beaten? But as they will have it so, I wash my hands of it; and, please God, in forty-eight hours I shall give them a severe lesson!' These last words were spoken in the hearing of a soldier of the 17th light regiment, and perceiving that this sentry was listening: 'Do you know,' said Napoleon, 'these people think that they are going to swallow us up!' Upon which the grenadier having replied: 'Let them just try it, we should soon choke them!' the Emperor began to laugh and his ill-humour vanished.

Then he commenced the retreat, following it himself on foot, either because he thought he was too much in sight, or with a view of increasing the enemy's presumption; the pace being taken at a speed which probably emboldened the Russians. One of ourselves, an old republican veteran, was misled by it, and said to me: 'This begins badly! young man, it is not enough to be always advancing; you have yet to learn what it is to fall back, and possibly even to be routed!' I was surprised at this free comment on Napoleon, such liberty of judgment having become rare. Most of us gave ourselves up to a conviction of his infallibility and executed the orders of the day without looking beyond, without any care for the morrow, sure of victory if we obeyed. Such submission places useful instruments in the hands of an extraordinary man, but is too often the reason why he leaves behind him few chiefs who are worthy to take his place.

This first retrograde movement was a brief one.

November 29th and 30th were spent in reviews and recognizances. Never was a battle-field more carefully gone over or better prepared. On the 29th, what seemed to concern him the most, was the defence of the Santon which he at once retrenched, armed and victualled like a fort. He sent me there several times either to repeat his orders, or to see that they had been executed, and was not satisfied without coming back himself and going up the incline on foot. He immediately posted there General Claparède and the 17th light infantry, ordering them to burn their last cartridge and get themselves killed there to a man if necessary.

Already, however, the march of the Russian columns, and their movements of cavalry from afar and beyond our right wing, indicated to the Emperor that they would make their greatest attempt on the other side of our line. Whilst watching them, he rejoiced at this, and allowed them to go on, knowing that one cannot turn a strong and well-prepared enemy without being turned oneself, and that the result would show which of the two had really cut off the retreat of the other!

This reflection was evidently in his mind, when on November 30th, having stopped on the great plateau of Pratzen which extends towards Austerlitz, he pronounced in our hearing these words which the event of the day after next rendered prophetic ones: 'As master of this grand position,' he said, 'it would be easy for me to stop the Russians here; but in that case, it would only be an ordinary battle, whereas, by abandoning it to them and withdrawing my right, if they dare to come down from these heights to surround me, they will be lost without resource!'

Consequently, already on that and the following day, 1st December, withdrawn behind this plateau, an oblique line of battle was taken up, the left thrown forward and the right refused, and as it were hidden behind the lakes Melnitz and Telnitz or Satschau. Our extreme left on the contrary appearing strong was thrown forward, and rested on the steep mound named the Santon.

This oblique position seemed only a defensive one, even showing timidity, negligently guarded in the centre and particularly on the right, it only seemed formidable on the left, but Bernadotte and our reserves could with a rush take in reverse any attack made against our centre or our right. The enemy's army on the contrary, weaker in front of our left on the road to Olmutz, and which was separated from the rest by the ravine of Blazowitz, was heaped together unprotected in the centre, on the plateau of Pratzen: its left was extended afar, towards Aujerzd, to throw it against our right withdrawn behind the lakes.

The forces were unequal: 90,000 men against 65,000. The advantage in number was on the side of the allies to an excess of 25,000, but was made up for by the accidents of locality. Of the two opposed lines, one was, fully in view, and the other masked, which was the first advantage. They formed as it were two arcs of a circle, of which ours was in the closest order, a second advantage, which was soon increased by an imprudent manoeuvre of Alexander.

On the one hand a thick screen of Cossacks, and a clear line of vedettes on our side within range of musket-shot, covered the two fronts. Whilst behind their outpost lines, the two armies about double gun shot range apart with their arms stacked, were tranquilly eating and reposing round their fires as if by tacit accord in preparation for the following day, Napoleon, followed by some of us and twenty chasseurs of his guard had advanced between the two lines, and was measuring their extent from right to left. He was making this last general recognizance so leisurely, at a foot's pace, and so close to the enemy, that when near Pratzen, Daumesnil, the captain of his escort of chasseurs, since celebrated by the defence of Vincennes, and myself, heedlessly provoked the line of the enemy within range of pistol-shot for which we were severely reprimanded: having drawn upon us several shots which whistled round the Emperor's head. I even remember that not being sufficiently alive to our imprudence, when we had got to the extreme left beyond the Santon, and whilst Napoleon was examining the approaches to it, an argument arose between us as to the distance which separated us at this spot from the enemy, and this very Daumesnil, who was an excellent shot, wishing to prove their proximity to us, took hold of the carbine of one of his men, resting its barrel on his shoulder, and with a single shot unhorsed a Russian officer who stood out from the others by the dazzling whiteness of his mount.

Towards three o'clock, having completed his recognizan the Emperor returned to his bivouac. He had established his quarters on the right near the high road, at the rear to the right of the Santon, and in front of Bellowitz, between the stream of that village and that of Ghirzikowitz. It was a woodman's hut, a great round place with a fire in the middle, lighted from the top, and which his grenadiers had built at the summit of a high hillock which commanded a view of the plain. His coach with the horses taken out, was close by, in which he had slept the preceding nights. There was also near here and the high road, a labourer's isolated abode, a poor cottage where his canteens had been established, and where we used to dine with him in the one low room, and at the one long table with benches all round which furnished it. The division of Duroc and Oudinot's grenadiers were encamped to the front, the guard was all round and to the rear.

He had just arrived there, when, about four o'clock, on a report from our advance guard he came out of his quarters with a telescope in his hand, which he directed towards the plateau of Pratzen in front of him to the right. A great flank movement of the centre of the Russian army was taking place there. Behind his first line the columns of the enemy could be seen extending themselves to their left and exposed towards Aujerzd and the two lakes. At this sight, with a thrill of joy, and clapping his hands, he exclaimed: 'That is a shameful movement! they are walking into the trap; they are giving themselves away; before to-morrow night this army will belong to me.'

It was indeed evident that the Russians in the pride of their inexperience, fancying that we were struck with fear, and resigned to a timid defence, imagined that they had nothing to fear in front of them, and only thought of throwing themselves upon our right, between us and Vienna so as to turn us and to cut off all retreat to our inevitable rout on the following day. Thus they ventured under our very eyes to converge their principal forces to this side, thus stripping their centre, and abandoning on their weakened right wing their line of operations or retreat. One would have said that conquerors already, with no other fear than that of letting us escape, they thought of nothing but despatching us, and not at all of the possibility that they might be forced to defend them selves.

In order still more to swell their presumption, the Emperor at once instructed Murat to issue from the ranks with some cavalry, and to make a feint of hesitation and anxiety, and then draw back as if frightened. Having given this order, he returned to his bivouac, and there, in a proclamation which he dictated from his carriage, and immediately sent round, after pointing out to his sol-diers the Russian army presenting its flank to them and offering an assured triumph to their valour, he told them that he was himself directing their battalions, and promised that he would not expose himself unless victory were uncertain, but after it was won they should have good cantonments and peace. Then going in with us into the neighbouring hut he gaily sat down to table.

Murat and Caulaincourt were seated next to him, then Junot, General Mouton, Rapp, Lemarois, Lebrun, Macon, Thiard, Yvan and myself. The meal lasted sometime, contrary to the habit of the Emperor who seldom spent more than twenty minutes at table, but the conversation was the attraction. As for myself, in the full persuasion that its subject would be the great event which was on the point of deciding his fortunes, I was all attention; but nothing of the kind happened. At the very outset, Napoleon addressing Junot, who piqued himself on being rather literary, led the conversation on dramatic poetry. The latter having answered by quoting several new tragedies, Napoleon, as if entirely oblivious of the Russian army, the war, and the next day's battle, disagreed with him, entered fully into the subject and, with some warmth, declared: 'That in his eyes, none of these authors had understood the new principle which ought to serve for a base to our modem tragedies. He had told the author of ' The Templars' that his tragedy was a bad one; he knew very well that the poet would never forgive him; and for the matter of that, the self-love of an author was inexorable. If you wanted any praise from these gentlemen, you must first praise them. In the whole piece there was only one sustained character which was that of a man who wanted to die. But that is not natural and therefore worthless; one must desire to live and know how to die!

'Look at Corneille,' he cried, 'what strength of conception! He would have made a statesman. But as for ' The Templars' there is no policy in the piece. 'He ought to have put Philip Augustus into such a position that it should be a necessity for him to destroy them; while interesting the public in their safety, he should have made it feel strongly that their existence was incompatible with that of the monarchy; that they had become a danger by their number, their riches and their power; that the safety of the throne demanded their destruction!'

'To-day that the glamour of the pagan religion no longer exists, our tragic stage requires another motive. Politics should be the great spring of modern tragedy. Policy should take the place on our theatre of ancient fatality; that fatality which rendered Œdipus a criminal although he was not guilty; which causes us to feel an interest in Phædra by throwing on the Gods part of the burden of her crimes and her weaknesses. These principles are both to be found in Iphigenia; this is the masterpiece of art, the masterpiece of Racine, who has been unjustly accused of being deficient in strength!'

He continued: 'That it was an error to imagine tragic subjects were exhausted; that there were any number of them in the necessities of politics; but it was necessary to be able to feel and strike this chord; that in this principle, which was an abundant source of strong emotions, a fruitful germ of the most critical situations, and of itself a fatality as imperious and dominating as the fatality of the ancients, one would find many advantages; it was only necessary to place your personages in opposition to other passions or other inclinations, under the absolute influence of this powerful necessity. Thus, whatever was called '*coup d'état,*' or political crime, would become a subject for tragedy, in which, horror being tempered by necessity, a new and sustained interest would develop itself.'

Then followed some examples, but none bearing on the recollection which possibly inspired him the most at this moment. One of them carried him back to the time of the campaign in Egypt; apropos of which, passing on to a subject more conformable to our present situation and to the habits of most of those who were around him: 'Yes,' he resumed, 'had I taken possession of Acre, I should have worn a turban; I should have put my army into wide trousers. 'I would no longer have exposed it except in the last extremity; I should have made it my sacred battalion, my immortals! I should have finished the war against the Turks with Arabs, Greeks, and Armenians. Instead of a battle in Moravia, I should have won a battle on the Issus, created myself Emperor of the East, and returned to Paris by way of Constantinople.'

These last words were accompanied by a smile, seeming to imply that he was yielding to an impulse which carried him away on the wings of some youthful dream of his conquering imagination. A dream which, nevertheless, might possibly have been realized; since, according to the irrefutable testimony of travellers who were at that time in Libanus, 100,000 Christians had expected him on that side, fixing all their hopes upon him, and ready to join his forces at the first signal of the taking of Acre.

At this moment I hazarded the remark in a low tone of voice: 'That if Constantinople were in question, we were still on the road to that capital!' I do not know if Junot overheard me, or whether, entertaining the same thought, he considered it advisable to repeat my words; but Napoleon answered: 'No, I know the French; they never believe themselves well off in any place where they happen to be. Long expeditions are not easy for them. Come now; collect the voices of the army; you will hear them all cry out for France. The French are like that, that is their character. France is too attractive, they do not like to be so far, or to remain so long away from her!' Junot having urged against this the manifestation of warlike ardour which broke out in all the ranks, General Mouton, with his austere voice, abruptly interrupted him thus: 'These acclamations prove the contrary, do not be led away by this, the army is tired out; it has had enough of it; and although it would obey if ordered still further afield, it would be with reluctance; only indeed manifesting such ardour on the eve of a battle because hoping to have done with it all the next day, and return home!'

The Emperor, who could not have been much pleased with these outspoken utterances, yet confirmed their truth; but he broke up the conversation, and rose up from table saying: 'In the meanwhile, let us go and fight!'

Day, however, was declining; the enemy's movement to the left was still going on, and Napoleon, whose arrangements were all made, after having renewed his instructions, visited his parks and his ambulances, assuring himself with his own eyes that all his orders had been executed. He was coming back to his bivouac, when, hearing some lively firing on his right, he sent one of us in that direction, and then throwing himself on the straw in his hut fell fast asleep. He was still sleeping, and the night of the 1st to the

2nd of December was far spent, when the aide-de-camp returned, and waking him up with some difficulty, informed him that a hot attack in the direction, of the lakes upon one of the last villages on our tight, had been repulsed. This confirmed his previsions; but, desirous of himself reconnoitring for the last time, by the light of the camp fires, the positions of the enemy, he remounted his horse, and followed by a few amongst us, adventured himself between the two lines. He was walking along them when, in spite of several warnings, having in the darkness directed his steps towards Pratzen, I think, he unwittingly came across a post of Cossacks. These sprang out upon him so suddenly, that he would certainly have been taken or killed, but for the devotion of the chasseurs of his escort, and had he not returned to our fires at full speed. His return was so hurried that being obliged to cross without picking his way the marshy stream which protected our front, several of the men and horses who followed him got bogged there, amongst them Yvan, his body-surgeon since 1796, whose duty was never to be away from his person.

Having crossed the stream, the Emperor regained on foot, from one fire to another, his own bivouac. As he approached it in the darkness, he stumbled over the trunk of a tree lying on the ground, and one of the grenadiers noticing this, conceived the idea of twisting his straw so as to make a torch of it, which he lit, and raising it above his head, used it as a torch to light the steps of his Emperor.

In the middle of the night which was that of the eve of the anniversary of the coronation, this flame which illumined and suddenly disclosed the countenance of Napoleon, seemed like a signal to the soldiers in the neighbouring bivouacs; one cry rose up: 'It is the anniversary of the coronation; *Long live the Emperor*!' an impulse of sudden enthusiasm which Napoleon vainly tried to check. 'Silence,' he said, 'till tomorrow; think of nothing now but sharpening your bayonets!'

Already the same thought, the same cry had spread with the rapidity of lightning, and was repeated from fire to fire: each one not to be outdone and grasping the idea, tore up his shelter; and fastening the straw at the end of every pole they could lay hands on, they set them alight, so that in a moment, over a line of two leagues, millions of sheaves of flames rose up to the reiterated cries of '*Vive l'Empereur!*' ... Thus was improvised under the eyes of the astonished enemy, the most memorable illumination, the most touching fête ever offered to its general by the admiration and devotion of a whole army.

The Russians, it was said, imagined that because we were burning our shelters, we were going to leave the ground, and their presumption went on increasing. As for Napoleon, who was first annoyed, but afterwards greatly moved and touched, he exclaimed: 'That this evening was the grandest in his life!' and he proceeded from bivouac to bivouac, some considerable distance from his own, to testify his gratitude to his soldiers.

During the rest of the night, in spite of his fatigue, either through emotion or because he had been awake to receive several reports of the march of the Russians upon his right, he slept very little.

At last when the morning of December 2 was beginning to dawn, he called us into his hut. Here we were served with a slight repast, which he took with us standing; then buckling on his sword: 'Now, gentlemen,' he said, 'let us go and begin a grand day!' Each of us then ran to his horses. A moment afterwards, on the summit of this hillock, which our soldiers had called 'the Emperor's mound,' from various points of our line we saw all the heads of our main body hasten up, each followed by an aide-de-camp.

Napoleon had desired that they should thus all come at once to receive his last commands. They were: the Prince Marshal Murat, Marshal Lannes, Marshal Bernadotte, Marshal Soult, and Marshal Davout. At this solemn instant these marshals formed around the Emperor the most formidable assemblage which imagination can conceive. What a marvellous spectacle! how many united glories were to be found in this redoubtable circle! How many warlike chieftains, justly and diversely celebrated, surrounded the greatest man of war of ancient or modem times! I think I can still see them, receiving his inspiration, as it were, like bearers of Jove's thunderbolts, scatter themselves abroad to shatter the united forces of two empires. Could my life last as long as the world endures, the impression of such a spectacle would never fade from my memory. Thus began one of the most celebrated days in our history! … How quickly the times have altered! In those days how grand was everything, what glorious times! what splendid men and what magnificent careers!

The Emperor's first words to his marshals gave them the key to his plan of campaign. He still felt so convinced, owing to the reports brought to him during the night, that the enemy was continuing his flank movement, and throwing himself on our right, with the sole thought of leaving him no chance of escape, that he once more exclaimed: 'Yes, it is a shameful movement! they must think me a greenhorn; but they will soon repent of it,' and on the spot he renewed his orders to each and all.

Davout, the head of whose harassed column was only just appearing in sight, received orders to stop the enemy on our extreme right, at the end of the defile which was bordered by the lakes, and towards which they were still pressing forwards.

Soult received the same order for his division on the right; and his other two divisions already formed in attacking columns beyond the stream at the openings of the two villages, were instructed to be ready to dash out upon the central plateau of the battle.

Bernadotte, who would come up obliquely from our left, was also to assail the plateau at the same time and on the same side.

This simultaneous effort of four divisions against the centre of the Austro-Russians, thinned by their movement to the front and left, was to be supported by the Emperor himself with his double reserve of the united grenadiers and his own guard.

At the same time, on our left wing, Murat and his cavalry were to charge in the intervals of Lannes' artillery; then drawing back behind it, they would attract the onrush of the enemy's cavalry which seemed strong on that side, and would bring it under the fire of our battalions.

The Emperor concluded with these words: 'In half-an-hour, the entire line must be in a blaze!'

Thus, whilst on the left, a defensive attitude would be adopted by our troops, withdrawn to the bottom of a valley into which the enemy was advancing and becoming entangled; the central plateau where the allies, by their movement to the left, opposed but a weakened front, would be carried by an attack in force. The two wings of the enemy would thus be suddenly divided by this decisive stroke. The one, attacked on the front and outflanked by our victory on the centre would be forced to give way; whilst the other, which had advanced too far, finding itself turned and over-come by the same central victory, would be completely hemmed in against the lakes in this cut-throat pass in which it had risked itself, and would there be crushed or taken. Here we have the battle as it was conceived and carried out!

After having repeated his orders to his marshals, the Emperor said to each one of them: 'Go!' and each in turn carrying his head high, full of eagerness, made the military salute and went his way. When it came to Bernadotte's turn, the Emperor's voice took a noticeably dry and imperious tone, and when a few moments after, the marshal's two divisions were starting for the point of attack, he harangued them himself. The proclamation of the night before was read by the light of the camp fires, and he added to it: 'That to-day, the Russian pride was to be brought low, and the war to be concluded by a thunderbolt!'

During this time the rising sun was obscured by heavy mists which seemed to the Russians to favour their flank movement forwards to the left; but on the contrary they veiled our attack, only deferred to surprise this imprudent and foolish manoeuvre in the very act.

They had already attacked our oblique line on the right, which was well to the rear and refused, from Telnitz to Sokolnitz in the direction of the low ground near the lakes, where, in their rivalry to get forward they had crowded together and assailed us as they were.

It was not yet eight o'clock and silence and darkness were still reigning over the rest of the line, when, beginning with the heights, the sun suddenly breaking through this thick fog, dis-closed to our sight the plateau of Pratzen growing empty of troops from the flank march of the enemy's columns. As for us who had remained in the ravine which defines the foot of this plateau, the smoke of the bivouacs and the vapours which, heavier on this point than elsewhere, still hung around, concealed from the eyes of the Russians our centre deployed in columns and ready for the attack.

On seeing this, Marshal Soult, whom the Emperor had kept last by his side, wanted to hasten to his divisions and give them the signal; but Napoleon, calmer than he, still held him back that the enemy might rush upon his own ruin; and pointing to Pratzen, asked: 'How much time do you require to crown that summit?' 'Ten minutes,' answered the marshal.—'Then go,' resumed the Emperor, 'but you can wait another quarter-of-an-hour, and, it will be time enough then!'

The moment having arrived, the divisions of Vandamme and Saint Hilaire springing out of the mist which enveloped them, suddenly appeared on the scene. It was then eight o'clock. The plateau attacked on the front and in flank was scaled at a quick step. The first cannon fired on that point was on the side of the Russians. The enemy was completely surprised; some were still marching towards their left, the others were facing us on three lines, holding their ground badly. Their first fire was disregarded, we attacked with our sidearms, and their lines one after the other turned tail, leaving their knapsacks on the ground before them, abandoning their artillery even, and flying before our bayonets. On our own side at nine o'clock the battle, which was painfully on the defensive behind on the right, already victorious to the front at the centre, and threatening to our left, was engaged on our whole front.

Towards eleven o'clock, all had succeeded according to the Emperor's previsions. The Russian centre had been broken and its two wings separated; but it was necessary to retain this advantage and profit by it; to maintain the centre against the Russian reserves and to surprise on the flank and rear simultaneously the masses of the enemy's left, whilst they threw them selves violently against our right which they were bearing down. From the height of the central position which he had just gained so rapidly we could hear their fire in the rear to the right of us.

Towards midday I rejoined the Emperor. I was returning by his orders from calling up his foot guard, and conducting the united grenadiers of the reserve to an eminence behind the stream and this plateau. He and his horse guards had taken up a position there, making Bernadotte remain on his left. He distrusted this marshal and sent me to repeat his orders to him, and to watch how they were carried out.

I found Bernadotte on foot at the head of his infantry, agitated and uneasy, expecting from his soldiers a calmness of which he did not set them the example. This anxiety was not, it is true, devoid of reason; pointing out to me the formidable masses of cavalry which were gathering in front of him, he complained somewhat too loudly that he had not a single squadron to oppose to them, and besought me so earnestly to go and beg Napoleon to send some cavalry to his aid that not being able to resist his entreaties, I undertook to convey them to the Emperor. Napoleon answered with some impatience: 'Why, he knows very well that I have not any to spare!' At this very moment he had just collected in front, of him all he had at hand, consisting of all the cavalry of his guard with one battery of artillery. At the same time forced in his turn to thin the central plateau, he threw out to the right Soult's two divisions which were also on the flank and rear of the left wing of the Austro-Russians, whom he thus completely cut off from the rest. In this movement an offensive return of the allied infantry supported by the Russian guard, very nearly shook Vandamme and Saint-Hilaire who repulsed it at the point of the bayonet: this was the critical moment of the battle!

It was now one o'clock, Napoleon from the summit of this commanding plateau, could see before him Alexander's guard advancing in a mass to drive him away and re-take it. At the same moment he could hear in the rear to his right the renewed firing of the Russians' advanced left. They were 30,000 men against less than 10,000 of ours who were endeavouring to hold their ground against them. It looked as if they were very nearly becoming masters of those very positions behind us whence we had advanced that morning. On this side the action in the hollow was hidden from him. The sound of its tumult, however, was becoming so threatening, that, withdrawing his glance from the decisive attack which was going to take place in front, and seeing behind him a black mass of moving troops, he exclaimed: 'What! can those be the Russians?' On my reply (for I alone happened to be near him at the moment) that it must be his own reserve, he ordered me to go off at full gallop and make sure of it.

It was indeed the division of the united grenadiers of our reserve. Duroc, having perceived the progress of the Russian left against our right was marching towards the lakes to come to the aid of Soult and Davout.

I had hardly returned, and re-assured the Emperor as to what was going on in his rear, when in front of him began the attack of Alexander's horse guard. It was so impetuous that Vandamme's two battalions on the left were completely overwhelmed! One of them indeed, covered with blood, and having lost its eagle and the greater part of its arms only got up to run away at full speed. This battalion was that of the 4th regiment, which almost passed over us, and Napoleon himself, our effort to arrest it being in vain. The unfortunate fellows were quite distracted with fear and could listen to nothing; in reply to our reproaches for thus deserting the field of battle and their Emperor they shouted mechanically 'Vive l'Empereur!' while they fled faster than ever.

Napoleon smiled pitifully; then with a scornful gesture he said to us: 'Let them go,' and retaining all his calm in the midst of the affray, he despatched Rapp to the cavalry of the guard.

It was time he did so, but a single moment is enough to change everything. Rapp reappeared on the scene, announcing almost directly to the Emperor the complete rout of the Russian guard by the French guard. He returned alone at a gallop, his head held high, his glance aflame, with a bloody forehead and sword, as a well-known picture represents him; but with this difference, that around Napoleon there was no wreckage of warfare, no shattered cannons, no dead men, no numerous staff, as the painter chose to depict. The ground worn by the passage of the combatants was perfectly bare; the Emperor was two or three paces in front of us on the summit, Berthier by his side, and behind him only Caulaincourt, Lebrun, Thiard, and myself. The foot guards and even the squadron on duty were at some considerable distance to the rear of our right. The other officers of the Emperor, Duroc, Junot, Mouton, Macon, Lemarois, were dispersed at distances over the whole line. Rapp on arriving said in a loud voice: 'Sire, I took the liberty of taking your chasseurs; we have overwhelmed and crushed the Russian guard and taken his artillery.'—'It was well done, I saw it,' answered the Emperor; 'but you are wounded, my dear fellow.' To which Rapp replied: 'It is nothing, Sire, nothing but a scratch!' and he came back to take his place amongst us. Savary then appeared at a foot pace, exhibiting his Turkish sabre, which had been broken, he said, in the same charge in which Rapp had just immortalized himself; but Rapp who hated him, and who happened to be near me at the moment, contradicted this, and being still very excited, said a great deal more.

This victory had indeed been decided by Rapp with the mame-lukes, whose colonel he was, and the mounted chasseurs of the guard. The cavalry and artillery of the Russian guard had been sabred and thrown to the ground; Ordener and his mounted grena-diers completed the work. A whole row of Alexander's unfortunate young horse guards lying on the ground with their death wounds in front, encumbered the spot where this terrible encounter had taken place. Other lines of dead and wounded, with the knapsacks of the infantry (which it is the Russian custom to deposit on the ground at their feet before the combat), indicated the other posi-tions where the infantry of the enemy's guard had succumbed, and whose defeat was to be now completed by Bernadotte. Just then a young officer of artillery, named Apraxin, whom our chasseurs had taken, was brought before the Emperor, struggling and weeping, wringing his hands in despair, and exclaiming: 'That he had lost his battery! That he was dishonoured!' Napoleon tried to console him, saying: 'Calm yourself, young man! and remember this; there can be no shame in being conquered by Frenchmen!'

From afar could be seen the remains of the Russian reserves abandoning the central plateau to us, and the left of their army retiring in close ranks upon Austerlitz. They were retreating under the cannonading of our guard, with which the commandant Doguereau (to-day a peer and general of division) was furrowing their routed ranks.

A few moments later in the midst of the noise of the firing which still thundered at our two wings, the Emperor despatched Lebrun to Paris to carry the news of his victory. In spite of the first pride of success, the choice of this officer was not displeasing to any of those around Napoleon. It was in our eyes a kind of reparation for some hard words which had passed the night before, relating to a financial error on the part of the minister Barbé-Marbois, father-in-law of this colonel.

The Emperor thus remained absolute master of this lofty and advanced centre of the battle. His attention was then withdrawn to his right at the rear in the direction of the lower end of the lakes. Twenty-seven thousand Austro-Russians, having blindly adventured themselves there, were still combating the 9,000 men at our right, whom they had not been able to force during the whole morning. Napoleon then pushed forwards upon the rear of this abandoned mass Soult's two divisions, which had been victorious at the centre and at Aujerzd, ourselves, his reserve batteries, and even his own special squadron on duty.

This unfortunate wing, overwhelmed on three sides under the simultaneous efforts of Davout, Soult, Duroc and his grenadiers, surrounded, forced, repulsed by Vandamme and ourselves against the lakes, sought a refuge there. Before reaching them the greater number were forced to lay down arms; 2,000 only escaping by the road dividing the two lakes. A few other thousands in their mad terror ventured upon the ice which covered, their surface, and in a moment this white and glistening mirror became suddenly black with the scattered multitude of fugitives, who had risked themselves on the dangerous foothold which gave way beneath their feet under the indentation of our pitiless bullets. From the heights where he had remained, the Emperor perceiving this, exclaimed: 'It is Aboukir!'

Indeed, we who were charging them, stopped short in pity at the sight of this terrible and novel spectacle; some of us even holding out a helping hand to these drowning men. As I passed by I pulled out a Cossack from the frozen water. Little did I then think that the following year, after having first taken part in the conquest of Naples and the Calabrias, then in that of Prussia, very far from these lakes I should meet with him again, and that, wounded myself, and a prisoner in the centre of Poland, I should be recognised and succoured in my turn by this Tartar!

It should, however, be told to the honour of this vanquished wing which was almost completely killed or taken, that its end in the trap into which it had fallen, was a glorious one. Hemmed in, and charged on all sides, it defended itself by squads to the very last. So much so, that after this disastrous scene, when some of us returned to these lakes, those who were still holding on there without hope, waited for us steadfastly till we were straight up to their pieces, discharging them at us point blank so that my face was scorched by the flame issuing from one of them.

A few hundred foot soldiers were still resisting our picked squadron, when Vandamme, perceiving me, cried out: 'Ségur, come and help me take this park of artillery imbedded in the mud, which a few drunken artillerymen alone are defending.' The capture was indeed so easy that the two of us sufficed for it. At this moment came up one of his battalions reduced to 150 men; and on my exclamation at the sight of so small a number, he replied: 'Yes, indeed; it is impossible to make a good omelette without breaking a great many eggs!' It was in fact his division which had borne the brunt of the battle.

Whilst this victory was being completed at our right, on our left, the Russian right wing had been conquered in front by Lannes and Murat with a loss of 6,000 men, it had been followed up on the road to Olmutz, whence, turning off to the left, it was nearing Austerlitz, losing its line of operations, and having no other refuge than by Holitch and Hungary. These Russians marched past our centre and Bernadotte, but the marshal, who was rather chary of giving himself trouble when it was a case of divided glory, having stopped too soon, allowed the defeated troops to pass by without molesting them, and did not even notice the singular direction they were taking.

Towards four o'clock the battle was at an end, and nothing remained to be done but to pursue and pick up the scattered and routed remains. While giving this order, the Emperor addressed a few pleasant words to the officers and soldiers who happened to be near him; then, leaving the lakes, he returned by our right to our left, as far as the road to Olmutz. Night surprised him whilst he thus walked over the whole line of battle, strewn with the wounded, stopping to speak to every one of them. The morning mist was then falling back in frozen rain, which rendered the night even darker; but ordering complete silence, the better to hear the groans—of his poor maimed soldiers, he would himself hasten to their help, making Yvan and his mameluke give them brandy out of his own canteen.

At last about ten o'clock at night, having then got as far as the road to Olmutz at the point where that of Austerlitz branches into it, he passed the night in the humble post-house of Posorsitz. There he supped off some food which the soldiers brought him from the neighbouring bivouacs, interrupting himself constantly to send order upon order for the wounded to be picked up and carried to the ambulances. It was there, that again meeting Rapp with the wound across his brow, he said: 'You now possess an added quarter of nobility than which I know none more illustrious!'

The next day (December 3) Murat, whose thoughts were solely concentrated on the side on which he had fought the day before, and who had seen nothing but what was in front of him, or perhaps was misled by certain reports, imagined that the whole of the enemy's force was in flight towards Olmutz, on account of which the French army was put in movement in this false direction. Napoleon, however, distrusting the rumour, took another road, and directed his own course towards Austerlitz, where he learnt through the unanimous replies of the inhabitants to his pressing inquiries, that the two vanquished Emperors had passed the night there, and that before daybreak, both Russians and Austrians had escaped towards Hungary by he road to Holitch. On this information, confirmed by a prompt recognisance of Thiard, it became necessary to change all the orders immediately, with the result that, for a part of the army, the day was nearly lost in marches and counter-marches.

The Emperor's irritation was extreme, but the previous day's knock-down blow had ended the war. The enemy's army no longer existed. At every moment and from every side fresh reports came in confirmation of the extent of this victory. This meant 400 artillery waggons, 186 guns, 45 flags, 10,000 dead, 30,000 prisoners and all the baggage! The two Emperors between them could not number 25,000 fighting men! The Emperor of Austria declaring that he withdrew from the coalition, had already sent to demand an armistice, an interview, peace; and at last submitted to the conditions which he had refused in front of Vienna.

Napoleon put all this off till the next day, and without arresting his course he caused the enemy to be driven to the front and outflanked by his two wings. He spent all the rest of the day in a state of conflicting feeling, sometimes anxious and sometimes congratulating himself. Towards evening, on a report which I brought to him of the position in which I had left the mounted chasseurs of his guard beyond the lakes which they had turned, he exclaimed, 'They must have fallen into the midst of the enemy; and probably had either allowed themselves to be cut to pieces or taken.' On the contrary these picked men had attacked and taken all that they had come across.

The Emperor could not have known at this time the extent of Russian discouragement. He was not aware that Alexander, misled by the answers of some of our captive officers who had been taken prisoner, believed that the whole of Davout's main body was before Holitch, waiting to make an end of him. The fact is that this marshal, who had been summoned rather late in the day from Vienna, had nothing but a harassed and half mutilated division to oppose on this point to the remainder of the defeated troops of the two Emperors. Napoleon knew the weakness of his right wing; he surmised that the Archduke Ferdinand was behind at the head of 20,000 men, who had obtained a victory over the Bavarians; he learnt that the Archduke Charles, with his army of Italy had just arrived on the Danube; and that elsewhere the coalition was master at the same time of Naples and Hanover. These considerations decided him on ending the war.

Having arrived at this decision, the next day, (December 4) began with a suspension of arms. About ten o'clock we were on horseback around Napoleon, galloping forwards on the road to Hungary. Having quickly reached an eminence beyond Urchutz, he drew rein there. A valley lay at our feet, and a road across the pools of Saruschitz approached by a mill. The French Imperial Guard with flying standards and scarlet plumes at their heads, in full review panoply, crowned on our side the elevated ridge of this valley where the war was to come to an end. The remains of the Austrian forces lined the opposite slope. The Emperor ordered me to go down into this hollow, and at about one hundred and fifty paces from the ponds and the manufactory to have a fire lighted by the chasseurs of his escort. A tree that the Russians had cut down the day before seemed to mark out a fitting spot, about ten paces to the left of the high road; and it was here I established the celebrated bivouac where the interview of the two Emperors was to take place The fire was burning up as Napoleon put foot to the ground, several of his chasseurs were trying who could best make him a carpet of straw, others were securing a plank upon the tree trunk, so that the two Emperors might be able to take their seats there, when, smiling at all this trouble he said to me: 'There, there; that will do; but it took no less than six months to settle the ceremonial for the interview of Francis I and Charles the Fifth!'

At this instant we perceived coming from Czeitch and issuing out into the road-way a single carriage without an escort. Two squadrons accompanied it, but they had not gone beyond the ponds which defined the line of the armistice. This carriage stopped on the roadway in front of the fire, and the Emperor Napoleon came up to the step to receive the Emperor of Austria with affectionate consideration, taking him by the hand to lead him to his bivouac. There was barely a trace of anxiety visible in this Emperor's listless aspect. As he descended from his carriage he seemed not to have perceived an impulsive movement of Napoleon, who I thought was about to embrace him, but who contained himself as if suddenly frozen at so solemn a moment by the cold and inexpressive gaze of this monarch. I could not even detect in the eyes of Francis II a single glance of curiosity, which would only have been natural in a first interview with so great a man!

His first words, however, were befitting. 'He hoped,' he said, 'that the Emperor would appreciate the step he was taking to accelerate the general peace.' Adding immediately, with a singular and somewhat forced laugh: 'Well! you intend to despoil me, to deprive me of my States?' To an observation of Napoleon, he answered, 'The English! they are salesmen of human flesh.' We did not hear the rest, having remained on the road, with the Austrian officers, about ten paces from the two monarchs and the Prince of Lichtenstein, who alone had been included in this conference. It was easy to see that Lichtenstein bore the principal part in the discussion.

The interview took place standing, and lasted an hour. We then thought we heard Francis II exclaim: 'Well, then, the matter is settled! I was only free this morning. I told the Emperor of Russia that I was anxious to see you; and he replied that I could do as I pleased.' We were surprised to hear this prince laugh outright several times in the course of his complaints concerning the plundering by some Cossacks of a farm which he seemed to hold in special affection. We may not rightly have heard what he said, but it caused us a painful feeling, that this monarch in the midst of the misfortunes of his empire should seem taken up with such an unimportant detail. The last words of Napoleon were 'So I have Your Majesty's promise not to begin the war again?' Francis II replied: 'That he swore it and would keep his word', upon which the two Emperors embraced each other and parted.

While mounting his horse, Napoleon said to us 'We are going to see Paris again, peace is settled!' But during his return to Austerlitz, after having despatched Savary back to the two Emperors, he seemed anxious and preoccupied with what had just taken place, letting fall some expressions full of bitterness; to which he added: 'That it was impossible to believe in these promises. He had just received a lesson which he should not forget; and in the future he would always have 400,000 men under arms!'

I am ignorant of the opinion that Napoleon conceived of Francis II, but it must be admitted, this prince possessed the respect of his subjects, who credited him with an enlightened mind and firm character; he was beloved by them; and I may even add that those of us who had known him, did not share the unfavourable opinion which this interview, no doubt a painful and embarrassing one, had left upon us.

About two o'clock, Napoleon was back again at Austerlitz. It was then that while giving thanks to God and his army, he commanded that thanksgiving services should be held in all the churches of the Empire. The previous evening he had dictated in one breath, and under the influence of one of his most eloquent inspirations, the famous proclamation which began: 'Soldiers, I am satisfied with you!' During the days that succeeded, the warmth of this feeling was ever present in his looks, his words, his bulletins, and in the generosity of the repeated decrees in which he desired to place on record his gratitude for the devotion of so many brave men.

The army on its side, proud of him, of itself, and of the victory which it had designated: 'Battle of the Anniversary'; 'Battle of the Coronation'; 'Battle of the Three Emperors', lavished upon him its love and enthusiasm. The greater part of the decrees, dated from Brunn, had been thought out at Austerlitz during the four days that he remained there. According to one of these, the price of all the magazines that had fallen into our hands, and a hundred millions of war taxes were to be the reward of the victorious army. Another granted generous pensions to the widows of those who had just fallen. By a third all orphans were to be fed, clothed, brought up, married, and provided for at the expense of the State. Napoleon expressed a wish that they should have the right to add his own name to their baptismal ones. He had said more than this in unmeasured language the day after the battle, when his delight caused him to break out in these remarkable words:—'Soldiers! you have won peace; you will once more see France! Give my name to your children; you have my permission to do so; and if amongst them there should be one worthy of us, I will leave him all my worldly goods, and declare him my successor!'

On December 5, the day after the interview, Savary was admitted at Holitch before daybreak to Alexander's presence. Davout, then reinforced, had only a step to take to make an end of the vanquished in their disorder. But the night before he had received a note from the Czar, informing him of the armistice, which had put a stop to this. Savary promised the prince to suspend the marshal's attack, making it a condition that the entire remainder of the Russian army should at once return to Russia by daily stages. He even dictated their itinerary, to which the Emperor Alexander assented without hesitation.

On December 6, the armistice which had been agreed upon the previous evening with Austria, was signed by Napoleon at Austerlitz.

XIX

THE SIEGE OF GAËTA

T HE WAR WAS HARDLY OVER in Germany before the Emperor
sent me into Italy, where fighting had begun for the conquest
of the kingdom of Naples. The grand affair at this moment was
the preparation for the siege of Gaëta or Gayette, the name of the
nurse of which General Gardanne, who did not trouble himself
much about ancient history, mistook for a surname, pronouncing it *caillette* (gossip); this was, he said, the nickname of a nurse
of former days, showing that they were exactly like those of the
present day and proving, according to him, that gossiping must
have been their original sin from time immemorial.

The traveller does not exist who has not described Gaëta as the
key of Naples, though many have entered that capital without
taking this fortress. It is a town built on a lofty rock at the end of
a peninsula. The sea surrounds it, with the exception of one side,
which is confined between two gulfs, forming a narrow isthmus of
some 400 yards, which connects the town with the mainland, and
offers to the assailant who should shape his course in this direction,
(the only available one) a loose soil on a bed of rock. The much
more developed front of the town dominates it, and the right of
this line of defence is bathed by the sea. On every other side it

is steep, and covered with batteries raised one above the other, forming a redoubtable amphitheatre whence a hundred pieces of ordnance converge upon and command the isthmus, forbidding all approach to it. The rest of the kingdom seemed under subjection; but it was impossible to expect its moral conquest, as long as the enemy possessed this centre of attack and revolt; all the more that throughout this long peninsula, which was nearly all coast, and within sight of the English, one found oneself as it were, at an advance post, in the very capital itself. It was therefore necessary to strike this last blow; Masséna insisted on it. However, before all was in readiness to come to extremities, an attempt was made to parley, but the first officer who was sent, received a charge of grape shot point blank and was killed on the spot. On the one hand it was said there had been some mistake; on the other, an inopportune recollection of my successful efforts in Ulm caused me to be selected to renew the attempt. I obeyed, but with the conviction of its futility, feeling much annoyed to be the means of giving the Prince of Hesse a further opportunity of braving our arms.

When, issuing from the outskirts, I appeared on the esplanade, the garrison, somewhat ashamed of having opened fire with all its batteries on a solitary man, allowed me to come up to the wicket which was opened; and in a kind of redan, I found the prince in the midst of a circle of officers. He had only agreed to listen to me out of doors, surrounded by his Council. Whatever one does against the grain is badly done. I felt that I was the bearer of an absurd proposition, ridiculous as far as concerned ourselves, and offensive for the governor of one of the most strongly fortified places in Europe, protected and victualled by a squadron which was mistress of the seas, and whose steady courage was well known. He was if I remember right, a little, thick-set man with an aquiline nose, whose grog-blossoms bore equal testimony to his prowess at table as well as in the breach. Fearing himself even more than he feared us, he had conceived the original idea of entrusting the key of his wine cellar to the Bishop of the town, exacting a promise from this prelate only to allow him a bottle a day. He had also been heard shouting himself hoarse, and repeatedly calling out from the top of the ramparts through a speaking trumpet: 'Gaëta is not Ulm; neither is Hesse a Marshal Mack!' I knew this very well; indeed we only exchanged a few words, which were rather confused on my side and ironical on his; upon which to cut short the sorry mission which had been entrusted to me, I concluded abruptly and took myself off, carrying away an indifferent opinion, not as to the determined character but the graciousness of our adversary, and leaving him probably with an equally poor opinion of my eloquence.

He was wrong on two points; first, by leaving standing an outskirt of the town a few paces from the fort, whose solidly built houses made our approach the easier; secondly, his sallies were not sufficiently frequent: he seldom ventured on any, that of May 15th, in which we lost a captain of engineers and a hundred soldiers not having given him sufficient courage to persevere.

These engagements had been intermixed with parleyings, during one of which the governor who had a pleasant humour, said to Gardanne, one of the besieging generals: 'That he thought his abode was unhealthy, and that he advised him to change it.'—'Unhealthy!' answered Gardanne, 'it is an admirable situation!'—'It is,' retorted the Prince, 'that very situation which makes it unhealthy!' Gardanne, whose intelligence was not of a very high order, and who thought that the air was excellent, would not agree to this remark of the prince. He had taken no steps in consequence of this warning, when the following night a deluge of bombs made him quickly understand its aim and meaning, rousing him hurriedly from his sleep, and barely leaving him time to go and seek a more salubrious domicile.

Mine was in the Royal quarters, situated between Mola, the ancient Formies, the country of the Lestrigons, and the fortress. This house was on the edge of the gulf, close to the road where Cicero, overtaken in his litter by Popilius, Lenas, and Herennius, perished under their blows. A ruin close by, which we had turned into a powder magazine, was reported to be his tomb. These royal quarters were so much exposed to the fire of the Anglo-Sicilian flotilla that one night one of their cannon-balls grazed the bolster on which my head was lying, and lodged itself, about a foot above, in the wall against which my bed had been placed. The sea bathed the garden of this quarter, which was defended by one of our batteries. I remember that from this redoubt and in the course of one of the attacks I could perceive under the waves the remains of some old buildings. After the combat was over, I returned to the ruins with the cicerone of the spot, who gave them out to be those of the baths and lecture room of the great orator whose name they had usurped, in the pride of a more than doubtful discovery.

That very day a spy in the pay of both parties proposed to us to poison the prince of Hesse. He was a Neapolitan priest. With a reminiscence of Roman history it was first suggested that he should be sent back into Gaëta, bound hand and foot, to the governor. He was, however, despatched to Naples, where with less of Roman austerity, it was considered sufficient to treat the wretch with contempt and send him out of the country.

We had to contend against the garrison of 8,000 men, seconded by a squadron of four vessels, four English frigates and thirty gunboats. The besiegers were more numerous than the besieged; that fact and the accidents of the locality made the approaches dangerous. By the correct aim of their cannon and small arms we recognised the skill of their English bombardiers and sharpshooters. Always sure of stores by sea, they so little spared their ammunition that since the commencement of the entrenchments without counting fire-pots, grape shot, etc., they sent us more than 130,000 cannon-balls and bomb shells. Frequently have I seen the latter aimed at some special individual amongst us, resting for a moment on the breastwork, fall about three feet only from its aim. In the third parallel if one showed one's head for a moment, twenty fire-balls would immediately hover over the crest, lodging themselves in the sand bag which crowned it and protected us, punishing our curiosity or warning us of our imprudence. Thus, although we only confessed to half the number, we really lost 2,000 men, killed or disabled in this siege.

It is quite true that on our side, use, vanity, and ennui had rendered us foolhardy. A battalion of blacks made itself very conspicuous, though from quite another motive. These negroes would follow through the air with greedy glances the enemy's bombs, for which they were paid sixpence; reaching them as they fell, they would dash upon them and draw out the burning fuse unless its premature explosion happened to kill them during this dangerous and not too lucrative sport.

Masséna however, well seconded by Dumas, by the whole of the engineers, and by the artillery generals second in command, had converted the blockade into a veritable siege. In order to move under cover and defile upon this isthmus, formed of rock covered with a thin layer of sand, where it was impossible to dig out trenches, it was necessary to bring up the material to form them of heaps of fascines and sandbags. Nevertheless when on June 14th, General Vallongue of the Engineers was killed, we were about two hundred yards from the place. At the end of the same month we were only one hundred feet from it; the breaching batteries being ready, they were armed. It was eleven o'clock at night on July 7th when in the midst of the profound silence of a beautiful night, at a signal from King Joseph, the simultaneous firing of our twenty-three mortars and our fifty 24 and 33 pounders, began to batter the fortress. For a moment it was struck dumb, but its hundred pieces of ordnance soon answered us. Imagine, if possible, these simultaneous and repeated formidable detonations, and worse still, the hiss and roar of these enormous projectiles, thrown from both sides, crossing each other and whirling through the air with infernal fury. Nothing can equal the sublime horror of such a spectacle. But it astonishes, nevertheless; such a disturbance of nature by the hand of man seems like a usurpation of the power of heaven, exceeding the latitude which is allowed to our passions.

The parapets and embrasures of the ramparts of Gaëta were overthrown by it. A great part of its guns were dismounted; three of its gunpowder and bomb magazines were blown up, and soon dumb from impotence as much as consternation, a long silence alone replied to our attack. But the next day the courageous governor with the aid of the English, restored order to his ruins and reorganized his defence, which he kept up with a constancy worthy of a better fate until July 10th, when, struck by the splinter of a shell, he was carried, dying, out of the place.

On July 12th two breaches began to be formed. On the 16th, under the breaching battery on our left, vigorously commanded by Clermont.Tonnerre, the falling-in of the enemy's works which protected the citadel, appeared vulnerable. This breach was accessible by the sea which was only about eighteen inches deep there; but the slope of the second breach more in the centre, made in a three-tier bastion, was incomplete. However, impatient to get on, we demanded permission to attack it, and as Chamberlhiac, the second general in command of the engineers, very properly refused, we persisted, pointing out to him where it had fallen in, saying: 'There are crosses of honour there!' But he, endeavouring to calm us, only replied: 'Yes, yes; I see plenty of crosses there—no lack of them, but they are wooden crosses. Listen to me, and let us wait forty-eight hours.'—Indeed, on July 18th, at the end of the second day, just as he had predicted, as we had feared, and as Masséna had hoped, the two breaches being practicable and the assault ordered, Gaëta capitulated. We entered it by the breach made by Clermont-Tonnerre. The terms of capitulation were that the armed garrison should defile before us, and embark for Sicily; but as it was not forbidden to tamper with the troops, who easily lent themselves to our enticements, by gestures accompanied with money and promises, we were able to draw away a part of them. A fair number thus passed over to the victorious side, in the ranks of King Joseph's army.

This siege must remain famous. It had cost us five months' blockade, four months of open trenches, eleven days' fire, and 2,000 men, of whom eight hundred privates and twenty-nine officers were killed or wounded, and from 1,100 to 1,200 lay sick or dead in the hospitals. We had fired 68,000 rounds of artillery, burnt 380,000 cartridges, made use of 171,000 sand-bags, 9,000 gabions, 32,000 fascines or bundles of fascines, and spent altogether nearly seven millions of francs!

XX

JENA

As for me, having been sent to act as aide-de-camp to King Joseph during the conquest of his kingdom, when Gaëta was taken, I had nothing further to do in Naples.

I obtained leave to join Napoleon in Paris again and to resume my post in his service. He received me with a kindly and even paternal welcome, of which I quote the last words only, because they prove that at that time the Emperor was very far from believing in the aggression of the King of Prussia aided by Russia, which was really so near. 'Take a holiday and get married,' he said, 'there is a time for everything, and there is no question of war just now.'

Only six weeks later, however, I left for Germany as a married man, and went on without a break from the campaigns of the coast, of Ulm, of Austerlitz, and of Naples to those of Prussia and of Poland.

The Emperor left Mayence and crossed the Rhine, October 3rd, 1806. His time was mainly occupied at Wurtzburg up to October 5th, in giving marching orders to his troops, receiving the homage of the Rhine princes, conferring with the Archduke Ferdinand, and a vain attempt at friendly relations with Austria; in settling the projected marriage of his brother Jerome with the daughter of the King of Wurtemburg, and denouncing the violent threats of Prussia against this new monarch, which greatly aggravated Napoleon's anger against Frederic and the Prince of Brunswick. On the date above mentioned I rejoined him in Paris where he had given me permission to remain till then.

One hundred and sixty thousand Prussians and Saxons had assembled, leaving the Rhine in the rear of their left wing. This magnificent young army was led by its beautiful queen on horseback, its princes, its king, and its ministers, all of whom were giving orders or advice; and lastly, by the old generals of the Great Frederic who were growing young again in the universal enthusiasm. This was manifested noisily, like a long restrained passion released from its bonds. One of these corps, detached and weak as to numbers, alone flanked its left, and leisurely watched Hoff and Franconia, whilst its masses accumulating around Erfurt, Gotha, and Weimar, already showed their advance-guards at Saalfeldt and even in the direction of Fuld, threatening the Main. They meant to attack, fancying that they would be able to surprise our army of 200,000 men, spread over its cantonments between the Rhine and the Danube.

However, before risking themselves further, they deliberated. The King and Luchesini alone still hoped for peace. The others—generals, ministers, princes, and especially the queen—were striving in emulation of one another to push on the war violently; as for any plan, they did try to originate one, but were unable to agree. Their unruly council at Erfurt lasted from the 5th to the 7th or 8th of October. A project of general recognizance over their left flank, and an insolent injunction to the Emperor at once to evacuate Germany, brought it to an end.

Whilst they were uttering their war-cry, and negligently leaving the Saal on their left, with no thought but that of throwing us back across the Main upon the Rhine itself, the whole of the Grand Army was already in motion under the eyes of its Emperor, silently leaving our frontier river to itself, having quitted its cantonments of Franconia and the Danube. It advanced in three columns from south to north-east, that on our left, by itself, was to meet their advance guard at Saalfeldt; whilst, unlike the Prussian army which had remounted and then left the Saal behind it on the left, Napoleon and his two other columns, moving rapidly between this river and the Elster, were descending it on the right bank in order to cross it suddenly between Jena and Naumburg, taking Frederic in the rear and on his left flank, interposing between him and the Elbe, and cutting him off from his magazines, his capital, and his retreat.

Our strategic march started from Coburg, Cronach and Hoff on October 8th. Five days after, on the 13th, the right bank of the Saal completely cleared was reached between Saalfeldt and Naumburg. The Prussian corps of observation was thrown back beyond Jena with the loss of a thousand men and its baggage. It had only taken part in an insignificant engagement, at Schleitz on October 9th; but on October 10th, before our left at Saalfeldt, Prince Louis of Prussia, the flower of the enemy's army by the beauty of his heroic form, his brilliant intellect, his chivalrous and daring valour, allowed himself to be overpowered by Lannes and Suchet, and was killed by one of our non-commissioned officers. Struck down in the *mêlée* of a desperate charge, he refused to surrender, and was run through by a sabre. He was left dead on our hands with 3,000 men, twenty-three guns, their carriages and all the baggage. Both armies lamented his death: Napoleon being so moved by it, that on October 12th he wrote to the King to express his sorrow at such a cruel loss, and to propose a peace.

However, on this very day of October 12th, Marshal Lannes, who had at first been called to Alma and Géra where the enemy had expected a battle, had drawn near to the Saal; his advance-guard having descended it as far as Jena which our infantry had entered. With the warlike instinct which they all possess, their position in this town was causing them some anxiety. As a matter of fact it was dominated by the left bank which was probably occupied by the enemy, for which reason several amongst them to make sure, before nightfall climbed up the slope; on reaching the top, what was then their surprise, instead of the mere post whose vicinity they had suspected, to perceive the Prussian army drawn up in three lines in order of battle.

The next day, October 13th, Marshal Lannes informed by them, himself verified their report, and taking possession of this dangerous defile which, was not very warmly contested, he summoned the Emperor there. Napoleon was then at Géra and his marching orders, to judge by those which he had given me, still tended towards Naumburg, but changing his mind at this news, he called up Soult, Augereau, and Ney; made Murat retrace his steps, and led them all upon Jena, where he himself, having rejoined Lannes and preceding his guard, arrived two hours before night- fall. He at once decided to offer battle beyond this town. Bernadotte and Davout, who were already near Naumburg, received orders to take the enemy's army on the left flank, whilst the Emperor, dashing out of Jena the same day, should attack it in front.

Whilst the Prussian army was reckoning on striking awe into Napoleon by the authority of its science and its manoeuvres, the corps of the advance-guard which flanked its left wing, and which it believed to be beyond reach of harm, had been surprised, beaten, and discouraged. The remainder had been seized with a panic of terror near Jena: on October 12th, on the false rumours of our appearance, they were seen flying through the town in disorder, throwing down their arms. The Saxon corps, already crippled, seeing itself cut off from its country, began to murmur; it thought it had been sacrificed, and threatened to desert the common cause. At such unexpected news, there was no longer a question of the forward march upon the Rhine or even the Main, in the frequent councils held at Prussian headquarters. They stopped short, they deliberated; they perceived that according to his habit, Napoleon had taken up his position in the most central point of his manoeuvre, whence he himself superintended the rapid and simultaneous execution of the movement which he had solely conceived and planned; they then understood that pivoting in this manner, with his right in advance beyond the left wing of his adversary he had turned it, gaining for his own side the advantage of numbers, time, and that of attack.

On October 13th, at the very moment when Napoleon was arranging everything so as to debouch the next morning at daybreak from Jena upon Weimar, the King and his 70,000 men, as if they had wished to leave the field clear to our Emperor, withdrew themselves from this plain. They departed marching to the left, summoning Ruchel and their right from Erfurt to follow them, and directing their course by way of Eckartsberg and Auerstaedt, upon Friburg and Naumburg. Their object was to precede us, not knowing that we were already there in full force; so that, by way of precaution and to cover their march, they left before Jena, only the Prince of Hohenlohe with his 40,000 men.

Napoleon, on his side, had on October 13th, as we have already seen, hurried up from Géra to Jena in advance of his troops and his guard, where he found Marshal Lannes already master, by his advance-guard, of the slope of the opposite heights crowned by the enemy. The Emperor and the Marshal, under the fire of the sharpshooters, pushed onwards from one bit of uneven ground to another, trying to reach some elevation whence they could make a recognizance of the ground to be conquered on the morrow. When night came on, he made the whole of Marshal Lannes' corps ascend the slope in perfect silence, these 20,000 men taking up their positions, line upon line, on this dangerous incline. Napoleon pitched his camp behind them. When the guard came up, he himself arranged their battalions in the rear of those of Lannes; and from their strengthened ranks, swelled the whole body to 25,000 men. Thus it remained all night, as it were fastened and suspended to the flank of this steep declivity. Its approaches, on leaving Jena are so difficult that certain works had to be carried out on the rising river bank to the left of the high road, to reduce the slope. The Emperor worked so hard that night to accumulate his means of attack on this ascent that at ten o'clock I saw him myself, candle in hand, holding a light to his artillerymen, encouraging them, and personally helping them to heave up their guns by the aid of ropes and main force, on the precipitous bank, before he went to take up his position with his guard.

Having seen after this, and given the order to Bernadotte, renewing it to Davout, to debouch from Kosen to Appolda on the king's flank, believing him to be opposite, he then betook himself almost alone to the heights beyond our advance posts. He was impatient to judge by what first movement on the morrow, he would be able suddenly to push forwards the mass which he was holding in hand, to make it emerge from this ambuscade with the last shades of night, and thus surprise his adversary, gaining enough ground to extend himself and engage battle.

During this last hazardous recognizance he got so far out of our lines, that on coming back, one of our outposts, knowing that the Prussians were only a little distance off, took him for one and fired upon him!

The remainder of the night passed quietly. Napoleon had reached his tent about midnight, and slept soundly. Our position, however, was such a perilous one that it was whispered amongst us that the enemy could have thrown a cannon ball by hand which would have passed through our entire ranks. So true was this that the first cannon shot the next day went over our heads, and killed a cook at his canteen quite a long way behind us!

The next day, October 14th, Marshals Lannes and Soult came to take their orders before five o'clock in the morning. The Emperor had just dictated them for the battle. There was no other course open than to attack in front, at dawn, with a view to gain enough ground to spread out about 40,000 men in two lines, for that was the only number Napoleon had at his disposition before midday. After which, counsel could be taken as to the locality which we only knew by the map, and the movements of the enemy whom we believed to be in force. Nevertheless, as a success on the left of this army would endanger the retreat of the whole of the remainder, and as Davout and Bernadotte were expected by that side, the village which had been noticed the night before, to the front of our right was fixed upon for our first attempt. Marshal Lannes with Suchet's division at the head, was to begin.

Towards five o'clock, Napoleon, who had remained alone with Marshal Soult, was saying to him:—'Shall we beat them?'—'Yes; if they are there,' answered the Marshal, 'but I fear they may not be!' Just then, the first musketry reports were heard, when the Emperor gaily exclaimed: 'There they are! The affair is beginning!'

and immediately proceeded to harangue the infantry, and to excite its emulation against the celebrated Prussian cavalry, 'which you must,' he said, 'destroy before our squares, as at Austerlitz, we crushed the Russian infantry.'

Up to eight o'clock, a bitterly cold and heavy fog prevailing, our sharpshooters could only grope their way, guided alone by the sound and light of the firing which answered their attack. They still advanced, but at haphazard, deviating to the left, in which they were followed by the battalions that came after them, until those of the 17th inadvertently ran up against the enemy's advance-guard, near Clozwitz. This line drawn up against a wood was steadily awaiting us; it was ready first, and at such close quarters it managed to disable a fair number of our men. But the fight soon became equal. It lasted nearly an hour, and was at the same time sanguinary and indecisive, consisting of a mere exchange of shots, the prevailing darkness hiding everything from sight, and preventing any manoeuvre.

But at nine o'clock, the freezing cloud which enveloped us, dispersed. Suchet immediately rushing on the nearest Prussian corps, which was in disarray, took it by surprise, overthrew it, and forced it back into the plain with a loss of twenty-two guns. A few minutes after, about ten o'clock, Marshal Soult appeared with Saint-Hilaire's division, which interposed itself between this part of the enemy's centre, already repulsed, and their left wing, which it drove aside and pursued off the battle-field. The cavalry of this wing was strong; its repeated attacks failed against the bayonets of the 10th light infantry, and when in its turn charged and defeated by Soult's squadrons, it lost heart.

The first double effort proved decisive. Soult had withdrawn his left wing from Hohenlohe; Suchet had left behind him a clear field for our columns. Both were already setting up our line of battle, with the right in advance, which obliged Hohenlohe to fight beyond his natural retreat. The sound of the firing had aroused this general in his singularly eccentric quarters at Kapellendorf. He had at first taken no notice, believing that there was nothing more than skirmishing on that side, and expecting the enemy on the right, when we had already overthrown his left. The two opposing chiefs were each under different misapprehensions: Napoleon thinking he was attacking Frederic's entire army, and Hohenlohe fancying that he had only to repulse an attack of the advance posts. The latter, in spite of the first noise of the combat, and of reiterated warnings, refused to believe in a battle. He was only busying himself about forwarding to his Sovereign the Emperor's proposition of peace. His persistence in the inaction to which he had devoted this day, lasted till about nine o'clock. At last, finding out his mistake, and forced by our aggression, he made haste to leave to the Saxons the defence of his right; to recall, against our right flank, his left wing which could no longer hear it; to summon Ruchel and his corps, then at Weimar, to take part in a victory which he seemed to consider a certainty; and to hasten with his centre to encounter our attack at Heiligen. He had time for this; because the Emperor, still imagining the King was in front of him, waited two hours for the arrival of his reinforcements. But Ney, hastening up too impetuously on Heiligen, and not closely enough followed, hurried everything!

It was here that the most determined effort was made. It was short but sharp, and the only moment of uncertainty was when Ney's first hasty movement was repulsed at several intervals, from the village in dispute, while waiting for Durosnel's cavalry and Marshal Lannes' left to strengthen it. The engagement which had begun about six o'clock, lasted ten hours; but this was because the first third of the time was wasted in the fog; the second sufficed in the first instance to rout the advance-guard and the left wing, and after arrival of the reinforcements, the centre. During the last three hours Hohenlohe was defeated, and the conquest was effected of Ruchel's corps of about 15,000 men, who had come up at the rear of their vanquished centre to take its place, and be destroyed in their turn; after which the Saxon left wing, deserted and surrounded, laid down their arms.

It was one victory after another in succession against an enemy taken by surprise, and fighting without concert, who was first cut off from his left, and being more and more outflanked on the left, found himself turned as well as defeated in front. Both forces were equal. Ours would have been almost double, but for the fact that our rear columns had such a distance to traverse through encumbered defiles before they could join us that half of them either arrived too late, or rendered no service. Such were the facts in their entirety; here are a few of the details:

About eleven o'clock when Hohenlohe appeared to contest Heiligen with us, his artillery having already begun their fire, the Emperor was at the head of his guard deployed on the plateau of Lutthbrode. One of Augereau's divisions was advancing on its left, and that of Lannes on its right. Several times when the fighting grew hot on one side or the other, at the head of this reserve, he would himself bear now towards the right, then to the left, of this lofty position. He remained there nearly the whole day; his glance taking in everything and commanding the whole plain.

Marshal Ney whose main body was still beyond the defile of Jena, had just come up. He had brought along with him three thousand of his own men in double quick time. Colbert's cavalry was following him. Carried away by his habitual eagerness, this marshal outdistanced Lannes' divisions; and leaving us all behind, he dashed into the thick of the fight, at its hottest centre, Heiligen itself. Soon, however, forced by the murderous fire of the enemy to stop short, he sent his squadrons at them. Their charge at first arrested the firing, but it soon burst out afresh, Colbert's squadrons having in their turn been thrown back by the Prussian cavalry, almost upon the Emperor himself, who was for a moment surrounded by their routed mass. The sight of him, and his glance and gesture of dissatisfaction alone was able to check them.

Whilst they rallied, the Emperor called up Durosnel with his two light cavalry regiments, ordering him to renew the charge. Then occurred a singular incident, although there have been other instances. One of this general's regiments which had been first despatched, had by a memorable onrush overthrown on their way three lines of Prussian cavalry and artillery; it was itself almost swallowed up in their defeat, when Durosnel ordered his second regiment to charge in its turn, to protect the first, and finish its work. But the colonel of this corps, up to that moment an intrepid warrior, hesitated; and although under the eyes of his men, his general, and the Emperor himself, he fell back into the ranks as if seized with a fit of vertigo, or under the influence of some fatal presentiment. Durosnel said that he seemed spell-bound, as if Death himself had suddenly appeared before him; and, in effect, he was killed by a cannon ball at that very moment.

His general, however, had had time to lead his regiment on the enemy's disordered battery, of which he remained master. At the same time Heiligen, which defined the centre of the battle, was carried by Marshal Ney, who an hour after in another rush supported by Augereau's right, conquered the village of Issertœdt.

The Emperor, then feeling sure of victory on the front and left, returned to concentrate his attention on the right of the plateau, to which he brought back his reserve. On this side and in front of him, Marshal Lannes was driving General Ruchel's left on the road to Weimar, but numerous squadrons of formidable appearance were showing themselves on the horizon; and seemed to be preparing to take this marshal on the right flank. When the Emperor perceived this cavalry, which he himself had called 'celebrated,' he showed some anxiety; and, pointing it out to me, sent me to Suchet's division with the order that they were to form up in squares against it.

This order having been transmitted and executed, I thought it right to go and inform the marshal of it. At this moment another and last line of infantry of Ruchel's, which had hastened up from Weimar, was checking him in front at about 200 paces distance and crushing him with its grape shot. Lannes then gave us a remarkable example of the accuracy of his judgment. When I had informed him of the Emperor's anxiety, and the orders he had given, he just threw a glance to his right, and upon this cavalry of which he did not seem to take any account. Two of his guns were firing on that side to keep it back; but pointing out to me the line of the enemy's infantry, of much greater strength than our own, which was facing him, he ordered me to go and fetch these two pieces of artillery, and to place them in position on his left, on a mound which he indicated. 'After their second discharge,' he said, 'you will see the whole of that line of infantry and artillery beat a retreat.'

I rather doubted this; but in spite of the enemy's fire which was directed against us directly we appeared, and notwithstanding the constant habit of artillery men to place themselves in position too soon and too far off, it only took ten minutes, after our second discharge, just as he had said, for the Prussian line to waver and fall back.

He was, however, very nearly killed at that moment by a discharge of grape shot: he was pointing out to me their retrograde movement with some self-satisfaction, when a shot tore his uniform across the chest which it grazed, and his charger was so terrified that he threw himself upon mine, very nearly unhorsing me; but, without taking any notice of his wound, he still gazed after the enemy, exclaiming: 'Look at them, how they are all flying to Weimar! The road is covered with their gun-carriages. Go at once to inform the Emperor.'

I found Napoleon still on the same plateau, but a little more to the left. It was about three o'clock; while listening to me, several Saxon bullets, aimed directly at him, rebounded almost between my horse and his. He interrupted me to say: 'There is no good in getting killed at the end of a victory; let us dismount.' He ordered me to bring up the artillery of his guard to this point, after which I thought it desirable to repeat Marshal Lannes' message to him. 'Very well,' he said, 'you may go, and follow their retreat upon Weimar; but before doing so, just give a look to our left front, and see what has become of those Saxons, and let there be an end of them!'

I rapidly crossed the plain which was covered with the defeated troops of Hohenlohe and Ruchel who were receiving the finishing stroke from Murat and our cavalry. Towards our left, Augereau was pushing the unfortunate Saxons on their front and flank, while one of Ney's battalions, marching in a square, was beginning to outflank them on the right; I joined it at the moment when a last charge of Saxon hussars broke up in front of it who received its fire.

A long and deep column of infantry, however, was advancing at the same pace as ourselves towards those batteries of position which had been firing on the Emperor Its last ranks were so mixed up with our battalions that they seemed to be issuing from them.

These were the Saxons. There were 8,000 of them; they were in full flight, but in an orderly mass, without a single sharpshooter on their flanks; and without particularly noticing them, thinking from their attitude and the course they were taking that they were our own men, I rushed up at breakneck speed to place myself at their head. It was only when within twenty paces of the first rank of this column that, on glancing at them, I perceived my mistake. Had I then called upon these poor Saxons to surrender, in their desperate position I might perhaps have had the honour of being the first to make them lay down their arms; but as their bayonets were directed against me, in my surprise I did not think of it; I even doubted if I should have time to turn round; but going beyond their front I yet managed under their fire to return by the other flank to some of our own men who were well up, with whom I almost immediately broke through this unhappy column which threw down its arms.

Murat got the glory of this; doing purposely what I had done unconsciously, in his chivalrous ardour, and quite alone, he had placed himself at their head the very moment after I had done so. When I came back myself through their disarmed ranks, I found him there with his sword sheathed, and only a cane in his hand, a smile on his face and his head held high, alone receiving as prisoners these thousands of men.

The first part of my mission was now terminated; Weimar was the second. The whole plain was cleared when about four o'clock I arrived at the elevation by which a quick descent could be made to one of the bridges over the moats of the town. Letort was forming up his dragoons into a column to force the entrance, which was being defended by a battalion of the enemy; but an impetuous charge through their fire rendered us masters of it. A few sword-thrusts had to be exchanged, as an infantry waggon was across the bridge and the Prussian grenadiers had retrenched themselves behind it; but they had lost their heads.

Whilst Letort was taking up a position beyond this town I went on to the Grand Duke's palace, where Rapp and Murat soon joined me, and where the Grand Duchess had remained.

The Queen of Prussia had only then left, and we were told that we had just missed capturing her. It was said that taken by surprise in Auerstaedt that very morning, as well as the king, by the beginning of another battle, she had yielded to entreaties to withdraw to Weimar, and it was only on perceiving the fugitives flying before us that she decided to leave it. We had to content ourselves with the capture of this town, in which Goethe happened to be, from the wounded General Schmettau with the 800 prisoners that we made there.

I was desirous of returning to the Emperor, but Murat detained me, asking me to wait for his report. It was late when he had drawn it up, having been hindered by his assiduous cares for the Grand Duchess, whilst Rapp and I were extinguishing a fire which had broken out near the palace. After a dinner of conquerors (though our satisfaction was restrained by the presence of the princess who insisted on doing the honours herself), I left Rapp and Murat only to arrive at midnight at Jena where Napoleon had retired after the battle.

As far as I can remember, his quarters had been established in an inn, and the bed which he was occupying was one already there in the corner of a pretty large room. The Emperor was not in those days surrounded by all the comforts which later on made war less fatiguing for him, and possibly too easy. I entered alone, carrying a light, and drew near his bed. Almost immediately the dim light woke him up from a profound sleep; he never could bear any light at night, the smallest lamp or the faintest glimmer prevented him from sleeping. As usual he woke up quietly, which is said to be a characteristic of happy temperaments, being wide awake at once without any surprise or agitation, which is also usual with soldiers.

As soon as he had read the report, I gave him an account of the taking of the Saxon corps which I estimated at 6,000 men. 'I saw them,' he answered; 'there were more, they were at least 8,000,' then when I added that we had nearly taken the queen, he answered in eager tones: 'It would have served her right, she well deserved it, it is she who is the cause of the war.' He continued with a preoccupied air: 'Did you not,' he said, 'whilst marching upon Weimar, hear heavy cannonading in the distance to your right?' On my reply in the negative, when I said that it would have been difficult to distinguish the sound from that of our own, he added: 'It is a singular thing, there must have been a considerable affair on that side?'

As a matter of fact, two hours later, one of Davout's officers named Bourck aroused him again. He came to inform him of the victory of Auerstaedt, a victory quite distinct from that of Jena, although simultaneous; for eight or ten hours after it was over the Emperor was still ignorant of this, and was making inquiries about it, not even having heard any of the firing. It should not cause any astonishment that in his next day's bulletin he chose to confound this victory with his own. It was at Auerstaedt that the pick of the Prussian forces, with their most renowned generals, their princes, and even their king, although three times more numerous than ourselves, had been overwhelmed by the Emperor's lieutenant; whilst at Jena the Emperor although as strong as the enemy, had only conquered two subordinates whom he had surprised when separated from the others. The glory was too disproportionate for him to let it go forth to the world, living on fame as he did. It will be seen that when less actuated by policy, he was more honest in his speech, and more just in his praise and gratitude.

He might, however, have attributed the success of the two battles to his first and great manoeuvre which had surprised the enemy on his flank and threatened his retreat. This manoeuvre, while suddenly upsetting his adversary's plans, had thrown the latter, who had to move such large masses, into the uncertainty and trouble of the unforeseen, and the disorder of counter-orders and of counter-movements in which union is lost, time wasted, and nothing done at the proper moment; whilst on our side, everything being concerted beforehand, the advantage of numbers, time, and attack, all, in fact, was entirely in our favour.

As for the great Saxon column which we had taken prisoner, I then learnt that it had been sent to the Emperor. It had defiled before him whilst he was lying on the ground with his maps spread out, pointing out to Berthier those bold movements which had followed up his victory. He was so overcome with fatigue that in the midst of his work he fell asleep. His grenadiers, perceiving this, on a sign from Marshal Lefebvre, silently formed themselves into a square around him, thus guarding their Emperor's repose on the plateau whence he had enabled them to enjoy such a glorious spectacle!

But the order of events must now, take me back to that moment of the following night (October 14th to 15th) when a second time aroused at Jena after my report, Napoleon received that of Davout with the news of the victory of Auerstaedt.

On this side, on the night of the 13th, the head-quarters of the two opposing armies, that of Davout with 25,000 men, and that of the king with 70,000, were, the one at Naumburg, the other at Auerstaedt. They were separated by a defile of about two leagues; Brunswick was close to it, he had only to take a step further on level ground to seize it. Davout was separated from it by the Saal and the whole length of the defile; but instead of sleeping during the night of the 13th to the 14th, he had pushed on Gudin and his division, whilst Brunswick had put off till the next morning the duty of throwing Schmettau and his advance-guard into it.

It thus resulted that in the midst of the fog of the three first hours of October 14th, when this Prussian advance-guard drew near to Hassenhausen, it ran against Gudin, who took its guns and repulsed it as well as Blucher and his squadrons.

Then the astonished chiefs held council in the Prussian camp. Brunswick was for deploying the army and waiting till the enemy was better reconnoitred; Mollendorf held quite a different opinion, he thought that the attack should be recommenced at once, which opinion was approved by Frederic; while Blucher again sent off and this time completely defeated, fled to the left towards Eckartsberg.

But behind him, three divisions of Prussian infantry were advancing. They opened out under our fire with the methodical slowness and scrupulous regularity of their man on parade. This orderly attack of 25,000 Prussians under a hail of bullets and grape shot gave way against Gudin's 7,000 men whose right had been just then supported by Friant's division. Our sharp shooters were especially brought into notice, and it was remarked with what war-like experience they made use of every advantage of the unequal ground. By a strange fatality, amongst the four chiefs of the enemy who took part in this second effort, two of them, Schmettau and Brunswick, were mortally wounded, and a third was unhorsed.

The King, however, persisted; holding out against his bad luck. His general-in-chief and his lieutenants were beaten, and his astonished infantry stopped short; he called to his aid the pick of his cavalry under Prince William. This time, Gudin who had conquered, but who was himself half destroyed, was on the point of succumbing, when Morand's division, led by Davout, hastened up to his left, forming its squares, and repulsed Frederic's third attempt. The vain and repeated charges of this renowned cavalry gave way under the cross fire of Morand and before his bayonets. By a similar fatality, the King himself was unhorsed on this occasion, and Prince William was carried off wounded from the field of battle.

Davout immediately rendered himself impregnable by crown-ing the Sonnenberg with infantry and artillery. Being as ardent in attack as he was obstinate in defence, whilst making sure of the conquered territory, he threw forward on Rehausen his two victorious divisions.

On his side, for the fourth time, the King already reduced to his reserves met attack with attack. But from the commanding posi-tion which he had just taken up on his left, Davout with his artil-lery was blazing away upon the right flank of the enemy; Friant was doing the same upon the left, so that Gudin and. Morand were able by a front attack to defeat this last effort of Frederic. There again by a fatality which was always against the Prussians, a mortal blow struck down their old and celebrated Mollendorf.

Frederic then stopped. Rehausen had just been torn from him; all his corps were beaten, disheartened, and in disorder; his two brothers and the greater part of his lieutenants were killed or wounded; his cavalry was flying to right and left; it was five o'clock in. the evening, and the unhappy king, driven back into his head-quarters of the previous night, resigned himself to his fate. Whilst the Emperor at that very moment was unaware of the greater half of his victory, the King ignored the half of his misfortunes, and at the very time that we were taking possession of Weimar, he had fixed upon Weimar as the rallying point of his defeat.

But during this day, in the midst of such an unequal struggle, and although he had been obliged several times to take refuge in the midst of his squares, Davout, who never forgot anything, and did everything at the proper time, had not thought only of conquering by a front attack, one against three, but he was also prepared to take advantage of his victory. Whilst doing everything to secure it at his centre and left, his right under Friant had pushed forwards as far as Eckartsberg, and had outflanked the king's left, turning it back upon the Emperor, and separating it from the Elbe and its retreat, by which last movement he completed and crowned his work. The King was thrown back into this plain of Jena and Weimar, where at that moment Napoleon was triumphant.

Here the left wing of Hohenlohe and the King's routed forces met each other. Where could they flee to? The victorious French were everywhere: Davout on the east, Bernadotte on the south, the Emperor on the west; Weimar itself, the spot chosen for their retreat was invaded. A single space to the north, but without any made road was still free from the enemy. In this direction the infantry, the cavalry, the guns, crossed and ran up against each other. Many soldiers threw down their arms, those of the artillery cut their traces, and all took flight at haphazard, helter-skelter across the fields. Erfurt was taken with 300 guns, 40 generals and 50,000 of the enemy killed, wounded, or taken prisoners, whilst all the remainder were disheartened, disorganized and routed. This was the immediate result of these two simultaneous battles and one single day's fighting.

We lost there 11,000 men killed or disabled; Davout lost 7,000 to 8,000 out of 25,000; the Emperor, 3,000 out of 50,000.

At the beginning of this grand day towards three o'clock in the morning, notwithstanding the last orders of the Emperor, and in spite of the offer of the commandership-in-chief made to him by Davout, Bernadotte separated himself from this marshal to

retire upon Dornberg. About ten o'clock and at the most critical moment, Davout, bare-headed, having been uncovered by a
bullet, sent to beseech him to come to his help. Bernadotte at that
moment had got as far as the bridge of Camburg which he had
only to cross, and a few minutes would have sufficed to bring him
at the head of 50,000 men on the enemy's right flank; his advent
would have decided the victory; yet he refused to come. Davout
called him, besought him, offered him the command; Bernadotte
knew that he was attacked by triple forces, and yet continued
his peaceful march on the opposite bank and withdrew. It was
not fear of the responsibility, nor any other fear, that held him
back. His own people said that he would have been a hero in his
own cause, but his disposition was such—thoroughly exclusive.
He only opened his heart when everything depended upon him
alone; then it became full of ardour, generosity, and devotion for
his own people who found in him all the seductions and fascina-
tions of a great soul. But to endure an equal or a superior; to help
on the glory of another, whoever he might be; such an effort was
always either impossible or intolerable to him. It was believed by
some, that a personal hatred of Davout had made him commit
this detestable action, which would explain it without rendering
it the more excusable.

As for Davout, who was a man of probity, of order, and of
duty above all, although he had already done good service, and
had obtained the rank of marshal, he had nevertheless in our eyes
remained an obscure individual. It was said that it was Valmy
which had made Kellerman a marshal of France; Fleurus, Jourdan;
Castiglione, Augereau; Zurich, Masséna; a hundred glorious
deeds, Lefebvre, Ney, and Lannes; and that others who had been
singled out had previously held the chief command; whilst as for
Davout, it would seem that the Emperor had specially desired to
reward his private services, and that his renown had less to do
with it than his devotion to Napoleon's person. Such had been
the general opinion. But by this single day of Auerstaedt, Davout
proved that his thorough going and tenacious genius had only
needed opportunity; that great circumstances make great men,

and that it is by their promptitude in grasping such circumstances and taking advantage of them, that these men gain recognition for themselves.

The choice of the Emperor was justified in Davout. In a few hours, he emerged from his unfair obscurity a justly celebrated man.

XXI

BERLIN

NAPOLEON'S FIRST CARE AFTER HIS victory and that of Davout was to dictate the bulletin. Davout received the highest praise, but the facts were not reported as they had happened; only one battle was mentioned, whereas there had been two. The Emperor also had the credit of the greater part of the victory, whilst the contrary was the case. It is true that there may have been some error concerning this last fact, for Davout's victory seemed almost inconceivable.

Napoleon then summoned the 300 Saxon officers whom he had taken the previous night and harangued them. 'He had only taken arms,' he said, 'to free Dresden from the yoke of Berlin, but for what possible cause had their Sovereign suffered himself to be led into taking up arms against France? Was it not to her that for two centuries past, Saxony, threatened by Austria and Prussia, owed its independence? Could not the Saxons see that even to-day in the Rhine Confederation, a similar protection was offered to their prince? Let them then swear no longer to serve against France, and free, together with their soldiers, let them return to their own country to carry back to their homes these promises of alliance.' Such was the gist of his speech, to which they responded with acclamations and all took the required oath, which they afterwards signed.

The Emperor then went on to Weimar, where his conduct was worthy of his victory; the instructions which he gave to profit by it were despatched from that town. It was there that he learnt from Ney and Murat, the capitulation of Erfurt and of 15,000 men, a first result of the discouragement which followed on these two battles. On his way from Jena to Weimar, he received Frederic's reply to the offers of peace which he had made on the eve of the combat, and the request for an armistice. He answered: 'That he had written to prevent the battle; that it had been fought, and that it only remained for him to reap the fruits of it.' Upon which coming to a conclusion from the King's letter as to the direction in which he had taken flight, he made use of this knowledge to pursue him.

He arrived at Naumburg on the 17th, after having crossed the still bloody field of Auerstaedt. The tokens of carnage that were visible here, seemed to make more impression upon him than at any other time: he was heard to exclaim: 'That a battle-field was an awful spectacle! That up to thirty years of age, one might be dazzled by victory to the point of considering such horrors glorious, but that later.' I do not know what he added, but he was under the influence of the same impression at Naumburg which he found full of our wounded, and from there he wrote to the Empress in similar terms.

There also he learnt the details of Bernadotte's conduct during this massacre: 'It was an odious act,' he said, 'a Council of war would condemn him to death, but the thing is so shameful that it is better to be silent about it. I hand him over to his conscience and to the opinion of the army; as for mine, he shall soon know what that is.'

On October 19th from Naumburg to Mersberg, while going over the battle-field of Rosbach he had its triumphal column taken down and sent away to France. Later on at Halle, then at Dessau, on October 20th and 22nd, seeing more and more of the results of his victory, in those sanguinary blows of fate which had so cruelly stricken the enemy's chiefs who had provoked this war, he felt that his own star was more than ever in the ascendant, and believed in it more firmly than ever: 'It was the finger of Providence itself,' he said, 'which had marked out these victims!'

It was, I think, after Wittemberg, that whilst crossing a pine wood, the Emperor, who had been obliged by a violent storm to take shelter in an isolated habitation, was surprised to be recognised by the inhabitant of this cottage. He learnt that although a Saxon by birth, having married a French officer in Egypt, and become a mother and a widow without being able to obtain a pension from the Directorate, she had been forced to leave France. Upon which Napoleon com passionately held out his hand to her, saying: 'That he would make reparation for this injustice by taking upon himself the bringing up of her son.' Whilst signing an order to this effect, he added: 'This was the first adventure that had ever befallen him in the midst of a storm and a forest, and that he thanked the fates it was such a lucky one!'

On October 24th, I preceded Napoleon to Potsdam, the Versailles of Berlin. Twice already during former missions, I, like many others, had gazed upon the relics that the Great Frederic had left there. But on this occasion, instead of drawing near with timid respect, I took possession of this royal residence and of Sans-Souci as one of our conquests. Being acquainted with the place, the first thing I did was to visit the room which had been formerly inhabited by the great king. I found everything in the same posi-tion under the care of the same servant. I venture to confess (for in the sudden whim that seized me, there was not a vestige of any feeling of profanation for which I should still blush) that at the sight of this celebrated seat whence had issued so many biting sarcasms, and so many redoubtable judgments; which had wit-nessed so many profound meditations in whose course Frederic, undazzled by fame, had been able to consolidate his conquests by so wise a policy, I could not resist the indiscreet wish to be able to remember all my life that I had for a moment occupied his place. I must therefore own, that with uncovered head, I sat down for an instant in this arm-chair, gazing with curiosity on everything that I could see from this position.

To the right of the seat, a door had been left open in the wall against which it was placed; amongst other objects in the cupboard I noticed a single eye-glass, and I ventured to touch and even to try it. The glass was a concave one: its number 8 or 9, it could only have suited an extremely short sight. 'What!' I exclaimed, rising up suddenly, for I was not feeling quite at my ease, 'did this glass belong to the Great 'Frederic?' The servant answered in the affirmative, adding that this object, like all those which were there, had always been kept religiously in the same place where they were found on the death of the great man. I tried it again several times, and, in spite of a temptation which I had to overcome, scrupulously restored to the same place from which I had taken it, the glass which seemed to me, and really was, so remarkable.

Thus on a field of battle where sight is of so great importance, Frederic the Great, afflicted with the same short sight as Alexander the Great, and the great Gustavus Adolphus, had not been hindered in his victories by this defect any more than had these two great warriors! In a lesser degree Davout at Auerstaedt offered another instance of this phenomenon. These examples prove that one must seek the source of great actions in character alone; that, as regards battles, men in such high positions who have once decided on their plans, recognised the important points and given their orders in consequence, need nothing beyond a general impression, and details may perhaps sometimes distract attention from the whole; such details being easily supplied by the subordinates whom they have selected, formed, or inspired.

I was absorbed in these reflections while placing my posts round the palace, when Napoleon arrived. He insisted on being immediately taken to see these relics upon which I gazed with a feeling of embarrassment somewhat akin to remorse! The Emperor examined them with attentive and silent curiosity. It was, I think, on the next day (October 25th) that meeting him on his way as he was leaving the end of the town on foot in a brown study, I followed him as far as the church which contains the tomb of the Great Frederic. He walked rather hurriedly at first but as he drew near the church, he moderated his pace, which became slower still and more measured, as he approached the remains of the great King to whom he had come to pay homage. The door of the monument was open; and he stopped at the entrance in a grave and meditative attitude. His glances seemed to penetrate the gloom which reigned around these august ashes, and he remained there nearly ten minutes, motionless and silent, as if absorbed in profound thought. There were four or five of us around him: Duroc, Berthier, Caulaincourt, the aide-de-camp on duty, and myself. We pondered on this solemn and extraordinary meeting, picturing to ourselves these two great souls in presence of one another, and identifying our thoughts with those which we imagined must fill the mind of our Emperor in contemplation before this other genius, whose glory had survived the overthrow of his grand work, who had been equally great in extreme adversity as at the summit of prosperity, and who had known where to stop!

I do not know whether it was before or after this pilgrimage that he caused the sword and insignia of the great man to be taken away as a trophy, for the consolation of those of our Invalides who had escaped the catastrophe of Rosbach. On the day of our departure for Potsdam, (October 26th) the Prince of Hatzfeldt came to bring the Emperor the keys of Berlin. During this audience those who accompanied Hatzfeldt censured their princes as the authors of the war, and answered for the submission of the capital. We shall soon see how this step compromised the Prussian nobleman, and nearly caused his ruin.

On that day the news of the surrender of Spandau had been received. Napoleon had gone to visit this fortress, whence he returned to sleep at Charlottenberg; but having lost his way he only arrived an hour before dark, on horseback, alone, and soaked with drenching rain. There was no inhabitant or care-taker on the premises, and the grass was growing in the court-yard of this royal residence which seemed entirely forsaken. I had only just arrived there, and was trying to open the door, when I saw the Emperor appear, he dismounted and united his efforts to mine, reproaching me that he had been left thus isolated, which was really an act of imprudence in the middle of an enemy's country:

'Why had I not posted any troops on his way? How was it that he was without guards?' I answered that it was not my fault, and he roughly told me to hold my tongue; but the moment afterwards, the door having yielded to our efforts, his humour changed. It was while walking through these apartments that he perceived a good number of letters which had been left by the Queen in a chiffonier which I had just opened out of curiosity. The Emperor made fun about this correspondence having been forgotten, declaring that it might be a lover's correspondence, and joking on the indiscretion which he might not be able to master, and which would make him a confidant of the secrets of the princess.

He then examined with curiosity all the evidences of this Queen's habits, making some observation or other on every object, with that caressing tone of voice which he knew so well how to adopt when he wanted to make reparation for a hasty or unjust movement of impatience towards any of us.

During the last year there had been a complete alteration in Napoleon's actions as well as in his speech. The preceding year, showing moderation in his victory, after having overthrown the third coalition, he had spared the conquered people the spectacle of a triumphant entry into Vienna. But with regard to the defeat of this fourth coalition—this new ally of England who had become more than ever his implacable rival—everything he did was a threat in which the conqueror asserted himself. Hence this solemn entry into Berlin. He received the authorities as a victor, took possession of the government, and also of the royal residence, where I received him on October 27th.

His anger, nevertheless, did not cause him to act blindly. Several princes and princesses of the royal blood, having been surprised in the town, thus found themselves in our power; he went to visit and comfort them, insisting that all honours due to their rank should be fully paid them; one of these, the young Prince Augustus, who was wounded and a prisoner, he set free, restoring him to Prince Ferdinand his father. The people were reassured; the police superintendence of the town was entrusted to the pick of the middle class; whilst his anger against the nobility, broke out in a threatening apostrophe: 'It had insisted on war in spite of its king; it should bear the whole burden of it.' He said a good deal more and kept his word to the letter. All his threats had been premeditated, the proof of which is seen in their publication under his directions. The same feeling was underlying the humiliation which he chose to inflict on the gendarmes of the guard. This whole corps taken with arms in their hands, was one of those which had most insulted the Grand Army and the Emperor by its scorn. Their arrogance had been displayed in Berlin, and he chose that this city should witness the sight of its young masters, who had formerly cherished such outrageous presumptions, passing through the streets, a long file of captives, on foot, disarmed, and loaded with universal reprobation.

But to return to his entry into this capital. An incident worthy of remark took place on that day. The Prince of Hatzfeldt had for the second time presented himself before the Emperor at the head of the defeated authorities. This painful position had been accepted by the Prussian general through devotion to his king, but either he did not sufficiently realize what it would entail upon him, or he had made up his mind to brave the consequences, for whilst with one hand he brought the keys of the capital to Napoleon, with the other he informed Frederic of the situation of our army in the midst of its conquest. Davout had seized his correspondence; but of this the Prince of Hatzfeldt was not aware, when the Emperor at sight of him exclaimed with a glance as black as thunder: 'Withdraw, sir! retire to your own estates, never dare to come before me again, I do not require your services.'

Hatzfeldt had drawn this upon himself, and a reception of this nature was perhaps a sufficient lesson. But the Emperor's anger was much increased after he had perused the intercepted dispatch that night: he gave orders that the unfortunate general should be immediately seized and brought before a military commission as a spy, even insisting that he should be conducted to the palace where he was himself residing, to be kept under watch night and day, and that, entrusted to my guardianship, I should answer for his person.

Napoleon was perhaps within his rights in arresting and bringing the guilty man to judgment, if such rights may be considered paramount to all humane considerations. But to turn his own residence into a criminal prison, to constitute himself in his palace his victim's gaoler, by the agency of his own guard and the officers attached to his personal service, was such an extreme measure that none of us believed matters would proceed any further. And what he had no doubt himself foreseen, came about.

Whilst he was that very day reviewing Davout's main body, and heaping praise and rewards upon it, preparing himself no doubt for a generous forgiveness, I had gone into the prisoner's chamber, not so much to be a watch upon him as to allay his apprehensions. A similar feeling had led the Grand-Marshal Duroc to endeavour to calm the anxiety of the Princess of Hatzfeldt, wife of the unfortunate general. Night had arrived and the review was over; the palace was a blaze of light; the grenadiers of the guard were already lining the narrow and winding staircase up to the door of the first room of the Emperor's suite, when this poor princess, who was on the eve of her confinement, trembling from head to foot, was confided to my care. Against all orders, I placed her at the very door of Napoleon's reception room by which he must enter. Unfortunately I was so engrossed in encouraging her when the Emperor appeared, that I forgot to order the drummer who was posted near her to keep silence; so that at the first sudden roll of the drum, she was as much terrified as if she had heard the volley of musketry which she feared for her husband, and fell into my arms almost unconscious. 'What does all this mean?' asked the Emperor, and on my reply, 'That is well,' he answered more by his look than in words, passing by so quickly that I hardly had time to revive the princess sufficiently to push her after him into his room, whose doors being closed immediately, separated us.

Half an hour later, she issued forth in great emotion and still half beside herself, but moved by sentiments; of the most lively gratitude. Grand-Marshal Duroc and I then led her to the very arms of the Prince of Hatzfeldt whom we had the happiness of restoring to her grateful delight.

We learnt later from her, and from Napoleon himself how she had obtained his pardon. Received with every consideration, her first idea had been to defend her husband by protestations of his innocence. 'Being a daughter of the Minister Schulemberg, one of Napoleon's greatest enemies, the Emperor doubtless,' she said, 'wanted to revenge himself upon her father through the man whom he had chosen for his son-in-law.' This supposition may have seemed offensive, but Napoleon took no notice of it; his only answer was to call for the incriminating dispatch which he made her read, and of which he constituted her the judge after explaining its consequences; but greatly touched by her extreme distress he hastened to add, pointing to the fire before which she was seated: 'Well, as you hold in your hands the proof of the crime, destroy it, and thus disarm the severity of our martial laws.' He had hardly finished speaking, before the happy princess had thrown the fatal letter into the very heart of the fire. The Emperor then proceeded to reassure her with a promise of his protection, and despatched her immediately to her husband whom he had enabled her to save from his own hands by this ingenious clemency.

This action of the Emperor, simple in itself, but fine as to its method, occurred, as we have said, at his review of Davout's main body. His nobility of soul manifested itself during this review by an act of justice of another kind. Since October 15th, his sense of honesty was suffering, burdened as he felt it to be by his lieutenant's share of glory which he had attributed to himself in the bulletin where, confounding Auerstaedt in Jena he had made one battle of these two victories. He had indeed seized every opportunity to restitute in detail the fame he had usurped, although his policy did not admit of a more open and complete restitution. Even at Jena during the night of the 14th to the 15th, when, two hours after the Emperor had received my report of Weimar, Colonel Bourck, one of Davout's officers, had brought him the news of our victory at Auerstaedt: 'My cousin,' he wrote to the marshal, 'the combat of Auerstaedt is one of the grandest days in the history of France. I owe it to the brave troops of the 3rd corps and to the general who commanded them; I am well pleased that it should have been yourself.'

The next day at Weimar, again returning to the subject, he concluded an order of the day with these words: 'Davout and his main body had thus acquired undying rights to his esteem and gratitude!' At Naumburg he had himself gone to visit and comfort this marshal's many wounded men. At Wittemberg, he had insisted that Davout should have the honour of being the first to enter into the enemy's capital; and in his order of the day he had gloriously justified this preference. Finally, on October 28th, at Berlin, during his review of Davout's main body, he had consecrated the whole day to the expression of his gratitude, and crowned its close by an act of clemency. In token of his satisfaction he bestowed 500 stars of honour and innumerable promotions to various grades. As for this last favour, it was indeed necessitated by circumstances, because he had to fill up the great gaps that had been created; but by distributing these promotions with his own hands, their value, which his kindly words still further augmented, was greatly increased.

From rank to rank he went, seeking out the private soldier as well as the officer and the general. These eulogies of the great Emperor, his attitude, his expression, his gestures while speaking, the intimate acquaintance which the humblest private imagined he had contracted with the great man, would henceforth form inexhaustible subjects of conversation in company, and in family correspondence. They were so many brevets of immortality, which would render each one illustrious for ever, whether in his squadron, his town, or his village.

Having produced this first effect of which Napoleon fully recognised the influence, his generals, his officers, and non-commissioned officers of all ranks were summoned to gather in a circle around him. Then with that voice which seemed to be the voice of Fame, the voice of History: 'Their valour,' he said, 'had rendered him most signal service at Jena. All the glorious results of this war were entirely due to their splendid and brilliant conduct. He regretted their dead comrades as if they had been his own children. All of you,' he repeated, 'have earned lasting rights to my benefits and my undying gratitude!' At these words which raised this main body of the army to the very first rank in the glory of conquest, the enthusiasm was universal. Davout in a transport of joy replied: 'Sire, we are your Tenth Legion, the 3rd corps will be to you everywhere and always what that legion was to Caesar!'

The grand scale of this comparison did not seem too ambitious, and was not considered out of place in the mouth of this marshal. Those who knew him best, said that there was something antique in his inflexibility, as severe to himself as to others; and above all in the stoical simplicity, superior to all vanity, with which he always walked straight forward to the undeviating accomplishment of his duty. In that day he did not give a single thought to the fact that in this chorus of praise he alone was still shorn of his full share. Napoleon repaired this wrong later on for in creating him Duke of Auerstaedt, he thus made restitution to his servant of the battle which belonged to him, the grander and more decisive of the two victories.

In the midst of so many cares in the present and the future, we all remarked during his stay in Berlin, that his disposition, which was so thoroughly and absolutely inflexible in the path of ambition, had become sensitive and generous as it was by nature under other conditions, and that he showed himself in conversation irresistible and fascinating, and of the most easy access. The Princess of Hesse-Cassel, Frederic's sister, who had been left behind in the disorder of defeat, had remained ill and ignored in one of the apartments of the palace. She was absolutely destitute, which Napoleon only heard of by chance. He immediately sent her 2,000 golden louis, gave orders that all her own possessions should be restored to her, and all her wishes granted, and he went himself several times to comfort her in her misfortune.

Humboldt and other less illustrious savants were invited to the palace, and they all departed fill of admiration and gratitude. One of them, the celebrated historian Jean de Müller, has thus recorded his reminiscences: 'Never,' he wrote, 'since his conversations with the Great Frederic, had he listened to such varied, solid, and energetic discourse.' With regard to the depth and breadth of ideas, he gave the preference to the Emperor over the great king. He said that in the charming expression of the mouth which distinguished both of them, he discovered the same gentleness and the same attraction. Müller adds curious details on the means which Napoleon employed to fascinate him; such as an exclusive converse with this most renowned historian of Germany in the midst of an assemblage of the very highest rank, and the delicate attention he showed him by ordering the national airs of his country to be played during the evening concert.

Thus did Napoleon and Frederic both pay court, in the person of the historian of their day, to one of the hundred voices of that fame for which they made so many sacrifices. And yet it has been said that these two great men despised the human species. What a singular contradiction between their scorn and their deeds; between their contempt for men, and the value which they attached to their praise and esteem; the care they took to gain their admiration and to survive in their memory! But every great man lives upon incense, and however he may despise it in small doses, he values it in the lump.

However it may be, the Emperor gained his end on that occasion, for Müller winds up by declaring: 'That this conversation of November 19th made that day stand out from his whole life, and that the natural kindness of heart and genius of Napoleon had also made a complete conquest of him.'

A deputation of the French senate then arrived to render homage to him. This body was his favourite instrument, that upon which he most counted to legalize his dictatorship; he gave it honours for honours; he commanded that the 340 standards which had been taken, and the insignia of the Great Frederic, should be given to the care of these senators, so that their return to France should be a triumphal one. As for the multitude of Prussian prisoners, he sent them away at the same time into the interior, offering the use of their disarmed service, for which a moderate salary would be sufficient, to our manufacturers and cultivators, to replace our conscripts, whose absence was making itself much felt.

The greater part of his army had now passed through Berlin under his eyes. Every day he could be seen on the palace square, reviewing the different bodies in succession; superintending their re-constitution, and by his voice and his victorious hand exalting self-esteem by his praise, and exciting emulation by his rewards. At that time certain inflamed imaginations around him conceived that madness of extremes which can only lead downwards into the abyss. Murat was the first in the pride of his dazzling renown, after having exterminated Hohenlohe and Blucher, he had hastened to the Emperor in Berlin, arriving there at the moment when Davout's letters were received from Posen, full of the fiery enthusiasm of Poland. The Poles at the sight of the French eagles, no longer doubted of their coming freedom.

XXII

I AM TAKEN PRISONER

On NOVEMBER 27TH, 1807, NAPOLEON arrived at Posen. The war with Prussia was at an end. The war of Poland against the Russians was beginning.

I had received at Berlin the order to precede Napoleon by a few days, first at Posen, then at Warsaw. I was not charged with any political mission, but the first arrival in these two towns of an officer attached to the Emperor, and the establishment of his headquarters which I superintended, had made some sensation there. Attracted as I was by the lively and brilliant intellect, and the patriotic and chivalrous enthusiasm of the nobility of this country, the demonstrative welcome of these ardent and open-hearted souls completely won me. I joined some of their gatherings, where in spite of the seriousness and reserve which was habitual to all those about Napoleon, I entered into their delight, and sympathized with the hopes of that brave and charming nation which was so worthy of a better fate. This will explain the exaggerated severity to which I was a victim during the captivity which awaited me in the midst of the Russian army.

The Emperor, almost alone, had unexpectedly entered Warsaw on the night of December 18th. Before day-break on the 23rd, I followed him to Davout's head-quarters on the banks of the Bug. He had arrived there about ten o'clock in the morning, and, impatient to resume his martial habits and as if weary of this whole month of abstinence from warfare, was to be seen immediately crossing the river and hastening to the advance posts upon the Ukra, there to examine with the most scrupulous attention, some times on horseback, sometimes on foot, sometimes even from the housetops, the positions of the enemy and our own. He had mastered them so completely, that on his return to Davout's camp, he had himself dictated the order of attack with a detail which would appear impossible, if the document were not still in existence. The close of the day had been designated for the commencement of this affair, and the signal that had been agreed upon was the setting on fire of a house.

The composition, the locality, the direction, not only of the attacking and reserve columns, but of each of their half-batteries, each company of skirmishers and the smallest cavalry pickets which were intended to support them; the indication of the various points and means of transport, of the manner in which each arm was to be opposed according to the nature of the locality and the calculated resistance; these were the arrangements which he had enjoined on our front. He had added others for two simultaneous flank attacks; he had even suggested that after the first volleys a thick smoke should be produced by setting fire to heaps of wet straw placed on the enemy's right with a view to harass their general by forcing him to select another passage.

All these minutiae had made those around Davout believe, that the Emperor meant to honour the army corps that had conquered at Auerstaedt by taking the command of it himself. That may have been the case, but one should not the less take note of this as a memorable example of all the precautions which are necessary to the preparation of a nocturnal combat. More than on any other occasion, everything must be foreseen by the general in this kind of warfare, for immediately the engagement has begun, the chances can no longer be seized at a glance. As a consequence, this operation was crowned with success, in spite of the difficulties of the locality increased by the opposing entrenchments, and by Ostermann's skilful and obstinate resistance. This conflict cost us about a thousand men; and the enemy, which had retired upon Nasielsk, lost double.

The principal thing to be noticed was our loss of officers, which was out of all proportion; this was attributed to the necessity in these night attacks of their going on in front of their men, to lead them, to encourage them, to make themselves better heard, and the easier to recognise the obstacles which have to be surmounted. The Emperor himself had established his quarters in a cottage, within reach of the Russian guns, intending to preside at the fight as well as to superintend all its arrangements. He distributed us upon the different points of attack, and took no rest until he had gathered from our reports that success was assured.

When I brought him mine it was about eleven o'clock at night. I found him as at Jena lying in a wretched bed which belonged to the cottage. Having made my report of the attack upon our left, I excused myself for being so late, on the ground that my horse, having been killed in an offensive return of the Russians against the 12th line regiment, I had been obliged to come back on foot. There was nothing very extraordinary in this accident, and I could not understand why the Emperor, lifting up his head, said to me eagerly twice over, 'You do not mean it? Your horse killed under you?' I left him surprised but grateful for this mark of interest; four days previously he had ordered me to assume the duties of his personal aide-de-camp; this accident probably made him still more desirous that I should be near him. I have every reason to think so. But in any case, being separated from him the next day by a stroke of misfortune, that good luck was retarded for the space of six years.

I cannot help relating here a rather uncommon fact, the recollection of which always moves me. I have said that during the nocturnal attack of the Ukra on December 23rd I was unhorsed. My animal had been wounded by a bullet in his chest from which the blood was streaming; and as he could no longer carry me, I had been forced to leave him, loading his equipment on my shoulders.

When I had reached our first out post about three hundred paces off, I sat down to rest before the fire, in some grief at the loss of my mount, when a plaintive sound and an unexpected contact caused me to turn my head. It was the poor beast which had revived, and had dragged itself in the wake of my footsteps; in spite of the distance and the darkness it had succeeded in finding me, and recognising me by the light of the camp fire, had come up groaning to lay its head on my shoulder. My eyes filled with tears at this last proof of attachment, and I was gently stroking it, when exhausted from the blood it had lost, and its efforts to follow me, in the midst of the men who were as surprised and touched as myself, it fell down, struggled for a moment, and expired.

Misfortunes, it is said, come in troops; it would seem as if isolation were not in their nature. A series of accidents now befell me. On leaving the Emperor's miserable bedroom, I passed through a kind of passage bestrewn with straw, which was the only other shelter to be found in this cottage. A Piedmontese officer, who afterwards distinguished himself greatly, was asleep there; awoke suddenly, he began to abuse me before he knew what he was about; and as he still persisted in his conduct when wide awake, I was obliged to fix the next day to settle the quarrel.

Behold me with my horse killed, and a duel on my hands! But this was not the end of it: the next day my adversary and I were separated for a time by marching orders, and I went off with Rapp who was the general in command of the cavalry of the advance-guard. As soon as we had arrived in sight of Nasielsk, we perceived the enemy on the opposite thickly wooded side of the valley in which this town is situated. At our first discharge of grape-shot the enemy's line partly opened, leaving a vacant space; I proposed to Rapp to charge it with one of his regiments, so as to prevent the Russians reuniting, of which Rapp approved, and asked me to put the manoeuvre into execution. I began it to the left of the town with Exelmans and the 1st regiment of mounted chasseurs which he commanded. I finished it with the 12th dragoons, Exelmans having been drawn to the right by the attack of Nasielsk. But the colonel of the 12th lost his head; instead of holding the plain which was already cleared, the heat of pursuit led him away to the woods of tall trees which bounded it. I joined him there, and made him realize his extreme imprudence. We were so absurdly out of place in this wood, that to get out we were obliged to go in single file, bent double over our horses to avoid the branches which caught on the helmets of the dragoons.

It was high time; the enemy's fugitives were reassembling by groups on the edge of the forest to slaughter us one after the other as we came out of this cut-throat pass. I was the twenty-fifth to escape their fire. Then with a view to facilitate the exit of the remainder, rallying the squadron, I overthrew the nearest group of the enemy. But in saving the regiment, I lost myself; and by a similar fault which I had just blamed in the colonel.

Up to then the manoeuvre which I had advised and was executing had succeeded. The line of the enemy's cavalry which had been separated in half was not able to reunite itself; some of them were flying to the left on the roads of Novemiasto and Wirziki; their general on the contrary with the bulk of his division was withdrawing to the right on the road to Srzégocin. As for us, placed between them, we discovered that we had turned Nasielsk, while Exelmans and Rapp were at that very moment attacking it on the front; there was nothing consequently for us to do but to take advantage of this by uniting our efforts with theirs against the town and Ostermann's rear-guard. The 12th dragoons, released from the forest by the charge which I had just executed, did not fail to make this attack. I alone with the squad which I had carried with me, was cut off from it.

Our first rush through the midst of these hussars who were escaping in confusion had been so energetic, that, pursuing them much too far into the forest on the road to Wirziki, I found myself surrounded by them. I stopped to return to the attacking point, when one of them passed me so quickly that he only just escaped a thrust from my sword. This irritated me so much that I started in pursuit, plunging blindly into the forest until I had reached and struck him down.

I must own that this was a mistake, and a most imprudent loss of temper on the part of a soldier. I soon recognised this, when I saw how far I was from my own men, in the midst of enormous pine-trees whose motionless silence was only broken by the movement of the flying Russians whom I could perceive seeking the shelter of these great trees to the right and left of the roadway; they were fortunately so scared that they allowed me to turn my horse and rejoin the few dragoons who had followed me, and had imprudently taken the same course.

These dragoons were returning on their steps; and two of their officers, seized with giddiness, and not perceiving the danger of their position, were going along at a foot pace, talking as if we were in a state of peace, without even thinking of rallying the small squadron which they commanded. They neither listened to my representations, nor to those of their non-commissioned officers, who pointed out to them a mass of every arm of the enemy barring the exit of the forest above Nasielsk, and preparing to contest with us its issue into the plain.

It was very evident that there was no hope for us except to get out as we had got in—by a desperate charge; but these officers (one of whom, the son of a Terrorist, had, I think, brought ill-luck upon us) had completely lost their judgment. In comprehensibly persistent in their thoughtless negligence, they seemed to me to be stamped by fatality, like the branded beasts led to the slaughter-house. In their default I hastened to join their dragoons, of whom there were twenty-two; but as there was no one to command them, they had gone on in front, so that when I wanted to rally them and take the command, it was too late. All this was the affair of a few seconds, for in these critical moments, action is quicker than speech. The dragoons who were furthest off without a chief, in disorder and repulsed, had abandoned the high road to throw themselves to the left into a swampy field which was contiguous to some canals. Notwithstanding my outcries and my imprecations, they carried on their officers with them, and, left alone on the high way, I was obliged to follow them on this land which had no egress.

There, surrounded and fired upon at close quarters, they allowed themselves to be shot down without seeking to defend themselves.

I saw the unfortunates dismount and plant their swords in front of them, showing that they meant to surrender. All perished except three dragoons, the only ones I was able to rally.

Once at the end of this ground, crossing the canal, we got out of the bog, all four of us flying in our turn, and followed up a track through the last row of pines which separated the road to Wirziki from that of Srzégocin. This road seemed to lead us at first towards the sound of our own guns, and though the enemy's rear-guard still occupied Nasielsk, which we were obliged to go through to rejoin our army, we had not yet lost all hope.

But I soon perceived that this unlucky road deviated to the left, thus increasing the distance to Nasielsk. We were, however, obliged to follow it and to get on quickly, for we again heard behind us the savage cries of a multitude of Tartars in hot pursuit. It led us in a few minutes out of the forest, but on the road to Srzégocin which was covered with troops marching in retreat. At this sight my dragoons, transported with joy, exclaimed: 'They are ours! we are saved!' 'Say rather, lost!' I replied. 'It is the enemy! We have fallen into the midst of the Russian army! There is only one thing to be done; we must join those first stragglers, take them prisoners, and surrender ourselves to them, they will protect us afterwards.' At that instant, seeing a foot soldier alone, I attacked him, and retrenching himself behind a ditch, he took aim at me.

I must confess, that in this desperate moment I lowered my sword, and swelled out my chest to receive the bullet which would have relieved me from an unbearable position; it was raining, and the shot missed fire!

As death did not choose to take me, I returned to my original idea. Not being able to reach this soldier, and hearing the shouts of the Kalmucks who were getting nearer and nearer to us, I left him to throw myself upon a frightened Cossack, on whose left side I had advanced, and whom I summoned to surrender; but perceiving his main body a few hundred paces in front and seeing that I was threatening him without striking, he continued his flight towards his own men, galloping by my side, and thrusting at me all the time until his lance pierced my right side.

Then, wounded, and not being seconded by the dragoons, either because they had not understood me, or because their exhausted horses had not been able to keep up with mine, I changed my tactics. We were just then near Count Ostermann's retreating division. Night was approaching, and the left side of the road for several hundred feet was still bordered by the forest: 'To the woods!' I exclaimed to my poor companions, 'let us lose ourselves there, till our advance-guard delivers us!'

A moment earlier we might have been saved by this inspiration, but such means of safety are so unpalatable that one only resorts to them at the last extremity; it was already too late. Our first enemies were then debouching from the wood into which they had pursued us, and now catching sight of us, and setting off at racing speed between us and the wood, they got up to us. These were about two score horrible Kalmucks and irregular Cossacks. One of the dragoons was mortally wounded by them, another was pierced through both cheeks by a lance thrust, and I do not know if he ever recovered; the third was taken without any injury, and seemed so rejoiced at this, that I could not help smiling; at least when I thought of it later on, for at that moment I had too much to do.

About fifteen of these savages fell upon me with repeated lance thrusts, one of which, rather better directed than the others, caught me in the neck and bore me to the ground. I got up again promptly, and gained a few moments by sheltering myself behind my horse; but one of these Kalmucks having seized my sword and displayed it to the others, whose fury increased at the sight of the blood upon it, my horse and my arms were powerless to protect me. It was in the midst of this rain of blows, that I first perceived their chief. He was one of those magnificent Cossacks of the Don with Persian features; his noble Countenance was calm and unmoved, and he seemed to disdain to slaughter a vanquished and disarmed enemy on the ground; 'Nikalé!' he said to these madmen, who did not seem to pay any attention to him.

I was ignorant of the meaning of this Russian word but I understood the intention, and at once repeated imperiously 'Nikalé!'

several times over. The effect of this command from my lips was magical. At the sound of this word which I have since been told signifies, 'do not strike,' surprised to hear me speak their language, their ferocious countenances expressed nothing but astonishment, and their arms remained raised in the air. I owed my life to this word; but my torture was not at an end.

The passion of spoil succeeded to their sanguinary brutalities, and throwing themselves upon me, they tore off my clothes amongst them, each one dragging at me from his own side, lifting me in the air, throwing me down and lifting me up again. I had no respite until after having stripped me and searched all over my body they disputed the spoil. It was especially my major's epaulette which one of them had torn off, which excited their envy. Their chief took no part in this plunder; he even ordered them to leave me an indispensable garment besides my shirt which was tattered and blood-stained.

I now thought that the worst was over, instead of which the last act and the most painful one was still to come. At this moment their attention was attracted by reports of firing, whose sound seemed to be drawing nearer. Afraid for themselves, and also fearing they might lose their prey, those who had come off worst in the pillage again renewed their ferocious treatment. Having quickly remounted their horses, I being alone on foot in the midst of them, they pulled me on by my arms and hair at the full speed of their animals. Those behind me did not spare their blows, and I was thus dragged on to Ostermann's rear-guard, where they at last drew rein.

I was panting, half suffocated, and almost fainting, and they were continuing to abuse, to buffet and ill-treat me, when, taking breath as I perceived a Russian regiment fighting with its colonel at its head, I snatched myself by a sudden wrench from their furious hands, and ran up to place myself under the protection of this chief. 'I am a colonel like yourself,' I exclaimed, 'and a prisoner. This is not how we treat yours. Save me from these savages.' My physical agony ceased from that moment, but it was the beginning of one of a different nature.

This colonel, whose name I should like to know, did his duty. I was naked, and hardly able to hold my up: he had a cloak thrown over me, and a horse procured for me, and gave orders at my request that my poor dragoons should be looked after; after which he sent us to Count Ostermann-Tolstoï who recognised me. The first reception of this general did not please me; it was too imperious. That is their manner when restrained by no special consideration, a consequence probably of their habits as masters in the midst of slaves; he was, besides, anxious about his own position. Having been beaten the evening before, and being eagerly pressed at this moment, it was important to him to know exactly whom he had to deal with. So, whilst making me go at a foot's pace at his side, he plied me with questions in the tone of a chief who exacts an answer. 'Is the Emperor there? With what bodies? What is their number?'—'Count,' I answered, 'you know me, at any rate you know my name; why uselessly insult me by these questions, when you must feel sure beforehand that nothing would possibly make me answer them.'—'How, Sir' he exclaimed with violence in a sudden impulse which was entirely Muscovite, 'you dare! …' But civilization at once regaining the ascendant, he recovered himself, held out his hand, and deplored my fate with concern in his tones; he even thrust aside his own anxiety, which was very natural in such a critical situation, to ask me news of those amongst us whom he had known in France. That evening at his quarters at Srzégocin, where we passed the night, and next day when we were leaving for Pultusk before day-break, his courteousness and kind consideration did not fail me.

The first night of my captivity has remained in my memory. We were in a room that was small but warm and sufficiently clean; a table in the centre, a few chairs and some straw in a bedstead, constituted its sole furniture. Fatigued as he must have been, the general insisted on giving up the bed to me. He first of all had my wounds dressed, one of which was rather serious, and at my request, he ordered that the wounded dragoons should also be seen to. He would not allow me to sit up to share his repast, which was a very meagre one, if I may judge by the short time he

spent upon it, and by the share which was brought to me by his
aide-de-camp.

A pale, withered personage of high stature and cold appearance,
with a scar across his face, had just entered. This was Beningsen.
There were four of them; he, Ostermann, and two other generals. They appeared extremely preoccupied, but their countenances
were calm; and their discussion, which was a long one, bore the
same characteristic. They held council during part of the night
around the table covered with maps which they frequently consulted. Their Field-Marshal Kaminski had just left them, ordering
at any hazard a general retreat upon Ostrolenka. It was evidently
while seated at this table, that they made up their minds to disobey
him, to struggle against Napoleon and defend themselves. Fate
willed it that I should be a witness of their decision which very
nearly lost them, although it did them honour, and succeeded in
the long run. They knew that I was attached to Napoleon, and
several times their glances were turned upon me, but however
important the least information from me would have been, they
respected my misfortune, and did not attempt to take advantage
of it, either directly or insidiously.

At two o'clock in the morning Ostermann, before resuming
his march, gave me a Polish pelisse to wear, and entrusted me to
the guard of an officer and six Cossacks. The first hours of this
march were very trying: I spent them on the straw of an open
waggon in the midst of the Russian columns, travelling slowly
and exposed to their threatening imprecations. Twenty times over
I thought they were going to pierce me with their bayonets; I even
parried some of their thrusts. This disagreeable situation, which,
however, was a distraction from my grief, only came to an end
on the morning of December 26th when we entered Pultusk. I
was confined there in a brick house of good appearance, one story
high, with a room in which there was a chimney, a rare thing
in this country; they left me for some time alone there with my
reflections, which were sad ones.

The first moments, however, were not the most trying. I
knew that Ouvarof, one of Alexander's aides-de-camp, had

suffered the same fate as myself at the same time. It was therefore possible to make an exchange, which indeed was proposed by Napoleon. Being in Pultusk, I felt that I was still within reach of my own people; I was soon even to hear the sound of their firing, and thus separated from them by sight I could at any rate hear them, which was a kind of tie. I was listening full of anxiety, and it seemed to me that the sounds of war were drawing nearer; evidently a violent combat was going forward. The guns were those of the impetuous Marshal Lannes, who unfortunately suffered a repulse. That had not then happened; his first attack had succeeded, the noise of his discharges was becoming more distinct; there was even a moment in which I thought I could hear around me the tumult which precedes a rout.

I had been left alone in this room for several hours, none of the men who guarded me having appeared. For all I knew, in the heat of warfare, in the midst of the disorder of a defeat, it was possible that I might have been forgotten! I had already opened the window and was sounding the chimney, seeking around for some hiding place where I might remain concealed during the first search, await the sudden irruption of our own men, and escape in the midst of the disorder of the vanquished. I reckoned on the inhabitants, who were Poles and would favour my flight. A woman entered whose moist eyes and compassionate glances evinced a lively interest. Some friendly hand had sent me, through her, an enormous loaf of white bread. I had had little or nothing to eat for twenty-four hours; that was not what troubled me the most, I entreated her by my signs and glances to help me in the evasion which I was planning, but by her demeanour, and her finger placed upon her lip, I could see that we were closely watched. I was still in hopes, even after her departure, when the Russian officer re-appeared with his Cossacks. They once more placed me upon a waggon, and I was rapidly conveyed along the high road.

All was over; that very night several leagues distance separated me from the battle-field. I could also perceive that although every possible consideration had been ordered to be shown me, there was none the less an unremitting watch kept up in this country, which was indeed an enemy's to them. It was carried to such a degree, that during our halts in the midst of these deserts, if any necessity obliged me to retire to a little distance, a Cossack with a naked sword always accompanied me. In the same way, during the long nights when I was shut in, stretched out on the straw in the midst of my escort, there was always a Cossack standing upright beside me, eyeing every movement, his lance in one hand, whilst with the other he was making an active onslaught upon the disgusting vermin with which they are infested, and which I had difficulty in keeping off my person.

Nothing then remained, neither hope nor danger, to distract my attention from my misfortune. I ought to have resigned myself; instead of which imagination augmented it by the weight of my own self-accusations. It carried me back oppressed with anxiety, amongst my own people: I thought I could hear them reproaching me for my foolish imprudence—as if they could have known it when all those who had shared it had been either killed or taken; then I would fancy that my order-book in which the situation of the army was written down, and which had been taken out of my pocket by the Kalmucks, had been preserved by them, and handed over to some chief, which was not likely, and happily was not true.

Thus I embittered my real distresses by creating imaginary ones. This was the more unnecessary, as the Emperor at that very moment, far from blaming or forsaking me, had said in his bulletin of December 30th: 'That, having fallen into an ambuscade, I had 'with my own hand killed two of the enemy before surrendering; that he had demanded my release, but that I had just been sent on to St. Petersburg.'

I had really done better than this, because instead of allowing myself to be surprised, I had only yielded after having made an attack and twice charged successfully; but the Emperor was unaware of these details, and in those which he imagined he tried to be favourable to me. More than this, he made a point of himself informing my father of my mishap, exonerating me from blame, extenuating it, and praising me at the same time. 'M. de Ségur,' he wrote, 'your son has been taken prisoner by the Cossacks. He killed two of them with his own hand before surrendering, and was only slightly wounded. I demanded his release, but these gentlemen had already sent him off to St. Petersburg, where he will have the pleasure of paying his court to the Emperor. You can easily make Madame de Ségur understand that there is nothing unpleasant in this occurrence, and that she need not alarm herself in the least. Upon which I pray God to have you in His safe and holy keeping.'[5]

'AT PULTUSK, DECEMBER 31ST, 1806.'
'NAPOLEON.'

Had I been informed of this at the time, such benevolence and paternal care would have spared me much anxiety.

XXIII

IN CAPTIVITY

ALONE THOUGH I WAS WITH my six savages, I was not yet down-cast, as my active thoughts could busy themselves with the movement of our march; to a certain extent with my ill-founded anxiety, and even, I may say, my material needs; for, whether the effect of so many violent emotions, or simply through my two days' fast, I was attacked by such an insatiable hunger that I really do not know what would have become of me without the enormous Polish loaf, which, the Russian officer to whose care I had been handed at Pultusk had not allowed me to leave behind. In any other circumstance this loaf would have sufficed me for four whole days, whilst I devoured it almost all in twenty-four hours; a sight which filled with astonishment the Cossacks of my escort.

The next night we arrived at Rozan. Perhaps the fame of my miraculous appetite had reached the ears of Colonel the Prince T—— who was lying wounded in the town, or perhaps this Russian nobleman thought it would be a diversion from the annoyance of his wound, but at any rate he invited me to share his dinner. I accepted the invitation with a gratitude which did not last very long, as he made me pay dearly for this meagre repast, which was interrupted by a quarrel.

We began by addressing reciprocal complimentary condolences to each other, I from a fairly well-served table, and he from his bed, but suddenly the old Tartar emerged from the half civilized Russian prince who thus addressed me: 'When does your despoiler of the world intend to leave off? When will he leave the human race in peace?' Surprised at this unforeseen and inappropriate attack, I answered quickly: 'From a Russian to a Frenchman, especially in this Poland in which we both find ourselves, such expressions are most unbecoming. In any case, even were they applicable, it could only be to the transgressors; and in the present quarrel these were not ourselves, but your Emperor and the King of Prussia.'

Surprised in his turn, the prince was silent; I arose and we parted coldly. Had he continued his invectives, he would have been merely brutal; but he was worse than that, for his silence was treacherous. It will be seen that on his complaint, I was very nearly sent to Siberia. He cherished a grudge against me, and represented me to his government as a rebellious prisoner, accusing me of having in his presence abused his Emperor.

Whilst he was cogitating to send me on this long journey, on my side, better pleased with my reply than with his incomplete dinner, I had returned to finish my repast at the inn. It was crowded with Russian merchants; one of whom planted himself in front of me, staring till I was almost out of countenance, and accompanying his exclamations with the most extraordinary gestures of joy and astonishment, repeatedly demanding to fill up my glass with the very best they kept in the house, so that at last I felt obliged to ask the officer in charge of me the explanation of this tender and gener-ous extravagance. 'He professes,' he said, 'to recognise you.'—'How unlikely!' I replied, 'I come from Paris, and he from Astrachan, you say; it is a far cry from one to the other.'—'Wait a bit,' resumed the officer, 'were you not at Austerlitz?'—'Certainly I was!'—'Was not your cap kept on by a white handkerchief tied under your chin?'—'That is true.'—'Did you not at the end of the battle stretch out your hand to a Cossack to help him out of a frozen lake in which he was drowning?'—'That is also true.'—'Well; having escaped that danger, then the war, and since then, from the hands of your soldiers who were leading him off, at the expiration of his time of service he became a trader, following your army, and this is he now before you! He recognised you, he said, by your features, which he had not forgotten, and also because your face is bound up in white linen just as it was last year with your pocket-handkerchief.'

There was no longer any doubt about it; the meeting was as extraordinary as it was agreeable, and I felt a sincere pleasure in shaking hands with this worthy Cossack.

It must have been on December 28th that we arrived early at Ostrolenka, the headquarters of the Russian army. I was conveyed into the best room of an inn which was crowded with officers like a hive of bees. Here I spent the rest of the day, seated at one end of the couch, more solitary than ever in the midst of this crowd which changed at every moment, growing larger and larger, and fatiguing me by a succession of curious gazers who were sometimes noisy, sometimes staring stonily, silent and contemplative. They called out to each other to come and look at me, interchanging remarks as one would do on some unknown extraordinary animal which had just been taken in a trap.

The movement at these headquarters which reminded me of our own; the curiosity, however natural, of which I was the helpless object, the contrast between my present sad inaction, and their free and lively enjoyment, strangers and enemies as they were, all this stung me to life again, and made my real and imaginary sorrows more unbearable than ever. Exposed to all this scrutiny, I had nevertheless to bear it with as good a grace as I could, and bring pride to my aid when at last dejection took the place of annoyance. How often, during that interminable day, above all when some manifestation of compassion took the place of this indiscreet curiosity, was I not forced to suppress a flood of tears! They seemed on the point of mastering me, I had to make such an effort to keep them back. I would have paid a moment's solitude with untold gold. I was suffocating, but eventually succeeded in concealing my weakness from our enemies. It would have been shameful had I given way; fortunately I was able to contain myself and maintain a brave front in spite of so many conflicting emotions.

The scene changed the next day; I had a more lively conflict to sustain, though a less difficult one, for this time it was not against myself. I had just been placed with an officer of the 13th chasseurs, also a prisoner, but so grievously wounded that he could not long survive. I remember that day we were shut up in a billiard-room together with two officers of the Russian Government. Colonel Swetchine was one of these. They had come there animated with sentiments of the most delicate and noble generosity, which Swetchine especially was expressing in the most amiable and courteous terms, when a little, lean, withered old man with a Kalmuck physiognomy, and apparelled in the plainest manner, entered abruptly and even rudely, without removing his hat, so that I drew myself up as stiff as a ramrod without offering to salute him. But Swetchine quickly took hold of my arm, whispering: 'Salute; it is Field-Marshal Kaminski!' I uncovered; and the marshal seating himself, at once told his aide-de-camp to take paper and pen and hold himself in readiness to write. Then without other preliminary he ordered me to reply on the spot to the questions which he would address to me concerning the French army. I refused politely, but he went on without paying any attention. Then I reiterated my refusal, adding: 'that I valued his esteem too much to make any answer.' He shrugged his shoulders, and getting up irritably, glared at me in a threatening manner, saying: 'you are a prisoner, you will obey!' and turning his back upon me, he went out as rudely and hurriedly as he had entered.

I was congratulating myself that this extraordinary freak had not been further prolonged, and Swetchine, who had seemed rather uneasy, was wondering at its tame conclusion, when the aide-de-camp came in again with a sheet of paper in his hand. 'Here,' he said, 'are the marshal's questions. He insists that I should at once take back your written replies.' I was not expecting this persistence and grew angry. 'Sir, 'I said, 'you heard my reply to the marshal; I shall add nothing to it, I have no other to make. Respect my position; and do not worry me any more by these unseemly interrogatories which, were you in the same situation, you would yourself consider perfectly useless!'

The aide-de-camp did not at all resemble his marshal; he was of a more civilized generation. 'I pray you to excuse me, sir,' he answered, 'I am executing an order; you do not know Marshal Kaminski. As much on my own account as yours, I entreat you to help me, answer just what you please; say whatever you think will best serve your army, whether true or not is of no consequence, so long as I have not to carry back to the marshal a refusal which I dread, and of which you are not in a position as I am to realize the fatal consequences.' Swetchine then joined him, entreating me to agree at once: he took my hands in his; he told me that I had to do with a man of the olden time, who was capable of anything, and whose furious bursts of rage were but too well known and feared by themselves and the whole of the Russian army.

This was so true, that it was fated this wretched old man should come to a miserable end by the stroke of an axe wielded in desperation by one of his own peasants whom his brutalities had exasperated. 'I understand you, gentlemen,' I answered, 'and I thank you from the bottom of my heart for your kind intentions, but I cannot possibly follow your advice; as far as concerns the interests of the French army, my inventions might perhaps not suit them; and as for myself, whatever may happen, nothing in face of your army or my own, should ever make me false to honour, either in reality or in appearances.'

I was in good company; the aide-de-camp held silence, shook my hand, and retired with downcast mien. Swetchine was inconsolable, foreseeing some outrage, still I did not believe such a thing likely, when my six Cossacks entered carrying their lances. They had received orders to bind our hands, and that very instant to drag us off on foot, in the midst of their horses, to the extremity of Russia.

For two days heavy snow had been falling in great flakes without any cessation, and the ground was already covered with it to the depth of a foot. The intention was evident; it was too atrocious a vengeance. 'Let us not submit to it,' I said to my companion in misfortune, who was not then prostrated by fever; 'let us defend ourselves here. Wounded as we are, we may just as well be killed in this room as infallibly to perish in the snow on the high road.'

Then snatching up whatever was nearest to us, and retrenching ourselves behind some benches in a corner of the room, we defied the Cossacks. They were advancing to seize us, when Swetchine, who had been almost struck dumb with consternation, threw himself between us and them, exclaiming: 'That it was an intolerable barbarity, that he could not allow an outrage that would dishonour the Russian name.' At the same time he ordered these nomads to go and fetch his own covered kibitcka in which he made us seat ourselves and set off at once for Byalistock.

Thus at all hazards, we were generously saved from the torture that had been intended for us by this odious marshal. We separated from Swetchine with tears in our eyes, full of a gratitude which I still cherish in this world, and which no doubt is also cherished in the other world by my poor companion, whose wounds carried him off a few days later. Swetchine could not have rendered us a greater service, his marshal had relied on the Russian winter as a sure means of vengeance. The weather indeed was so awful that the officer of our guard and the Cossacks themselves could not stand it and were obliged to wait three days at Tycoczin. Thence we went through. Byalistock, all the more rapidly because the person of highest rank in the place came to express his wishes for my success, and heaped upon me many touching proofs of his sympathy with my misfortune. I took advantage of this to confide to his generous care my poor dying companion, whom he was not able to save, but whose last moments were soothed by him.

On January 6th we crossed the Niemen; we entered Grodno; I was in Russia! General Abrewskow was in command there. I was taken before him; and his frigid reception disgusted me. I was almost naked; I had nothing on but my tattered uniform trousers which had been despised by the Kalmucks, and that Polish half-pelisse, a kind of vest in bad condition, which was the only garment that Ostermann had been able to procure me. Such a miserable appearance was far from being imposing; but, as you make your bed, it is said, so must you lie; and as nobody appeared willing to take the trouble to make mine, I felt that I must lend a hand to it myself, and that I must meet this harsh reception with an appearance of pride which would serve as a mantle to cover my wretched and disreputable garments.

Consequently I complained bitterly of the merciless treatment which wounded, disarmed and beaten as I was, I had received. I wrapped myself up in my rank, my position near the Emperor, my father's name and the remembrances which he had left at St. Petersburg; adding that having been plundered, I had a right to expect from those who represented the Russian government that they should come to my help with an advance whose repayment would be quite sufficiently guaranteed by my signature. This tone succeeded. I cannot say that it was very gracefully done, but the general did let me have fifty ducats on my receipt; I even obtained from him that instead of being incarcerated in some prison, I was merely confined in a decent kind of house belonging to a Jew, where, thanks to some gold pieces, I was able once more to attire myself suitably. But I was kept in such seclusion that the Jew himself was hardly allowed to come near me. During the four days that I was there, if he came in for a minute in the night, it was with such extreme caution that I asked him the reason. I then learnt to my great astonishment that I passed for a very dangerous person, formerly chosen by Napoleon to excite the whole of Polish Prussia to revolt; that since then even as a prisoner I had insulted the Emperor Alexander; and that I was the object of strict watch and the most stringent orders.

I became aware at the same time by several presents that the Jew mysteriously offered me, such as money, various travelling comforts, and other objects, that the Lithuanians of this province had friendly feelings towards me, and that they were as impatient to be freed from the Russian yoke, as the Poles of Posen and of Warsaw to shake off Prussian domination. This Jew, in fact, did not leave me in doubt as to the interest which I inspired, or the efforts which might be attempted to help me to escape from the hands of the Russians. I recognised the impossibility of this, and expressed my thanks, but accepted nothing, distrusting such an agent, and being equally afraid of exciting, uselessly as far as I was concerned, and dangerously for these worthy people, their generous imprudence. It was well I did so, for I subsequently learnt that the Jew had betrayed them!

This durance vile, as far as my solitary imprisonment was concerned, lasted up to eight o'clock on January 9th. I do not know if it was by chance, or to overthrow the kind intentions of some inhabitants of the town, but it was at that hour when night had well set in, that an officer and three grenadiers came to take me. The cold was keen in the extreme; two harnessed sledges were in the street, a soldier got into the first with our luggage; I was made to get into the second; the officer seated himself by my side; placing two grenadiers in front and making them sit on our feet, which they crushed with their weight, saying that it would keep them warm, but much more likely with a view of preventing me from making use of mine if occasion offered. The signal was then given and the start was effected.

We travelled at full speed on the way to Smolensk, perhaps even to Siberia. We passed the 11th at Nowogrobeck, the 12th at Minsk; and on the 13th, at Borisow we crossed the Beresina which I gazed upon with all my might, thinking only of Charles XII.

During our rapid six days' track through the frozen snow, the frequent overturnings of our sledges, and the very short time spent at the relays were our sole stoppages. I was only allowed to get out at two stations, at the first where I remained alone for about five minutes, the poor Lithuanian mistress of this miserable post-house, managed to find means to approach me. Her signs and her compassionate looks had attracted my attention, when she slipped into my hand a piece of paper yellowed by age, which I quickly opened and found to contain four ducats. This was the widow's mite. I gave her back her poor little treasure with tears in my eyes, but kept the old bit of paper which I pressed to my heart in an endeavour to make her understand my gratitude, all the value which I attached to her generous intention, and the remembrance which I should always retain of it.

Our second stoppage did not last half an hour, it was before coming to Borizow, I think, in a burg in the midst of a forest. There whilst my officer was otherwise occupied, the mistress of the house quickly took me into a retired room which was full of Lithuanian noblemen of the neighbourhood. Had this gathering assembled there by accident, or from anxiety to hear news of a war upon which their freedom depended? I know not, but I was received as a compatriot. I told them that I had left our army powerful and victorious. These worthy gentlemen showed some excitement; they began by pointing to the forest and seemed to be concerting some plan amongst themselves to carry me off from my escort; in spite of the fatigues and dangers which awaited me, and the bonds in which I was held, I was ready to brave all in the hope of gaining my freedom, when the Russian officer appeared again with his soldiers and I was obliged to follow them. My arrival had been too unforeseen; there had been no time for these excellent people, eager and enterprising as they were, hut their kind intentions were evident I even noticed that they did not attempt to conceal their disappointment: defying the Russian officer, they overwhelmed me in his presence with marks of regret, which he appeared not to perceive, though he nevertheless withdrew me in precipitate haste from such audacious manifestations.

The only benefit, which accrued to me from this incident was that I was a little less bored in the company of my four Russians. In the midst of the monotonous extent of this frozen land buried under heavy snow, and shadowed by dark pine trees which seemed to wear the livery of its own mourning, my imagination had warmed itself at the spark of hope which had been lighted in my breast. I abandoned myself complacently to a thousand reveries which bore me away from sad reality. From one relay to another I dreamt of the possibility of deliverance. In imagination I saw myself in the prompt kindly hands of my protectors, pressing the sides of their light and fleet-footed horses, crossing their vast plains, penetrating into their forests, hiding myself in their sanctuaries, assuming their disguises, and finally escaping from their frontiers in the teeth of a thousand adventures, bringing back to the Emperor with my freedom, the proof of the support our army would find in the midst of such a courageous nobility, and a people so impatient to break its bondage.

These lively illusions vanished one after the other as the Lithuanian ground disappeared all too rapidly under the advance of our sledges. I had to renounce them altogether on January 15th near Lyadi, where Old Russia begins. We were approaching Smolensk, and we arrived there at nine o'clock in the night of the 15th to the 16th. My officer, Major Petchskin, of whom I can only speak in praise, conducted me at once to General Count Apraxin, governor of the province.

I knew him to be a grand nobleman of the polished and charming court of the Great Catharine where my father had left behind him so many brilliant and pleasing recollections; I was wounded, my head was still enveloped in blood-stained bandages, I was unfortunate, I therefore expected at any rate a fitting reception. Everything in this residence attested the luxury of modern civilisation: a numerous service; warm and well-lighted rooms; a large reception-room sumptuously furnished, where, glancing round an assemblage of army officers of rank I immediately singled out a personage whose elevated stature, noble countenance, and manners of the highest distinction, recalled my best recollections of the relics of our own former Court, and all I had heard related of the grand times of Catharine's splendid century.

This was Count Apraxin himself. But I was greatly surprised after having been handed over to him to be accosted in the hardest and most imperious tones: 'It is you, sir, then,' he said, 'you who, respecting a nothing, have dared to speak evil of our Emperor!' I answered, that whilst defending my own, and refusing to satisfy unbecoming questions, I had only done my duty, and that besides I had not spoken ill of anybody. But he, interrupting me, resumed still more rudely: 'that an unfavourable report had been sent to St. Petersburg, and that I deserved most rigorous treatment.' Then folding my arms in my indignation I answered that I repented of nothing, that there was no necessity for false and unlikely pretexts to proceed against me, that I was in his hands, and that he could do with me what he pleased, as he was the master.

During this colloquy, poor Petchskin seemed on the rack. He threw upon me a glance of commiseration, and I think that he even ventured to say in Russian some words in my favour to the governor. The latter, however, for all reply, dismissed him by a sign; then with another imperious gesture, opening the door of an adjoining room, he ordered me abruptly to enter it.

I think I can still see that little study: it was lighted by two wax candles, and some logs of wood were burning in a chimney built up in one corner of the room. He followed me in the same rough manner; but hardly had the door closed upon us than to my extreme astonishment, he turned round and opened his arms to me: 'Now that we are alone,' he said, in the most sympathetic voice, 'come and embrace me; let us sit down beside the fire and converse together, as I have so often at St Petersburg conversed with your father, whose memory I shall always cherish.'

The metamorphosis was complete. What a change from one side of this little door to the other! In the reception room, no doubt before some awkward witness, I seemed to hear a hard and haughty Tartar chief taking pleasure in threatening a wounded and disarmed enemy; here, in the same individual suddenly trans-formed, I encountered the most touching, amiable and expansive sympathy, and the delicate attentions and kind consideration of an old and beloved family friend. After these preliminaries, with what an easy and fascinating grace, with what elegant and noble politeness, and the conversational charm of the last century, he entered into the most interesting matters: first touching on the recollections of a much regretted society, and then on the present war, the common interests of two Empires and the character of the two Emperors; all this in a spirit of conciliation which in the general interest, as well as my own, I was careful not in any way to oppose. After having thus tried me: 'We shall understand each other perfectly,' he said; 'I shall keep you here, I shall not let you go any further; I shall allege your wounds; we will see each other frequently, we have a great deal to talk about; my aide-de-camp's house shall be your residence; go out little, you will be accompa-nied by a sergeant, an indispensable formality, but it will be more useful than inconvenient to you. You will want books; you are in Russia, read its history; here is Levesque; but do not display

that map which it contains: however reduced and incomplete it
may be in this duodecimo edition, it would compromise me; it
is ridiculous, but they would say that I had betrayed to you the
secrets and the plans of our Empire. That is the reason why I
have kept back the volume where a few pages are to be found
treating of the history of our Great Catharine; it is forbidden as
too modern. I am myself subjected to the same restrictions; that
is how we are situated.'

During the next fortnight I only went out at night to go to his
house, he sending for me almost every evening. In these interviews we made reciprocal acquaintance with Russia and France,
each dwelling on the good points of the two nations and their
Emperors. As to whether their policy was a policy of ambition or
not, we agreed that, in any case, war between them was contrary
to all their interests, whilst they would gain everything by a peace
in spite of England.

On retiring to my solitude at night, I used to reflect on these
conversations. Did the governor provoke them merely for the
pleasure of touching on topics which he could not discuss with his
compatriots? Did he snatch the opportunity of opening his heart
to the son of one of the former friends of his youth? Or had he a
more serious end in view? However this might be, and whatever
might happen, as a matter of principle as well as in my special
position, I felt sure that the expression of my desire for peace was
at any rate becoming, even if it were futile, coming as it did from
a prisoner, the son of a minister plenipotentiary, whose name was
connected with the grandest memories of Russia, and the first
treaty of commerce granted between France and that Empire.

One evening, it was, I think, February 1st, 1807, that I was there
playing my part as usual, we were sitting in closer converse than
ever in this same study where so many pleasant hours, (doubly so
to a prisoner) had been spent by me, when it happened that after
a short recapitulation of the gist of our former interviews, Count
Apraxin said to me with even a more friendly glance than usual:
'My dear Ségur, do you know all the anecdotes relating to your
Emperor's history when he was Consul? There is one which ought

to have a special interest for you at this moment. Do you remember that a short time after his accession to the Consulate, a peace was concluded between himself and the Emperor Paul; that this was through the medium of a Russian officer who had been taken prisoner; that your Consul having sent for him dispatched him to St. Petersburg; and that from this mission resulted the separation of Russia from the coalition, and the alliance between the Emperor Paul and Bonaparte? Tell me, what do you think of this officer's position, and of the part which he played in the matter?'

At this preamble, whose intention it was not difficult for me to divine, I was seized with such lively emotion that I could hardly restrain it, 'Verily,' I answered, 'what mission could be a more honourable one, what event more fortunate in any position, but above all in that of a prisoner! That officer must have blessed the captivity that put it in his power to be so useful to two Empires!'—'Well, then,' resumed Apraxin, taking my hands in his, 'you would accept a similar mission; I hardly doubted it after our conversations, and I have possibly paved the way for it.'

He then explained to me that the Emperor Alexander's Council was divided into two parties; the one French, the other English: that the first which was for peace, although beaten, was still struggling, resting its hopes upon the Emperor's character and inclinations; that Apraxin, being of this opinion, had written to St. Petersburg, describing me to his friends according to the judgment he had formed of me; and that they were even then acting with the view of having me summoned to that capital. 'When there,' he said, 'the Emperor will wish to see you. Do not fear to use the same tone to him that you have used in speaking to me; I know him: be yourself; you will produce the most favourable impression on his mind, and, in all probability, peace will result from it!'

It was midnight when we separated. I remember that at the thought of this happy prospect which was opening before me, the agitation which I had restrained before Apraxin became so violent that before going in, as I was not able to calm myself down, I took a rapid walk round the ramparts of the town without noticing that there were eighteen degrees of frost. During this stretch, my imagination travelled much further still: to St. Petersburg in place of a probability of Siberia; instead of an inert, wearisome and painful captivity (a kind of eclipse, a long and annoying interruption of my career), a sudden glimpse of a new destiny a hundred times more useful and more brilliant than even the position from which I was torn at Nasielsk and which I had ever since so blindly regretted! I pictured my arrival in the Imperial residence still full of the illustrious recollections that my father had left behind him. I was touched at the thought of this remote paternal protection which was at the same time so sweet and so glorious, and not without trepidation when I thought of the difficulty of rendering myself worthy of it; but after all, a first success predicates favourably for a second, and if I had succeeded in Smolensk, might it not be the same in St. Petersburg?

I was mistaken; but I was not the only one. From that moment, Count Apraxin, giving way to the tender and generous sentiments which he felt for me, and possibly trusting too much in these hopes, constantly showed me in public a friendship and consideration in defiance of the consequences and dangers that might result to himself. One day he would allow me to assist at the reviews of the troops on their march through his government; another day from a place of honour he would enable me to witness the oriental splendour and majestic pomp of the ceremonial of the Greek Church. Many times, one of them being a public market day, in spite of the excitement of Russian patriotism which his government was kindling against the French, he was not afraid of being seen with me sitting beside him in his sledge, whilst he pointed out the whole town on either bank of the Borysthenus, as if he were doing the honours of it to me.

A confidence so extraordinary in this country, and so opposed to his previous precautions, augmented my own. The letters which he received from St. Petersburg confirmed him in this assurance. All concurred to redouble it: the rigour of the season had suspended war, the moment for negotiation seemed opportune; more than ever I indulged in this delightful hope of being able to dispose the mind of the Emperor Alexander favourably towards the

Emperor Napoleon, and of making my appearance at our Imperial headquarters, not only as a free man, but as one miraculously transformed from a poor, useless, forgotten prisoner into a kind of minister of peace between the two Emperors and the two greatest empires of the world.

I was cherishing this dream, when on the morning of February 11th, about ten o'clock, someone came to summon me to the governor's with all speed. I hastened there at once, when he opened his arms to me and pressed me to his heart, and I saw that his eyes were full of tears. 'All is lost,' he said, 'we have been betrayed!' From some words that he let fall I saw that he even suspected the Countess Apraxin, who was then at St. Petersburg, and who belonged to the opposite camp to his own. However that may be, the count's distress was so moving that it caused me to forget my own. 'Good heavens!' I exclaimed, 'I trust your good intentions on my behalf have not compromised, you.'—'I think not,' he answered; 'but what causes me real sorrow, is that we must separate.

'Our adversaries have foreseen everything. I have the strictest orders to send you off at once, whatever be the state of your wounds. You are to go to Vologda, 'a species of Siberia, towards the White Sea, by way of Vladimir, but without entering it; you are not even to be allowed to go through Moscow. Depart then, if it must be so, to make your preparations for this long journey. The young Prince Moustaphine will convoy you there; I have chosen him for the duty, you may therefore feel sure that you will be pleased with this officer. But I cannot let you go like this; come to dinner to wish me farewell, so that at any rate your last moments here may be spent with me.' This dinner, before inconvenient witnesses, when both of us were unable to eat anything, was one of the most trying moments of my whole life. For some time past I had been so accustomed to sudden emotions of all kinds, that I had been able to bear myself with calmness and resignation on receiving the news of this stroke of fate which had destroyed so many brilliant illusions; but on this occasion, Count Apraxin's sorrow, his tearful farewell, and all the evidences of tender solicitude which he bestowed upon me up to the last moment when the sledge was ready to carry me away, caused me to break down completely. My heart was bursting with suppressed feeling which I was powerless to master during his last embrace, and in spite of the many Russian glances fixed upon me, I hid my eyes on his shoulder, and after a last shake of his hand, threw myself into the half-covered sledge which was waiting for me. My young Russian officer jumped in after me, placed two soldiers in front, gave the signal, and we set off at a tearing gallop.

I soon recovered myself, partly owing to the motion and fresh air, partly to the high spirits and heartiness of Moustaphine, and the little incidents of travel. I accepted my fate; renouncing the role of a mediator, of which I had been so abruptly divested, and entering into that of the traveller, I resolved to get as much out of my new situation as I could from that point of view. But this was another disappointment: we went at too quick a pace, and the snow which concealed all outlines made everything look alike. As for the towns, I saw none of them, our relays being posted outside. It was only on the rare apparition of a hill with a noticeable stone house on the top of it, which was another rarity, that I was able to recognise the celebrated Vladimir.

I know not whether Moustaphine was obeying orders transmitted from St. Petersburg, or whether he wished to astonish my stranger eyes with the fabulous rapidity of Russian sledge travel, or whether it was simply the vivacity of youth which glories in doing everything by extremes; but during our journey our sledge annihilated space. Fields of snow, half buried towns and villages, immense forests of black pines, of sad larch trees, of pale birches, especially between Jaroslaf and Vologda, were all passed by us, and vanished in the distance in the twinkling of an eye. This would have been quite natural, and even amusing and suitable enough, in spite of my curiosity which was not the question in point, if the weather had favoured such a rapid transit; but an unlucky thaw had set in after the first hour or two. A thousand little rifts had already formed themselves in this deep sea of snow, so that every minute our sledge, which was travelling at lightning speed with our three horses abreast, incessantly spurred on by the guide and the soldiers, became engulfed in it, and imbedded in the earth, stopping suddenly with such a horrible shock that the traces would break, the horses be flung back upon their haunches, and ourselves frequently turned out, rolling over into the snow, bruised and aching in every limb, and with our faces torn and bleeding.

And yet we suffered less from these accidents than our soldiers, who being placed in front, were the most exposed, and the guide also; but his agility and skill always saved him, and his damaged harness would be patched up in a second. Then up again immediately, sometimes standing on the front part of the sledge, sometimes almost on the horses' cruppers, as eager as ever, he seemed to think that his whole duty consisted in making us fly through the air at all risks, and at breakneck speed from one relay to another.

As for us, both young, and both soldiers, our vanity was concerned in seeing who could keep up the gayest demeanour under these trials. During our rapid transit we did not fare badly on the provisions with which Count Apraxin had generously loaded us; and we hardly ever spent three minutes in any of the peasants' houses which consist merely of a kind of bakehouse, and a room which is almost all stove; they are all alike, and too well known to render any description necessary. We only stopped at Jaroslaf, a real town. I arrived there about nine o'clock at night; and was immediately presented to Prince Galitzin, the governor of the province, and to the Princess. This was a fine and handsome house, a kind of palace, where every resource of comfort and even luxury was united. I was received in secret by these illustrious hosts, alone and without witnesses, but with the forms and ceremonies, and extreme politeness of the courts of Louis XVI and Catharine II. After a somewhat constrained interview of ten minutes, of which certain former family relations were the text, Moustaphine brought me back to our hostelry, a brick house built in two stories, which was very clean and comfortable.

There whilst I took my rest sadly and alone, he went off gleefully to spend the whole night at a ball; this capital fellow would have been very glad to take me with him, but I did not envy him in the least. I did not feel my fatigue so much at that moment as a kind of oppression, as if weighed down by the enormous space, each instant becoming greater and greater, that cut me off from my return to my own people. I thought that my captivity would be a long one, as they had spared nothing to send me so far off. And even had the government in its anger sent me to Siberia, I should have been pitied without being much more deserving of pity, it would have been a distinction I should have derived a species of renown from that exile, the only one which I could now hope for. I should have seen the Ural, Asia with its nomad races, those countries which have been rendered celebrated by their ruggedness and the sorrows of exiles; how much I should have had to relate! I should have suffered for my country, for not having allowed its chief to be insulted. That would have been a combat in itself. Instead of which I was confined in a neighbouring region which was almost as distant, by the roundabout way I had been sent there; situated on the descent to the same Sea of Ice, but in an obscure province where there was nothing to strike the imagination. It was, alas! after having been so rudely despoiled of my diplomatic hopes that I was thus reduced to the insignificant position of a prisoner, and forced reluctantly to accept the fact that I had no cause of complaint and that I was not even interesting.

My self-love thus put out of countenance, had to console itself with the reflection of the sums of money that had been spent on the escort of a single captive, and the singular precautions which had been judged necessary to prevent all communication, as at Smolensk, with the other towns and the principal personages of this Empire. That is why, no doubt, my interview with the Galitzins had been so embarrassed, so short and so mysterious. I at any rate found some pleasure in persuading myself that this was the case.

Off again at break of day, still at full speed, we passed several hills beyond Jaroslaf which I should not have noticed anywhere else. These undulations of the soil, however, mark the division between the great waters of the south and north of the Russian Empire. In a few moments without slackening speed we found ourselves at their fall into the White Sea and the Sea of Ice.

We were nearing the place appointed for my exile. During the few days of six hours in length and nights of eighteen hours' duration, which had been spent in this long and too rapid journey, I had been able only to make observations on some exterior objects. I had seen that beyond Jaroslaf the country became more and more of a desert, and of sombre and severe aspect. But in the midst of these more or less wild solitudes, I was surprised to find that the men and their habits were always the same. All bore the same imprint of a universal and eternal uniformity of servitude. I had passed through the governments of Smolensk, Kalduga, Vladimir and Jaroslaf, and had now arrived in that of Vologda; nevertheless from the centre to the north of this vast Empire, nothing had changed in the rural habitations of this people of serfs, neither in their dwellings, their furniture, their food, or their apparent characteristics. It was always the same primitive immobility of brute customs, of superstitious faith, of uncouth habits; everywhere the same conscient submission under the level of the same yoke, the same docile and pliant alacrity, the same tactful and obedient eagerness, and the same devotion in their slavery. These poor people obstinately repeated, with no progress whatever, the lives of their fathers before them; believing only what they had believed, and no truths but old ones, as if ideas were the fixtures instead of the furniture of theft heads, which had been hardened under the double despotism of the climate and theft masters.

On February 19th, after nine days and as many nights of this rough journey, towards the middle of the day, we at last perceived the domes of the churches of Vologda, and the great brick buildings where the governor of this province resides. Moustaphine handed me over to him, and on taking leave of me, this excellent young man was quite moved; he insisted on writing a simple and touching farewell in my pocket book which still remains there, and which I cannot read even now without emotion: 'Remember me, and God grant that we may meet again!' Russian as he was, accustomed to the frozen deserts of his country, it went to his heart that he should have been forced to conduct, and then leave me in this desolate country which was certainly not embellished by its governor. He was a big, long German, sickly, phlegmatic, and taciturn; but if he had some of the disadvantages of his origin, he also possessed its advantages: a placid kindness and unvarying gentle simplicity of character, fitting in very well with my situation, which he did not seek to aggravate, merely leaving me to my own devices and to patience.

The quarters which he selected for me consisted in a pretty wooden house of elegant and picturesque construction, which stood alone and was the property of a rich trader. Like many other houses, it had by way of dependencies a kitchen garden and a yard enclosed by a wooden wall and by some out-buildings. Imagine a house built with big pines, stripped of their bark and painted, not set square, but just laid one upon the other. These solid walls calked and tarred on the outside, are covered inside by a layer of painted plaster, furrowed by twenty degrees of heat with innumerable cracks, in which immense hordes of vermin find a lodgment. This is their only drawback, and in similar houses, the superior classes have means of remedying this. The habitation was composed of a low-pitched ground-floor of some extent, but of only one story; the largest and best part was assigned to me. My suite included a narrow vestibule, a pretty bed-room, and a well-lighted and fairly well-furnished sitting-room. The proprietor himself with his wife and family were relegated without ceremony to the rest of this ground-floor habitation.

Everything in the way these two rooms were furnished was reminiscent of German domestic belongings, except the bed, which is not much thought of in Russia, where a couch is its frequent substitute. Beyond that I only saw three characteristic objects: in the vestibule or ante-chamber, there was a narrow circular wooden bench, fastened to the wall, where an old sergeant who was entrusted with my watch and ward, had to sit all day, and sleep at night in his clothes without any other covering; in the sitting-room was a great stove built up from the floor to the ceiling and lighted from outside; this mass of brickwork covered with china tiles, filled up an angle whence it warmed at the same time all my three rooms; in the opposite angle a framed and illuminated picture of St. Nicholas was hanging behind a lattice with a night-light constantly burning in front of it, forming a kind of oratory before which the master of the house would come every day to cross himself repeatedly with the most prodigious rapidity, evidently invoking curses on his lodger with all his might and main.

I was not brought into any relationship with him and his young wife. The latter was very handsome, although too stout, which is a common disfigurement with persons of her class, arising from the little exercise they take and from the kwass, a kind of insipid light beer, which these women, through their want of occupation, and the thirst produced by heating foods, and the temperature in which they live, drink continually.

Such was my young hostess, whom I seldom saw; like her fellows she wore on gala days a kind of elevated tiara or open crown adorned with pearls, gold, and precious stones, whose height, without being as great or resembling it in form, recalled to my mind the head-dress, which is also of Scandinavian origin, of our Cauchoises. These merchants' wives on holidays thus decorate their handsome faces, Persian in contour, and with complexions of dazzling whiteness, but unfortunately heightened by a crude mineral rouge, a colouring imported from Asia, which I at first imagined to be an exaggerated imitation of the style in which the ladies of the former French Court used to get up their faces.

It is said that the manners of ancient Russia are to be found in this class of traders who were at that time serfs of the Crown and much esteemed for their business negotiations. In my own elegant domicile, I noted nothing of this kind, except in the habitual seclusion of the wife, the superstitious ignorance of the husband, his bushy beard, his Asiatic garb, his daily drunkenness and his brutality. A locked door alone separated me from this couple. Every evening the nocturnal arrival of my host was made known to me by a horrible storm of curses, repeated blows, and the cries of my hostess: an appalling uproar which was soon succeeded by another sound, the filthy and disgusting wind-up of the drunken condition in which this Russian of former days regularly returned to his home.

I do not know if I should judge of the rest of his class—this kind of *tiers-état*—by this rich trader, but such coarse habits were not an exception. I remember one day seeing an inhabitant, who was wallowing in the mud in a state of drunkenness, picked up at the door of the Cathedral, and learning that he was the pope who performed the duties of this church. His parishioners who had come to his help seemed neither astonished nor scandalised at the shameful example he set them, which no doubt formed a precedent for them to follow.

I did not, however, notice in the people the resigned sadness which is attributed to them. Indeed, I was often struck with the alertness and decision in the expression of these peasants. The Russians are still what they have been made; the day that they are free, they will be themselves. Then woe to Europe, if this vast empire, more populated and better provided with means of communication, does not divide itself. As they are indebted to their long superiority over Asia, to their superstitious faith, and the concentration of power in a single hand, for the most haughty and exclusive of national personalities; and as at the same time, their trying climate makes them easily bear pain, and their wretched lives cause them to brave death as easily, they will go far some day!

XXIV

MY RETURN

I REMAINED AT VOLOGDA UNTIL JUNE 30th, 1807, at this date the attitude of the Russians caused us to suspect the victory of Friedland: certain semi-avowals were rendered complete in my eyes by the officiousness of a French *émigré*, a vagabond of low degree. It was the second time that I had met with this man. By his insolence I inferred that we had lost at Eylau; by his servility that we had conquered at Friedland. This was, however, only conjectural, for I received him the second time as I had done the first, with a disgust which was not encouraging. At last came the day of our deliverance, and our farewell to our new allies. I parted from them with sincere regret, and well deserved gratitude, for I am really glad to repeat, that whether victorious or conquered, enemies or allies, always the same, I found them the most pleasant, kind, and generous of hosts.

On the orders received from St. Petersburg we were divided into several convoys. But I was set apart. I was sent by post, or rather by long days' marches of twenty-four hours, with Major Deschamps, who having been taken prisoner at Eylau had come to share my captivity. Our kibitcka was a covered one, we ourselves occupying the back seat, and a *feld-jäger* the front. The constant attentions of this non-commissioned officer bore testimony to the kindly instructions which he had received.

Our delight in returning, however, was alloyed by the bitter regret that we had not been able to take an active part in the glory of our arms, and by the fatiguing prospect of the great space to be traversed before we could see France again: an enormous distance which would be still further increased by the slowness of locomotion in summer, compared to the swift flight of the sledges in the winter. But we had to resign ourselves to the common law, which ordains that good should be as long in returning as evil is quick in arriving. And this we entirely demonstrated, for our return was as tedious as our exile had been rapid in its accomplishment.

As our itinerary was the one by which we had come to Vologda, we could not allay our impatience by curiosity or interest in the localities we passed through. Doubtless their aspect had changed, but at the first glance it would appear as if there were little difference between the Russia of winter and the Russia of summer: in the heart of the country, especially in its boreal region, there was always the same monotonous uniformity of solitude, the same sad and sombre verdure of the pines and larches, and the plains of uncultivated and desert sand which took the place of the plains of snow.

The vast expanse of Russia is grand in itself, a despairing grandeur increased by the habitations which one catches sight of from afar. We might have found it otherwise at St. Petersburg and Moscow, or in military stations; but at first we were only allowed to go through fields, forests, and villages. Our *feld-jäger* was ordered to take us outside the towns, without entering them, so that we could only see Jaroslaf from a distance as we passed it by. We could see the disproportionately wide streets which were lined with flat and low wooden houses, intersected by gardens. At that distance they looked like an assemblage of huts of savages in a desert. Man seemed to have changed the face of nature but little, except in the building of a few stone or brick houses, and especially a good number of churches capped with gilded domes and painted in rich colours; trophies of a religion which was at first vanquished and then victorious. These monuments represent the history of the Russian people, its long dependence on Asia, its triumph over the Golden Horde[6] and the victory obtained by the cross of Christ over the crescent.

We soon saw Kalouga, which was the first town that we entered. With its more numerous habitations and the movement of the population, we felt as if we were again in a European town, and with the same vice around us, if we might judge by the precautions of our guide against a throng who surrounded us with officious eager hands whose dexterity he evidently suspected.

Between this town and Smolensk, if I remember rightly, the hilly soil which is also frequently wooded with aromatic trees, and fairly well populated, reminded us of that of France. When at last we had reached Smolensk, where I had experienced such lively emotions, I felt that I was in my own country and amongst compatriots in its inhabitants; but Count Apraxin was absent. The town, animated as it was, seemed then empty to me, and I only asked our guide for time to address to this governor a few lines of thanks and tender regrets. After which we started again, and continued our day and night journey by Minsk and Vilna where the Russian headquarters were then installed. Their generals received me with open arms, Prince Gortchakoff especially was the foremost to display the caressing manners which they would seem to have imported from Asia. As new allies, this line of conduct may have been prescribed by their Emperor, or it may have been inspired by the still lively remembrance of my father. Thousands of Kalmucks and Baskirs swarmed upon the road. My companion, the major, and I purchased some of their weapons out of curiosity. We did not then think that we should put them to sorry use by turning them against each other.

The best understanding had always existed between us, and had I been told that, just as I had gone into Russia with a duel hanging over me arranged the preceding night, I should leave it with another duel in view, I could not possibly have believed it. This second quarrel, however, was destined to have a more prompt and happy issue than the first. We had just thrown ourselves into each other's arms in our delight at having at last crossed the Russian frontier; but from that moment left to ourselves in the midst of the malevolent distress of the Prussians who had been so heavily taxed, pillaged, and humiliated, we found ourselves without the necessaries of life. If, as is said, hunger brings the wolf to the door, many of us have experienced the truth that it entirely changes a man's character. That of my companion in captivity had been up to that moment remarkable for its equable and kindly gentleness; it changed suddenly and in this manner:

On August 8th we were approaching Friedland, when pressed by an insatiable hunger, we hesitated in sight of a castle and a cottage. He wanted to address the lord of the domain to beg a breakfast of him, which this Prussian nobleman would probably have refused; and I, dreading this humiliation, resisted with all my might, dragging my famished companion into a cottage, where for a little money we might obtain a probably less succulent repast, but at any rate without running any risks. Unfortunately, as ill luck would have it, in spite of our appetite and the poor woman's good-will, the feast of sour milk and detestable bread which she set before us was really not eatable. Thence ensued an altercation, in which the major carried away by brute instincts, and beside himself with hunger, covered me with abuse. I tried to recall him to a sense of his age and his superior rank; I invoked his habitual moderation; but he had lost his head, and instead of apologising, he raised his hand against me.

This was too much; we ran to our waggon where three non-commissioned officers who had been exchanged like ourselves, were awaiting us. We took away without their knowledge the Kalmucks' wretched sabres, and disappearing into the orchard, selected the ground for our encounter. This was a narrow clearing where stood a pretty isolated cottage which at that moment was closed and uninhabited. We had hardly divested ourselves of our outer clothing, when, in his rage, the major threw himself upon me with such impetuosity that I fell back slightly wounded in the arm. He was at the same time abusing me with such violence, that furious in my turn, I charged him, forced him to give way, and cut his wrist with a sabre stroke. Falling to the ground backwards, he lay there disarmed and disabled, his mad exasperation still increasing, calling me an assassin and a scoundrel. He only came back to his senses, on seeing me extend my hand to raise him up, then run to the neighbouring well for water to wash his wound and his clothes, which were already covered with the blood that issued freely from his wound. Then alone did my poor companion resume his real character. As soon as his wounds had been dressed as far as was possible, and all traces of blood washed off, we returned to our waggon, and got back to our places without our non-commissioned officers having any cognisance of this adventure. This was my battle of Friedland.

The same day the major's wounds were more carefully dressed in the town, and the next day, August 10th, better friends than ever, we parted from each other at Konigsberg. On the 14th I reached Elbing, and the 19th Berlin, after another quarrel very similar to this, with the difference that the wrong was on my side, but in which I acquitted myself very much in the same manner. Finally, on September 1st, I again saw Paris, the Emperor, and my family, to whom alone, perhaps, this narrative of my captivity may not appear out of place, or altogether wearisome by its length.

XXV

IN SPAIN

AT THE END OF THE year 1807, after my return from Vologda, having been made major, that is to say lieutenant-colonel, and weary of my inaction at Fontainebleau, I received orders to go to Poitiers to take the command of a marching regiment. It was a temporary agglomeration of recruits from seven hussar regiments, such indeed being the too youthful and weak composition of a great part of the first army which was destined to take possession of old Spain.

We entered there as allies in March, 1808. The division of the advance guard to which I belonged stopped at Aranda on the Douro. We were peacefully occupying this position at the time of the revolution of Aranjuez about March 19th, when Ferdinand VII usurped the throne, and Murat entered Madrid to protect the former sovereigns and their overthrown favourite against this prince.

Up to then everything remained apparently peaceful, and when Ferdinand, as we have seen, gave himself up at Bayonne in the middle of April, he passed through our cantonments when I was then in command of the furthest one, without causing the least stir on his passage; after which we reformed in his rear in Aranda and up to May 2nd, Spain remained inert. With regard to the relations of the army with the inhabitants, discipline was strictly kept up on our side; but we lived as complete strangers the one to the other. The difference of habits, of language, of character, the constraint of military life, the national pride, in revolt at this invasion disguised under the form of an alliance and whose aim was becoming more and more suspected, all separated us. As for religious observances, as we had no orders in that respect and made no profession, this fervent Catholic land of Spain must have thought we had no religion at all; so that what might have been at any rate a common tie between the two nations, became an additional obstacle to their mutual approach.

The departure in succession of the princes of the reigning family, especially that of 'the Prince of Peace' rescued from the national vengeance, increased the general irritation. The attitude of these people, which is always grave, became sombre; their patience was visibly only maintained through astonishment at the docility of their princes, through the habit of obedience, and a remnant of uncertainty regarding an event which their loyalty and the high opinion they had formed of the Emperor made it difficult for them to believe.

But when doubt was no longer possible; when Murat, taking the place of the last Bourbon who had left for Bayonne, became head of the government, the universal anger only waited for a signal, and the Junta of Madrid not daring to give it, the people of that capital took it upon themselves. Such was the revolt of May 2nd. It occurred on the occasion of the departure of the Infants, Don Antonio and Don Francisco. In the tumult 500 Frenchmen perished, either stabbed, or killed while fighting. This first symptom, however, was disavowed by all those who had anything to lose. Murat quenched this rising of assassins in a few hours in the blood of 160 insurgents. The slaughter of our men was avenged the following night by the military execution of thirty-five of the most guilty; a vengeance which promoted hatred, on the ground that these wretches had been shot without having had Christian preparation for death.

Napoleon experienced a fallacious joy at the first news of this rising, of whose details he was still ignorant, and he took advantage of it without sufficiently fearing its consequences. This was, however, the first spark of a conflagration which was only to be extinguished under the ruins of his Empire. It was the first signal of a new struggle in which the parts were to be reversed; where right was no longer on the side of our standards, and all moral powers, justice, public faith, individual rights and national pride which had been aroused, had turned against us; in which the war of a nation for its independence, a similar war to that whose impetus had saved us in our own revolution, was now to be found on the contrary side.

The counter shock of this revolt was not long in being felt from the Mançanarès to the Douro. A week after, we were warned of this by several assassinations, then by the bribery and desertion of several of our conscripts. Soon escorts became necessary; an atmosphere of hatred surrounded us, we felt on the edge of a volcano. Badajoz and Oviédo answered on May 22nd to a signal given by Madrid, Valencia on the 23rd, Seville on the 26th, Aragon on the 27th and from Bayonne to Aranjuez nothing remained free except the town in our occupation and the high road.

There, as in La Vendée in 1793, it was the people alone who had begun; the great, the rich, the civil authorities, even the Spanish army, all, in fact, who calculated and had an interest in order, and understood no force but organised force, hesitated and temporised.

Our marching regiments were then pushed on to Madrid, where the detachments dispersed to rejoin their numbers. I was thus left without a command, at Murat's disposition. Another throne was awaiting him, his disappointment at seeing himself deprived of this one, his responsibility in the midst of a general insurrection, the climate, the food, more nourishing in this country than in our own, had upset his temper and his health. Ill and dejected, when pressed to go and reign over Naples, his only wish was to leave this kingdom. He begged me to inform the Emperor that this was his desire.

The evils of the battle-field are the least of the evils of war. These are the sufferings of marches, of camps, of privation, want of regular rations, the absence of medicaments and hospitals by which armies are decimated, our own especially, where everything is done in haste without sufficient care for the thousand details on which the health of the soldier depends; but at that date, although the title of general comprises a knowledge of administrative science and prescribes its practice, few of our generals knew how to be administrators. Amongst the exceptions, I can, however, quote three really worthy to be so called: Davout, Saint-Cyr, and above all Suchet. It was not such a chief as he who commanded us at Aranda. It would be impossible to form an idea of the horrible spectacle presented by the hospital which had been started in that town for our regiments. All was wanting: fresh air, medicaments, even beds, for two, and sometimes three, sick and dying occupied the same. In the visits which were part of my duty, I had contracted the germ of typhus which was mowing down the ranks of our young recruits, and when towards the middle of June, Murat gave me my instructions to rejoin the Emperor, I was more ill than he was himself.

The fever gripped me just as I was getting on horse-back at Madrid, whence I was to proceed straight to Bayonne. Nevertheless such was the power of duty, the habit of braving everything, and my strong desire to quit this country, that, putting spurs to my horse under a burning sun, I accomplished the 160 leagues in fifty and odd hours. Several times, however, the illness asserted its sway, three times I fell down unconscious; fortunately this happened at relays where I found compatriots or pitiful women. I was hoisted up again into my saddle and went on.

Near Aranda a fresh danger nearly brought my mission to an end, as since happened to many others. I had noticed on the road when nearing a village, traces of a violent struggle, shreds of blood-stained uniforms, and at a little distance off, in the vines to the left, an assemblage of the enormous vultures so common in this country. These traces and fragments, these birds of evil omen, and their eagerness over a prey, the nature of which I could not specify, only too plainly pointed to the approach to this village as the scene of some horrible murder, and the vultures indicated, the spot to which the victims had been dragged. Had I stopped or gone back at the sight of this den of assassins I should have been lost myself, or failed in my mission; there was no choice for me but to go through it at full speed. But at the very minute when I was entering this cut-throat place, my guide slackened his pace and barred the way against me; I threatened him with my sword, a whistle was heard, and suddenly a multitude of furious men with atrocious countenances, or at any rate I thought them so, sprang out from various buildings, surrounded me and menaced me with their daggers, uttering cries for my death. Having fallen into this trap, I thrust my feet more firmly into the stirrups, and was trying to choose the weakest point of the circle which I might perhaps break through with a desperate rush, when from that side an old priest ran out towards me. He came up with extended arms, covering me with his body, and with a few rapid words, arrested the tumult. In a moment the daggers disappeared, the expression of their ferocious countenances altered; the murderous circle opened, and I was allowed to make my way through.

I only took time to shake hands with the worthy priest, endeavouring to express my gratitude by a look, and passed on, but this glance and the first sight of the village as I galloped through, at once explained the cause of the happy issue of this adventure. It may be remembered that at the time of the departure of Ferdinand VII, I had been detached in advance of Aranda, on the road which the prince was following. It was in this very cantonment and at the residence of this very priest. He had recognised me; and having been satisfied with our pleasant relations, and remembering how well discipline had been observed, he had gratefully come to my help with such happy results at the very nick of time.

After several other accidents, serious enough, but of too frequent occurrence in Spain, and in such headlong rides, to deserve mention, I arrived at the Imperial headquarters, conquered by my illness and utterly prostrated. I was just able to enter and hand my despatches to the Emperor, expressing to him the good wishes of the Grand Duke of Berg. More dead than alive, I could not have answered his questions if he had waited for my replies; but he saved me the trouble, for while enquiring as to the pacific spirit and the submission of the Peninsula, it was in such a. way that I felt the necessity of saying nothing which might shake a security that could only have been assumed. He promptly dismissed me, but only just in time. Otherwise I should have fallen at his feet: in a dead faint, which happened outside his door before a sentry of the grenadiers who picked me up.

I was taken to Bayonne to the house of Madame de Ravignan, my relative, and mother of the Jesuit preacher, then a child, who has since become so celebrated. There I was twice believed to be dead and a sheet thrown over my face, but I managed to struggle back to life under the unremitting care of the family, and was sent back to Paris to complete my convalescence.

Having returned as an invalid from Bayonne to Paris, I had not been able to accompany the Emperor to the Congress of Erfurt. On his return he had taken me back again and I had entered Biscay in his suite I rejoined him at Vittoria.

Up to then nothing in Spain seemed to me to have altered. The green, picturesque, and laborious Biscay still intact, seemed a stranger to the passions and the general upheaval of the rest of the Peninsula. This was the third time I saw it; but on this occasion, even more than the first two, I was struck with the abrupt dissimilarity of aspects, manners, and character which separates the two countries far more than the narrow Bidassoa. Our troops astonished me, above all those who had come from worthy and comfortable Germany. All was unlike our other frontiers. There was no shade of similarity, nothing in common, and the transition was abrupt, without any beginning of fusion of habits, language, and manners. Our soldiers felt ill at their ease from the very first frontier village, that of Irun. The serious and reserved countenances of the inhabitants, their costumes so different from ours and so dark in colour, their narrow, winding streets with the barred windows of the houses, and their closed doors, their little carts of antique form with large creaking wheels; a nauseating smell pervading every inhabited place, of which dirt alone could be the cause; in fact the whole of this serious, severe, alien, and inhospitable aspect had saddened and oppressed their hearts.

It was still worse beyond Vittoria when the first army of invasion informed the second of its defeat, and of the horrors which had accompanied it. Sadness was then changed into indignation, which was perhaps too evidently manifested in the light of subsequent consequences. Our French army indeed had realised only too well the atrocities of monkish anger and the hatred and vengeance which fill the soul of an insulted Spaniard.

It was related how these people had preluded their general insurrection with fearful massacres of their own generals; how their priests had with lies set them upon our companions of the war. The pleasant manners and the personal charms of the new king might have won them over, so they represented him as blind of one eye, a mean drunkard of the most repulsive aspect. Then using heaven as a lever to raise the earth, they had inflamed these superstitious minds by pretended miracles: they declared that a thunder-bolt had extinguished the sacred fire which burnt before their Virgin of Battles, they said they had seen the images of the saints weep. From that time and everywhere, the most *fortunate* of our sick, our laggards, our orderly officers surprised and seized, had been slaughtered on the spot; whilst others had been thrown into cauldrons of boiling water, and some even sawn between planks or burnt at a slow fire. Amongst a thousand victims of such atrocities our soldiers mentioned one of their own most excellent and humane generals, whom they had found still alive, but fastened by the neck to one of the trees on the road, with his four limbs sawn off by these monsters.

Overcome with indignation at these narratives our armies issued forth in raging fury. The Spanish army, with the exception of their regular troops, everywhere about the same, were principally composed of these ferocious insurgents; they were much less prepared for the defensive than for the offensive. Their principal thought had been to prevent our flight; intoxicated by the remembrance of Baylen, by national pride and monkish predictions, they were taking with them as much iron to enchain us, as to fight with.

Even their smugglers, formed into a regiment, carried after them great masses of merchandise with which they intended to inundate France, already conquered in their eyes. We have seen how, from their left to their right, a few hours had been enough for us to change all this oriental braggadocio into a contemptible flight. For, like the Turks, whose defects and qualities they possessed, these people can only defend themselves steadily from behind walls; they do not hold their ground in the open, feeling no shame in turning their backs, scattering themselves, and running to hide in their mountains.

However, as they have no great attachment for their miserable habitations, and live upon very little, if they take flight and find refuge in their rocks, they do not lose heart and abandon their cause, but they go there to multiply the warfare, to transform it into a succession of incessant struggles on the enemy's flank and rear, which are all traps, surprises, and assassinations. It is true that then in their turn surprised and seized, they are able to die proudly like martyrs, without condescending to murmur or to implore grace.

It also happened that in their defeats, many of them, escaping by a thousand by-ways would go great distances to rejoin their flag; this was why their armies, constantly scattered, would as constantly reappear in almost equal numbers, on new fields of battle. Later still, others got into the habit of being taken and retaken, and compounding with their conscience: they would take the oath to the new monarch, simply to gain time and an opportunity of deserting with the arms which the king would have given them, and which they would faithfully take back with them to serve their own worthy cause.

A great people! But destitute of great men during six years of events the most fitted to create them. It must, however, be allowed that in this country it was not then so very easy to be a great man: that could only have happened by a series of victories which would have been impossible for a mass of insurgents confronting an experienced army like our own; so that, in spite of the aid of all kinds lavished by the English, the constant efforts of these people produced nothing more than some rather remarkable partisan chiefs with out ever being able to create a general. To this, one might add other considerations; such as the configuration of the country, its parcelling out into provinces, animated by different local spirit and interests; whence a multitude of chiefs, each of whom exalted his least successes in such hyperbolical language, that it would be difficult to say whether Fame could have found other voices capable of overpowering these, and proclaiming actions of less imaginary grandeur.

Beyond Brivesca I was not in a position to judge of the country, because at the time when the advance guard of Soult and of Bessières were overwhelming the army of the centre at Burgos in a first onrush, I had been sent from one to the other of these two towns at full gallop during the night. By chance I still have at hand the order dictated and signed by the Emperor. Here it is: 'Start at midnight with my personal attendants so as to arrive at Burgos before five o'clock in the morning, and establish me there. My intention is to leave from here at two o'clock in the morning and to arrive at seven at Burgos. If the army and the marshal are at Burgos, I shall go straight to my headquarters but incognito; if on the contrary there is any disorder, I shall go out of the town. You must inform Marshal Soult so that he may be there on my arrival, also Marshal Bessières if he is still in the town. But if he is in pursuit of the enemy, he must on no account be disturbed. All my chasseurs and dragoons who have been here for some time will start on the march at three o'clock to-morrow morning, for Burgos. I shall arrive there in strict privacy. But as long as I can manage my business, I do not care! Leave, yourself, at midnight, so that you can be at Burgos by day break. I imagine that you will get there at four o'clock, or five o'clock at the latest. I shall arrive at seven. I wish to find, about a league from the town, someone to show me the way. On which I pray God to have you in His good and holy keeping.

'Cubo, this 10th November, 1808,
7 o'clock of the evening
NAPOLEON.'

This order which I did not receive till after midnight could not be obeyed by the Emperor's personal attendants. But leaving everything behind me, and going post haste, saddle and bridle, through the very darkest night, I reached Burgos towards six o'clock, at day break. In the early light I could discern the high road and the neighbouring fields covered with the Spaniards who had been killed the night before; monks lying there in their frocks with weapons in their hands, horses struck down, and many of the beautiful sporting dogs, so frequently seen in this country, either lying dead beside their masters, or howling as they sought those whom they had lost.

As for Burgos itself, taken by force and almost entirely deserted by its inhabitants, it was given up to the most active pillage: the doors of the houses were battered in, the streets were strewn with torn clothing, and broken household utensils and furniture. Our soldiers were prowling about, bent double, some under masses of valuable effects, others under sacks of *quadruples*;[7] all were so eager at this sport, that it was almost an impossibility to collect a battalion to take possession of the Archbishop's palace, and establish the Imperial quarters there.

I had not yet placed the first posts when I saw the Emperor himself arrive, accompanied only by his Mameluke and Savary. He had galloped all night as I had done, and arrived at full speed covered with mud, and dying of hunger, cold, and fatigue. The archiepiscopal palace had been no better treated than the rest of the town: the rooms intended for the Emperor were still in disorder, soiled by burst bottles and spilt wine, with the furniture all battered; we tried to set things a little straight, then Savary went off with Rustan to get some food ready, leaving me alone with the Emperor, who helped me to light his fire.

I was doing what I could by the light of a single candle, when Napoleon, whose delicate sense of smell was offended by the odour of the broken viands, called me to open the window near which he had sat down. I luckily ran up to pull back the curtain; when what was our surprise! Behind these curtains three Spaniards, fully armed, upright and motionless, were pressed up as close as they could be against the shutters, either with a view to escape from our plunderers or having come there to plunder themselves, a practice of which their army was accused as well as ours. During the ten minutes that Napoleon, suspecting nothing, had been there alone with me, sometimes seated, and sometimes leaning over the fireplace with his back towards them, they could a dozen times over with a single blow have put an end to the war. But, fortunately, these were not insurgents, but soldiers of line regiments. The wretched creatures when they found themselves discovered were petrified with fright and glanced towards us terror-stricken. The Emperor never even thought of putting a hand to his side arms, but smiled with a gesture of pity; I disarmed them and handed them over to our soldiers; then having assured myself that no other enemy was hidden in this chamber and its neighbourhood, I made haste to go and reconnoitre, with even more care than usual, the rest of this vast building.

It was like an entire town, the celebrated cathedral and its dependencies being united to the Archbishop's palace. I was transfixed with admiration at the aspect of this magnificent church when I thought I saw human shadows gliding about at the top of the enormous pillars. This recalled me to the duty which I had come to fulfil, and having soon discovered an entrance in the base of one of these gigantic blocks, I quickly reached the top by the winding staircase which it contained. This staircase led to a rotunda. I was quite out of breath when, emerging into this cupola and raising my eyes, I found myself surrounded by twenty of the enemy's officers ranged in a circle, and seated in silence against the wall. At sight of me a murmur arose which was half supplicating and half threatening; several swords even were drawn, and perhaps I should have been sacrificed to their safety, if I had not had the happy idea of promptly calling out 'Help! help, grenadiers!' and ordering them to surrender immediately. They did so after a moment's hesitation, luckily for themselves as well as for me, for I should have been avenged at the selfsame instant, as some of ours, having seen me disappear in the pillar, had at once followed me up.

The next day and the day after that, pillage continued all over the town. Our own rations had failed, and none of the inhabitants being there to supply us, and our pressing need of food serving as a pretext, nothing escaped this destruction, which was renewed with the successive arrival of the different corps. The chiefs by way of shutting their eyes to it, justified themselves by the Spanish atrocities which had been perpetrated against us. It was thought necessary to strike terror; and from the Ebro to Madrid it was one vast military execution. The soldier was allowed to enjoy this vengeance and to take his fill.

The contagion spread even to the Imperial headquarters in Burgos; it could not be stopped until after the Emperor had made a severe example by way of a warning. I remarked one curious fact in the midst of this disorder. I had been told that a troop of pillagers had been seen to enter the cathedral, and hastened there at once; but it was unnecessary, the imposing majesty of the sacred building had sufficed. Before its grandeur and beauty, the astonished marauders, seized with sudden respect, remained confounded. They were in positive admiration. Their audacity had been turned into humility, and anyone witnessing their silent contemplation and abashed demeanour as they retired, would have thought that at the unforeseen aspect of the sublime immensity, crushed by their own nothingness, they had felt themselves transported into the presence of God Himself!

It happened differently in Lerma where I was sent about November 20th. This town is built on the incline of a small hill, a kind of truncated cone whose table-land is surmounted by an abbey and a palace, with their esplanade. Everything was sacked during the first night, and half the town was set on fire; I was powerless to do anything, having been almost asphyxiated by a brasier which had been left in my room all night.

Besides, what can be done in such times of universal delirium? It is well known that a long succession of victories ruins the soldier as well as the general; that too frequent forced marches are fatal to discipline; that the irritation produced by hunger and fatigue, and the darkness in which they arrive at their cantonments at night, lead and embolden to every excess, also the absence of distributions which are impossible to be made in such haste; so that there arises each night for the soldiers, the need of scattering themselves abroad to provide for their own wants, and as they receive no money, the habit of helping themselves to everything. Why then be astonished at these disorders? Our soldiers considered themselves in the right. After the miracles of Jena and Friedland they had gone over 500 leagues at double quick march, and had conquered on their arrival. Their life was one long superhuman assault against fatigue and danger; in which pillage seemed their right as one of the fruits of victory. To contest it would have been to dishearten them. Besides, by what right could so much be expected from them, if nothing was tolerated?

The inhabitants, however, had taken care not to wait for our arrival. Their flight was of itself a sufficient proof that they made common cause with their army, and much worse. It had been said that during their first success, they and even their womenkind had disputed with each other the horrible enjoyment of putting the finishing stroke to our sick and wounded. Frightful details were added which were only too true: how some had been deprived of life by a series of odious mutilations, others by countless stabs with scissors, stuck into their eyes and into the most sensitive parts of their bodies. It was known that at Valencia 200 French who had been inhabitants of the town for years and had become almost naturalised, had been martyrised; and it was reported that there as elsewhere the signal for these massacres had been given by monks. To this was due the excesses of our men, followed by sacrilegious profanations of which Lerma offered the first and most terrible example; hence this long orgie of forty-eight hours, and these conflagrations, caused by wine, which they wanted to extinguish with wine. Hence also, on this elevated table-land, in view of these people, religious to fanaticism, who were contemplating the sight from their sheltering rocks, the spectacle of our soldiers trebly intoxicated by wine, mirth and anger, going round their fires in a procession with tapers in their hands, travestied in the frocks of these monks whose sacred chants they parodied by the least edifying of barrack-room songs.

The Emperor did not witness these excesses which he would not have tolerated. He had even tried by a proclamation to recall the populations to their own centres, and to their hearths, and to rally them to his cause, giving them a month to come back. He promised them his protection at this price, with the exception of several grandees who were to bear the whole brunt of his anger. He left Burgos November 23rd, and did not stop that day until he had reached Aranda. Here, of all the inhabitants the Alcalde alone had remained. He declared that the resources of the surrounding country would admit of his feeding 80,000 men for a whole month. But here as at Burgos there reigned the same pillage and disorder. Every door, every bed, every piece of furniture in the houses, either adorned the bivouacs or fed the camp fires of the centre of our army united around this town.

On the next day, the 29th, Napoleon himself pushing straight on to Madrid by Sommo-Sierra, with Victor and his own guard, had no more pressing care than to precede the arrival of the Spanish remainders of Tudela, and promptly to astonish the Peninsula and Europe by the news of his entry into the capital.

Consequently I received the order to go and wait for him on November 29th[8] at Boceguillas. This is a rather pretty village about three leagues from Sommo-Sierra, a strong position of which the approaches and the defile were occupied by the enemy's reserve. On that day the Polish light horse of our guard formed the advanced guard. They drove the Spanish from Carajas, another village situated at the entrance of the gorge of Sommo-Sierra. This regiment took up its position there and thus protected the Imperial quarters.

The Emperor arrived at Boceguilas at the end of the same day. At that moment endeavours were being made to extinguish a fire which had caught to a house situated on the village market place. It happened to be the only one which could accommodate him. During the night an icy fog, and the smell of the conflagration of the previous day, together with his own impatience for the morrow's fight, agitated him and he slept badly. The smell of fire at last drove him out of his quarter into his tent, whence he came out several times to warm himself at our camp fires. This caused him to get too early into the saddle, directly the morning report was to hand, and as soon as he thought Victor's infantry was at the head ready to engage battle on the mountain.

XXVI

SOMMO-SIERRA:
I AM WOUNDED

Sommo-sierra was the last obstacle to be conquered before arriving at Madrid. The remains of Castanos having escaped Lannes at the front, and Marshal Ney in their rout, were dispersing behind this screen, which the Emperor was anxious to break through, so that he hastened the march. Nevertheless, having arrived about eleven o'clock abreast of Carajas, and finding that Victor's infantry was not ready, nor the enemy sufficiently reconnoitred, he drew up on a hill to the left of the road, where he breakfasted.

There Major Lejeune of the Engineers, one of Berthier's aides-de-camp and well known since as a painter, by his remarkable picture of this affair, came to give him an account of the position of the enemy's corps and announced that Victor's skirmishers were already engaged.

In front of us, in fact, this marshal's advance guard could be perceived entering a defile on the high road, which was rendered still more narrow by two steep ridges. At the bottom of this gorge, on the side to the right of the road was an enormous rock. This rock defined and concealed the foot of another slope, which was steep though short, and the last that had to be scaled in order to reach the top of this plateau more celebrated than it deserves to be. It was a blessed, almost sacred position, and believed to be invincible. The summit was crowned by a redoubt with sixteen guns, defended by 12,000 Spaniards who were in position in two lines between the rocks, and commanded by Brigadier-General Saint-Juan. A cloud of their skirmishers was extended to their front on the spurs to right and left, whence they directed their fire down into the defile.

Victor's main body was numerous, compact, and supported by the Imperial Guard. They had fewer men on their side, but they had the advantage of locality and were animated by such hatred to us, and such faith and confidence in their position, that even after it had played them false, still believing it sufficiently strong of itself to have needed no defence, they declared that there had been treachery at work, and became guilty, as will be seen, of an abominable murder.

The Emperor in his astonishment that they should have dared to await him, and growing more and more impatient, made us remount. Distancing the infantry he ventured too soon into this gorge, where the enemy's fire arrested his progress at about 400 metres distance from the right of their line of battle. Them taking up a position in a bend to the left of the road he let our foot soldiers advance. But either contemptuous of these insurgents, or annoyed at having so uselessly exposed himself, and the fog hiding the obstacle from him, in his growing irritation, he ordered his escort squadron to advance, charge, and carry the position without waiting any longer. This squadron was composed of eighty Polish light horse, commanded by seven officers: MM. Korjietulski, Rudowski, Dziewanowski, Rowiczki, Krazinski, and Niegolewski. At their head went also Generals Montbrun and Piré, the Prince of Neuchâtel's aide-de-camp. At the same time he ordered the 9th regiment of light infantry to scale the spur on the right, the 24th that on the left, and he pushed the 96th forwards on the high road.

This well-planned infantry attack needed time; for there is often some hesitation at the outset of a manoeuvre of this kind when the features of the ground, varying at each fresh step, have to be conquered as well as the enemy. Their chiefs do not hold the united bodies massed under their hand; the ensemble fails; the one body waits for the other; and the combat broken up into insignificant skirmishes, languishes without coming to an issue.

It was beginning in this way when the Emperor was informed that the charge of his escort squadron had been suddenly checked; that it had come across an insurmountable obstacle which it would be impossible to carry from the front. It could indeed only be overcome by a flank movement and by infantry only. But there was no time to be lost, Napoleon had placed himself in a dilemma; he would not retreat in sight of his troops, though from the top of the crest above him, the bullets were raining round his head. It was, of course the duty of the Poles as guards to protect his person from this danger; nevertheless, as Piré and Montbrun were ignorant of the Emperor's peril, they acted rightly; and we shall soon see that from a military point of view their charge, ill-timed at the moment, was impossible.

But, on hearing this word, the Emperor who was in a fever of impatience, became furious. Violently striking the pommel of his saddle he exclaimed: 'How, impossible? I do not know the word! There should not be anything impossible for my Poles!' whereupon Walther, the general in command of the guard, endeavouring to calm him, replied: 'Sire, a moment's patience, I pray; the infantry is already ascending on the flanks, both wings of the enemy will be encountered on level ground, and then a charge from the centre will finish him; he will not have lost anything by waiting.' The Emperor would not listen to him, and in the midst of his explosion of anger, I could hear these exclamations: 'Impossible! What! My guards stopped by peasants! by armed bands!'

The enemy's bullets were falling more thickly every moment, and by a natural movement I came forwards to place myself between them and Napoleon, watching him, in fear every instant lest he should be struck, growing excited by his danger, and too much roused up by his words, for indeed Walther was in the right. But he, seeing in my glance a reflection of his own impatience, replied as if I had addressed him: 'Yes, yes; go you, Ségur! Go at once, make my Poles charge, make them take everything, or bring me back prisoners!'

Speeding off through the moving forest of our bayonets which bristled on the road, and which I had even to thrust aside not to be struck by them as I rushed by at a gallop, I arrived at the foot of the rock under shelter of which the Polish squadron was drawn up alone, in front of the infantry. 'Commandant,' I cried to Korjietulski, 'the Emperor orders us to charge home, and at once!' Upon which, Montbrun made an exclamation and a gesture of astonishment without venturing to contradict me; but Piré answered: 'It is impossible!'—'The Emperor has been told that,' I retorted, 'and he will not hear of it.'—'Very well,' resumed Piré, 'come and see for yourself; the devil in person, pretty well used to fire as he must be, could hardly stand that!'

Then to prove the truth of his words, advancing beyond the rock through a hail of bullets which rained down upon our equipments, he pointed out to me the steep slope of the road up to this amphitheatre bristling with rocks, the redoubt of sixteen guns which crowned it, and twenty battalions deployed in such a manner as to converge their front and flank fire on an attack which could only be effected in column and along the road.

This made 40,000 discharges of musketry and more than 40 discharges of grape shot to be received in a minute. Without doubt nothing could be more convincing, but the order had been too imperative, it was impossible to go back upon it. 'It does not matter,' I exclaimed; 'the Emperor is there and he insists on the thing being settled. Come, Commandant, the honour will be ours, advance by squads, and forwards!'

This colloquy carried on aloud would have intimidated any other troops who would have hesitated; but there was not a sign of this with these heroic Poles: I had hardly had time to draw my sword from the scabbard, before they had begun their charge in a column from this road.

We charged at full speed, I was about ten paces in front with my head bent down, uttering our war-cry by way of distracting my attention from the din of the enemy's fire which was all breaking out at once, and the infernal hiss of their bullets and grape shot. Reckoning on the rapidity of our impetuous attack, I was hoping that in their astonishment at our audacity the enemy would aim badly; that we should have time to dash into the midst of their guns and bayonets and throw them into disorder. But they aimed only too well!

Very soon, in spite of our clamour and the detonation of so many arms, I could distinguish behind me the sound of smart reports followed by groans, with the thud of falling men and horses, which made me foresee defeat. Our warlike cries were becoming lost in the cries of pain of the unfortunate Poles; I did not dare to turn my head, fearing that the sad spectacle would cause me to give up. I knew that I had been myself struck several times; different bullets had gone through my hat, the collar of my cloak, and all my garments, but so far had hardly bruised me. One had dinted the scabbard of my sword on my left side, for on both flanks, as at our head, the more we advanced, the more we were assailed by the enemy's fire. A grape shot ball then grazed me on the heart which was left almost denuded of covering. I took counsel with myself; but quickly realising that such a wound must be either mortal or insignificant, as I did not feel like fainting, I went on. (It took me, however, six months to get over it.) Almost at the same moment a bullet catching me on the right side and taking away my breath forced me to stop and look around and behind me.

I was alone within thirty paces of the redoubt I had outstripped two battalions of the enemy, placed obliquely, behind a ravine on our right flank. One officer alone was following me, Rudowski, I believe, a colossus, like most of these picked men. He was still on horseback, but wounded to death, staggering, and on the point of falling off with his face to the enemy. Distance and the rocks prevented my seeing anything more. I made a vain attempt to turn back my horse, which was itself wounded; but the Spaniards advanced to seize me, shouting cries of victory. Then I jumped to the ground trying to collect what strength remained to me, and while retreating to shelter myself from their fire needlessly directed

against a solitary man, I pressed as close as possible to the rocks
to the right of the road. A cruel retreat! first, whilst rapidly passing by Rudowski, the poor fellow in his death agony almost fell
upon me; after which I had to leap over, or avoid our unfortunate
comrades, either dead or in the agonies of death, who were lying
on this glorious but most sad field of battle.

Nearly the whole of the squadron was laid low. Out of six
other officers, three more were either killed outright or mortally
wounded: these were the lieutenants Rowiczki, Rrzyzanowski and
Captain Dziewanowski. The three others, Lieutenant and Captain
Niegolewski and Krazinski, and Major Korjietu were wounded.
Forty non-commissioned officers and lancers, killed or mortally
wounded, were lying on the ground. Twelve others were wounded
but less seriously; twenty alone had escaped this massacre safe
and sound. These had assisted their wounded to retire, so that,
over the whole of the remaining ground covered by our charge I
only saw one trumpeter left standing, motionless in the midst of
the firing which was still going on. The poor child was weeping
for his squadron, and over one of his officers stretched upon the
ground, whose horse he was holding, and which he helped me to
mount. I was then suffering a great deal: I could no longer drag
myself along, and it was impossible to stop under this rain of
bullets and grape shot, so he led me to the foot of the sheltering
rock whence our brave Poles had dashed forth so full of life and
ardour which death alone could have extinguished. The advanced
guards of our infantry had stopped behind. This last journey down
a rapid descent at a foot pace, was terribly painful, and appeared
to me of interminable length!

Having at last reached our men, and being no longer held up
by the danger, I fell into the arms of the grenadiers of the 96th.
Colonel de la Grange happened to be there, and I owe to him the
first care bestowed upon me, and the preservation of my sword
which up to that moment I had had sufficient strength to retain.

It was he who caused me to be carried off directly by four grenadiers. A few paces off, Savary met me on his way to arrange the
attack; he made an exclamation of pity, but, still under the influ-

ence of that fiery ardour without which such self-sacrifice could not exist, I answered: 'Do not think of me, but forwards, forwards! and may our infantry avenge our Poles on these wretches!'

A little further on, as we passed near the Emperor, the little group which we formed attracted his attention and he sent to inquire. 'Ah! my poor Ségur!' he exclaimed, 'Yvan, go off at once and save him for me!' It was from Yvan himself that I heard this. Yvan hastened up, and by the help of some grenadiers was carrying me away, when another Spanish bullet aimed from the crest of the defile, picked me out in the midst of all the heads which were bending over and covering me, just grazing without wounding them, and entered my right thigh.

Surprised at the relentless ill-luck which seemed to pursue me, they stopped short. 'Oh, the poor fellow!' said Yvan, 'here is his leg broken now!'—'No, no,' I said, as I moved it; 'but go quickly and get me out of this, for it looks like one of my most unlucky days!' The bullet in fact after running round the bone without breaking it, had pursued its way to the other side where it remained.

This rather remarkable instance of bad fortune was at that moment followed by one of quite a contrary nature. Turenne, an officer on the Emperor's staff, on perceiving me had hastened to come to my help, which proved a very fortunate thing for himself; for hardly had he got off his horse, before the saddle was demolished by a cannon-ball. Resuming their way, about a hundred paces more to the rear, they set me down by the side of the road, sheltered by a rock, and now began the most unpleasant part of the business, that of sounding the wounds.

Yvan, accustomed as he was to this kind of thing, while taking off my clothes, which were torn and literally riddled with shots, as in a military execution, could not restrain the expression of his astonishment. My contusions, the large wound which was over my heart, and that on the thigh, which he had to enlarge to extract the ball, did not seem much to trouble him; but by the contraction of his countenance when he saw the course of the wound which had entered my bowels beneath the liver, and whose depth he was unable to sound, I could see that he had no hope of saving me. I perceived this even more by his gestures in reply to the numerous and eager inquiries of the officers ot the Old Guard, who were defiling almost on my feet, and by their exclamations and regrets, the last farewells offered by their friendship, whose remembrance still touches me.

Thus convinced of my approaching end, Yvan being obliged to leave me, I begged him to convey my adieux to my family and to the Emperor. Vanity must retain a very tenacious hold upon us, or Napoleon must have raised it to a high pitch, for I must confess that in these last words which I addressed to the Emperor, my principal thought was to increase his esteem, even consoling myself for death by thinking how I should best make a fine end.

I had felt assured of the success of the battle when I saw our reserve march onwards to the front. In fact whilst our charge had drawn and concentrated upon itself the whole fire of the enemy, Barrois, the infantry general, had taken advantage of this diversion, and had advanced as far as the rock which had been our point of departure and retreat. There, like myself, pushed forwards on the road by the Emperor, he had no sooner left that shelter to renew my charge, than thirteen of his grenadiers were struck down by the firing from the redoubt. Then retreating behind the rock, he had sent on some companies to scale the heights on our right, to turn the obstacle; and later, becoming impatient at their hesitation, he had himself gone up at the head of his brigade. There, on level ground at last, in face of 10,000 Spaniards ranged in two lines, he had attacked them. But they, although four against one, seeing themselves about to be attacked, after discharging their arms, had rushed off helter-skelter as fast as their legs could carry them. At the same moment he adds (for I hold it from him and have his note under my hand) the noise of the cannonading on the left ceased.

Our troops were on the point of reaching the burg of Buytrago and a last troop of the enemy; they could even perceive in their midst a group of French soldiers whom they had taken prisoners and were dragging along; and were straining every nerve to overtake and deliver them, when a sudden halt followed by a discharge and the simultaneous fall of all these captives, filled them with consternation. The crime was consummated; the unfortunates shot down at arm's length were slaughtered; vengeance alone remained. It was an ample one in spite of the flight of the assassins who hoped to escape, and it was found possible afterwards to raise up and restore to life a few of their victims.

The whole of the Spanish corps which had been defeated at Sommo-Sierra was not dishonoured by this infamous act; but the same corps completed its dishonour about ten days later, and twenty leagues further on, by a still more odious outrage. Talavera de la Reyna was the theatre of this misdeed. The rout of these wretches had only come to an end in this town, here it had not been believed that they could possibly be beaten on the Sommo-Sierra which bore the reputation of being sacred and impregnable. This it certainly was not, though it was easier to defend themselves there. But in order to absolve themselves from the charge of cowardice by imputing their defeat to a betrayal on the part of their general, they threw themselves upon the excellent and unfortunate Saint-Juan whom they had abandoned; and fastening him alive to a stake, during an entire day of agony made him the aim for their execrable skill. After they had been shamefully scattered by our advance guard, the terrible sight was revealed to us of the corpse in. its Spanish general's uniform, riddled with a thousand bullets, still fastened up.

Our main body had passed by during the two hours that I was lying stretched on the damp ground, and the Emperor having entered Buytrago, where the Duc de Bassano had joined him, said to him: 'Before this day is over, I shall have sustained a loss which grieves me deeply,' but learning that I was still alive, he dispatched his own carriage with Yvan, his surgeon, and orders that if possible I should be conveyed to his headquarters. This journey of several miles over the encumbered ground was a very painful one. They were forced to stop every moment as I was suffocating; and often Yvan, who was escorting me on horse-back, would bend his head over to see if I was still breathing.

But I remember even then, that perceiving by the road side several groups of Spanish prisoners, I was struck by the menacing pride of their attitude, their sombre and ferocious physiognomies, and the thunderous glances full of rage and hatred which they still dared to cast upon us.

The next morning, after having left one of his surgeons beside me, the Emperor, who was riding on the road to Madrid with Berthier, said, calling up Larrey the surgeon-in-chief: 'You have seen Ségur, can you answer for his life?' On his response in the negative, after several inquiries addressed to Duroc and Berthier, he turned round to the other officers who were following, and asked: 'Does anyone know where and how Ségur was wounded? Was it in carrying an order?' Nobody could reply, for Walther was not there; but Piré like a Breton, as he was, ever to the fore, and perfectly fearless, feeling surprised at this question as I myself was afterwards, spurred on his horse. 'Why! Sire,' he said, 'it was whilst charging by your orders at the head of your own special Polish squadron, I heard it and I saw it!' Upon this, it would appear that General Montbrun, since celebrated, added a few words of such a flattering nature that it is not for me to mention them. Yvan also repeated some of the words which he had heard me utter. The Emperor then, so they said, fell into a very thoughtful mood, and after that he made Yvan bring him every day a bulletin of my condition.

Nevertheless in the bulletin of this battle and the following one, although the Emperor did me the honour of daily public notification of my condition, and also announced that he had made me a colonel, he judged it necessary to confound the most of these details here related in one single charge. But it will also be seen, that as far as I was concerned, he did not stop short at the preceding marks of his esteem, a personal fact which would not be worthy of mention, were it not on account of the calumnies which accused this great man of hardness, and a want of kindness and gratitude.

During this march forwards of the Emperor I had been left at Buytrago alone with my surgeon, I should rather say alone with myself; not that this doctor was without merit, for the future proved the contrary; but being then very young and having little practice in his art, or faith in himself, he was of those who fear to attract the enemy by attacking him. Never daring anything, for fear of killing, he allowed one to die, and would temporise in a state of indecision whilst the patient was in the grip of his malady and there was not a moment to lose.

This timid doctor was all the more emboldened in pursuing his system because the farewells of my friends and the prognostications of his masters had convinced him that my doom was sealed. Therefore on the 1st and 2nd of December when the danger which Yvan had momentarily prevented by bleeding me, returned with the fever, thinking that he was only there to keep up appearances, he allowed it to take possession of my whole being; with this result that on December 3rd by the first rays of daylight I saw him packing up his portmanteau, as if, seeing me speechless and breathless, and probably believing I was almost unconscious, he was every moment expecting our simultaneous departure: his own for Madrid, which he was in a hurry to reach, and mine for the other world, in which, I must confess, I was not so anxious to suit his convenience.

I was suffocating all the time, and, unable to make myself heard, I could perceive my *valet de chambre*, Le Grand, sitting on the ground by my bed weeping bitterly; but not feeling at all in a melting mood, I was hanging on to my last thread, when I heard the doctor dictate to this excellent servant the last things that were to be done for me: 'He was to take care of my property; to keep some last souvenirs for my family, and to have me buried suitably.'

I was not so resigned but what I could be angry! Were these the only prescriptions which I had a right to expect from this doctor? His neglect enraged me, and with a last effort I called him by a gesture; he came back and leant over me, and I was just able to articulate, that if there were any last chance to try, he had better resort to it, 'Not bleed you!' he replied, you are so feeble! I could see, by his eyes raised to heaven, that he was afraid lest I should die under his lancet. But stretching my arm out with an imperious sign and word, it decided him: the blood spouted out, and I was saved!

That very evening the doctor proclaimed with pride that I was out of danger; but in his inmost heart, although glad of this, I think he was very much mystified at my coming to life again. I did so with such promptitude, and he was in such a hurry to reach Madrid, that three days later, the carriage of the colonel of the 54th being there, he placed me in it and we started for that town in the middle of an icy snow-storm. He did not even hesitate to instal me that night, shivering with fever and cold, under a miserable open shed on some damp straw, where, during twelve mortal hours, a thick bed of snow lay on the rug which he had cast over me. One cannot forget such sufferings, though one ought rather to feel pride than regret, glory consisting as much in enduring them bravely as in confronting them. We did, however, reach there at last.

I fear I may perhaps have somewhat too much descanted on these details, but would like to add yet another fact of which I was almost a witness during this journey, a fact principally interesting by the discussion which it provoked. We had halted in a village where there was one of our stores officials, as well as a depôt of prisoners. This *employé,* a man of sense, with whom I was acquainted, after having asked how I was going on, accosting my doctor, exclaimed: 'That if it could be affirmed by a material proof, that it is the mind alone which feels in us and not the body, a fact which he had observed with one of the officers taken at Sommo-Sierra, would suffice. This prisoner,' he added, 'had had an arm amputated in the affair, and had hardly recovered before he got into a quarrel with some other prisoners and very nearly lost the other arm which was wounded in some way in the scrimmage.'

Up to that point metaphysics do not seem to have entered into a purely physical accident, but it was remarked at the time that in the exasperation of his anger the prisoner did not the least seem to feel the violent blow which he had received on his remaining arm, whilst he was always complaining, like others who have had amputated limbs, of the pain in the other arm which had had left on the field of battle. Our *employé* argued from this that feeling can only exist in the mind, because by it alone this unfortunate man could suffer in a missing part of his body, whilst, on the other hand, the mind entirely given up to passion, had withdrawn the sense of feeling from the healthy part of his body which was still alive!

Upon which I saw the doctor smile. Having more to do with the body than the mind, he explained this fact more materially; attributing the effect of the pain of the missing member to a continuity of sensation in the common origin of the nerves, and the contrary result, that of want of sensibility in the remaining arm, to a sort of contraction, a concentration produced in the brain by anger.

For my part very much interested as I had been lately in not separating the mind from the body, this solution which appeared satisfactory, physiologically speaking, seemed to me, philosophically, incomplete and insufficient I did not think it went sufficiently back to the principle in question; I therefore added to complete it, a quotation of the passage from Malebranche where he says: 'That the mind resides immediately in that part of the brain to which all the organs of the senses lead;' either because God has chained it to this summit like Prometheus to his rock, or that, imprisoned in our body of which it is the life, this spot must be its centre of action; the precise spot where God has willed that, in an ever impenetrable mystery, this emanation of his immaterial immensity and eternity should undergo a passing personification, at one and the same time spiritual and material.

However this may be, in the midst of these reflections I had arrived at Madrid on December 7th. During my stay in this capital up to the 27th, both before and after the Emperor's departure, I was overwhelmed with marks of his interest. He informed me through Berthier that he had made me a colonel: and after my letter of thanks he said with a smile: 'Well, if he is ambitious, that is a proof that he will live; but in the future I desire that he should expose himself less. I have been in fifty battles without a single wound; and here he gets wounded twice running. One should really have some luck in war!'

Thereupon they discussed the matter; not seeming to have remarked that where I had only been wounded the greater part of those who had followed me had perished. But they came to the conclusion nevertheless from a general observation already quoted by Louis XV, as may be seen in my father's memoirs, that I offered a fresh example of those strange and systematic blows of fate which alternately strike one generation and miss another. Thus my grandfather, the Marshal de Ségur, had been constantly struck, my father spared, and myself struck like my grandfather!

The Emperor added that he would console me for this. On the eve of his departure he sent me word by Duroc that he entrusted me with the duty of bearing and presenting to the Legislative Assembly all the standards taken in the campaign. He was good enough to request General Belliard, the governor of Madrid, not to let me go till I was quite strong enough. Then, notwithstanding the haste with which he again entered on his campaign, on mounting his horse, he handed over the letter which will be read below; such a letter as in conjunction with so many marks of attachment to those around him, can hardly, I think, leave any grounds for the accusations of coldness and ingratitude.

'M. PHILIPPE DE SÉGUR, I was truly grieved to know that you were for a time in danger. I learn with much pleasure that the state of your wounds allows of your entering upon the convalescent stage, and that you will soon be able to complete your recovery in Paris. You must be under no kind of anxiety as to your future; you have given me every possible proof of your zeal, your courage, and your attachment to my person. Your principal care at present must be to get cured of your wounds so that you should feel no evil effects from them. This letter having no other purpose, I pray God that He may have you ever in His holy keeping!'9

'At Madrid, December 21st, 1808.'

'NAPOLEON.'

XXVII

I PRESENT THE STANDARDS TO THE LEGISLATIVE ASSEMBLY

To finish with these details, which are too long and doubt-less too personal, I will only add that on December 27th, 1808, lying full length in a carriage with the conquered standards under my care, I left Madrid for Bayonne, by Sommo-Sierra, Burgos, and Vittoria. A company of infantry escorted me, camping at night around me and the standards. This was indispensable, and an officer carrying dispatches, having insisted in spite of our advice in going a little in front of us, was killed as soon as he got beyond the protection of our bayonets.

At last on January 7th, 1809, leaving for the second time this country of Spain which had proved almost as fatal to me as it was to be to the Empire and the Emperor, I returned to France and soon rejoined my family. My wounds, which were still open, having kept me on my back some months longer, it was necessary to put off to the next session, that of 1809 to 1810, the presentation to the Legislative Assembly, of the trophies conquered by our armies of Spain in 1808. But as this last scene almost exclusively concerns the subject which occupies our attention, why delay the narrative? I therefore give it here.

It would certainly seem that to a young colonel, above all eager for glory, such a day should appear the finest and happiest of his whole life. But one has to pay for everything; and it may be considered a singular fact that the moment which preceded this presentation, redounding so much to my honour, was perhaps one of the most trying moments that I have ever spent. Such are the secret anomalies of the soul, when imagination excites itself, and self-love is bound up with more elevated sentiments.

May I confess that, in this moment, the public honours which Napoleon had lavished upon me, the pleasure of associating my father with them, of enabling him to be at once a spectator and an actor at this memorable sitting, (that of January 22nd, 1810) when the most celebrated orator of the time, M. de Fontanes, in reply-ing to me was to speak for the last time; the public composed of princes and foreign kings who would be present; these standards, these picked soldiers of renown who surrounded me, finally, and above all, the honour of speaking before the representatives of the greatest of nations, in the name of its Grand Army and in that of the grandest of men; all this instead of inflating me with presumption, had perfectly overwhelmed me.

I had left the château of the Tuileries on foot feeling then in good spirits, at the head of eighty grenadiers of the Old Guard, and the Spanish standards which they were carrying. But when, after having traversed the gardens of the Imperial palace up to the Place de la Concorde, I found myself in the antechamber of the legislative precincts, to wait there till the doors of this chamber were opened for the moment when the historical scene should begin, I must confess that all the joyous pride of my soul vanished in the fear which assailed me lest I should badly sustain my part and destroy all this pomp by not rising to the proper dignity of the occasion. With what kind of an air should I present myself before such a considerable assembly? How should I show a sufficiently steadfast demeanour when confronted by so many glances? and, worst of all, when I should have to ascend that tribune, for me so novel a position, what attitude should I assume? How should I render my voice sufficiently steady, distinct, and assured to be heard? What a humiliation, what a disastrous situation it would be, were my memory to fail me, should I not be sufficiently master of myself to remember the discourse learnt off beforehand that I had to deliver; if I were to stop short in the midst of the universal silence and attention!

During half an hour of suspense and ever increasing anxiety, my excited imagination brought it to such a pitch that even now I cannot conceive how I managed not to break down. I felt as if my whole being was disordered, when the doors opened at last. Imperious necessity alone enabled me to enter after several others and go up the whole length of the room in an absolutely mechanical manner, although the ground seemed to be giving way beneath me. Having arrived at the foot of the tribune—so redoubtable a spot that the most eloquent orators have declared they are never able to ascend it without an emotion which shortens their lives—I felt incapable of pronouncing a single word, when a false movement of my grenadiers restored the power of speech to me. The order which I gave them, an every-day matter, roused me from my stupor. The sound of my own voice reassured me, my being underwent a sudden revolution, and all my fears took flight. This transformation was so prompt and complete that once in face of the Assembly I spoke with such assurance as to delight myself, enchant my grenadiers, and quite surprise the legislators, one of whom, M. d'Aguesseau, my uncle, told me afterwards that he would have preferred a greater semblance of modesty. This criticism, which was really so little deserved, was received by me in a lively spirit, as I infinitely preferred it to a reproach of an opposite nature, which I esteemed myself very happy to have escaped.

XXVIII

INTRIGUES AT PARIS: FOUCHÉ AND BERNADOTTE

Having been obliged to remain in France to get cured, I was the witness of numerous intrigues. The campaign of the malcontents of the interior had been re-opened with the campaign of Austria in 1809. Once again, and more than ever, as we have seen, the chances of the one had excited the activity of the other. Indeed, the Emperor's wound at Ratisbon; the disaster of Essling; the sudden illness followed by the attempt of assassination at Schoenbrunn; the risings in the north and south of Germany; the evidently fallacious element in the co-operation of the Russian Emperor; the violences committed in Rome, and the excommunication; the English descent; our reverses in the Peninsula; all these vicissitudes in short, of a religious, a naval, and continental struggle engaged at all points of the horizon, were so much food for the calculations of those who had grown weary of attaching their destinies to the precarious and compromising existence of a single man.

It should, therefore, not cause astonishment that in the interior, everyone was not resigned to this hand-to-mouth existence, and that amongst men whom these revolutions had created and worn out, a certain number desired to feel some security for the future.

We have seen that at the head of these uneasy speculators were Fouché and Talleyrand; two personages of very different origin, looking upon themselves as the representatives of the old and the new society, a circumstance which they considered useful for the furtherance of their ambitious views, and all the greater reason that they should draw together; for the rest, having no morality to inconvenience them, agreeing as to the necessity of holding themselves ready to meet any event, and having quite made up their minds to extract every kind of profit therefrom for their own personal interest.

Although present in Paris, where I was detained by my wounds, not being a very fitting historian of such details, I will only relate such of the facts as came directly under my knowledge by reason of the part which I had perforce to take in them.

On July 7 the day after Wagram, a lying proclamation of Bernadotte had attributed to his Saxon main body the honour of the victory. It was the skilful habit of this marshal to endeavour to win hearts and gain partisans on all sides. This, however, did him very little good, his corps being immediately disbanded, himself censured, brought to book, and sent back into France where, being taken up in his disgrace by Fouché and Talleyrand, he associated himself with their intrigues.

Fouché, the Minister of Police, was then also in temporary charge of the ministry of the interior. An ever restless and audacious courtier of Fortune, skilful in taking up such a position as to remain her indispensable minister in whatever direction she might turn, he always had one hand hidden in those of the malcontents, and the other eager to display itself before the eyes of the reigning power as the most devoted and useful of servants.

It was at that moment that the English descent had suddenly threatened Antwerp. On this news, notwithstanding the hesitation of Cambacérès, Fouché had taken upon himself to call the National Guard to arms, to mobilise part of them, gain over the officers, and incite Bernadotte to ask for the command. But Clarck, who was then Minister of War, had mistrusted his colleague. As a man of order and of aristocratic inclinations, he detested the antecedents and the revolutionary spirit of Fouché; he suspected his intentions and transmitted his doubts to Schoenbrunn.

The Emperor, in spite of the distance which separated him from such grave complications, did not take alarm. Just as on the battle field he could discern decisive points with an unerring eye, he appreciated every danger, he assigned to everyone his part, and was able to guard against everything. In order to make the descent miscarry he multiplied the necessary orders, adding that it would be sufficient to hold it in check, crowded up as the troops were in the marshes of Zealand, where they would be decimated by fever, which was exactly what happened. The King of Holland and Bernadotte each offered to take the chief command at Antwerp: he refused his brother, whose zeal he suspected, besides considering him inefficient; while with regard to Bernadotte, as this mission would cause the Marshal to leave Paris, he entrusted it to him, on condition that he should only place under his orders officers of incorruptible fidelity. With regard to the calling out of the National Guard, at first only partial, he approved of it, he even encouraged this demonstration which augmented the idea of his power and his means of recruitment. He had, therefore, in the first instance, praised Fouché for this measure; upon which the latter, by way of increasing his importance, extended the call to the whole of France although the danger was over, thus drawing upon himself well-deserved suspicions, which the Emperor did not try to conceal. Amongst other grievances he disapproved of this minister's haste to nominate the officers of the National Guard. Nevertheless, with regard to this, he only took notice of Clarck's warning as far as concerned Paris. It was only there, that looking closer into the matter, he insisted on Fouché retracting one of his selections, Louis de Girardin, whom he had appointed colonel of the Horse Guards in that town.

I was then about again, and nearly cured of my wounds, when on the 9th or 10th of September, Clarck sent for me. 'You see,' he said, 'what is going on, Fouché has just levied 30,000 men in Paris. He is arming the people, even domestic servants. It is a levy of '93 that he wants to have at his disposal. He is preparing to play a great part in certain anticipated cases, such as a more serious illness than the indisposition which has just attacked the Emperor, or a more severe wound than that of Ratisbon, or a more complete reverse than that of Essling. Thirty thousand armed men in Paris! An army would be necessary to guard us from this guard. He continues to organise it in spite of us: he has nominated the officers, although he knew perfectly well that the Emperor had reserved the right to himself. His aim is evident, it is a betrayal. But I am looking after him. That is why the Emperor has just given Marshal Serrurier the command of this fine National Guard; as for the cavalry, he wants you to be its colonel, and we shall then see if Fouché will be able to do what he pleases with it.'

I did not like Fouché any more than he did, but I must confess that this sudden announcement of the role which was being prepared for me in this conflict was as if a slate had fallen on my head. I, in the National Guard! My career thus cut short by a veteran's brevet, when I was anxious to return to active service! No piece of news could possibly have been more displeasing to me. But the circumstances were imperative, and the Emperor, more imperative than they, never allowed the least objection to be made to his orders. I did not attempt it, but returned home very much annoyed, and found awaiting me there an invitation from Fouché to go and see him on the morrow.

Everybody knows this personage; his medium stature, his tow-coloured hair, lank and scanty, his active leanness, his long, mobile, pale face with the physiognomy of an excited ferret; one remembers his piercing keen glance, shifty nevertheless, his little, blood-shot eyes, his brief and jerky manner of speech which was in harmony with his restless, uneasy attitude. Directly he perceived me, all these features were accentuated by an ill-restrained discomfiture. Being obliged to inform me that the Emperor had cancelled his selection and nominated me in its place, he could not hide his annoyance from me. This I shared, agreeing fully with the Minister of War; but with a quick change of front in Fouché's company I declared myself honoured by the Emperor's trust, eager to obey his orders, and consequently to be promptly recognised as the head of the National Guard.

Possibly this minister may have hoped that I should hesitate, perhaps refuse. My alacrity augmented his confusion; he tried to evade the matter, putting it off to the next day, and when the time had arrived he said to me: 'That he had referred it to the Council of ministers, but that they had not come to any decision, and that I must wait; that he must write to Vienna where no doubt it was not known that Girardin had been actually recognised as colonel; and finally, that he should continue to fill the post for the time being until the Emperor, better informed, should send him fresh orders; that indeed a second regiment might be formed, and that he would propose me as general of the brigade.'

Two regiments! when they had hardly been able to get together a hundred volunteers for the first; when this little number, almost entirely composed of bankers and stockbrokers, very decided not to go outside the gates, had not even the leisure to exercise themselves in the indispensable manoeuvres; this was such a palpable fraud that I at once denounced it at head-quarters. I hoped that when the Emperor knew the whole truth he would be too disgusted to entrust me with this command.

The fact is that in the Council the discussion had not concerned myself at all. Clarck and Fouché had had another passage of arms. The former had exclaimed: 'That it was only a confounded Jacobin of who would have entertained the idea of raising and arming the National Guard in Paris.' To which Fouché had answered: 'That it was only a stranger who had sold himself to the English who could oppose the formation of this guard.'

Hulin, Commandant of the capital, spoken out pretty plainly telling me: 'He could no longer answer for Paris. His patrols were unexpectedly coming across unknown posts and patrols: it was impossible to tell if they were citizens or evil-doers: He would disarm them; he would fire upon them!'

Such was the exasperation, when on December 28th I was recalled by Fouché. This minister handing me my commission, said that the Emperor persisted, that he had confirmed my nomination. Then unfolding the letter he had just received, he read me this passage: 'That other sovereigns nominated to the command of their regiments those only who could prove quarters of nobility; that quarters of nobility for him were wounds received in the service of the country; that I was covered with them, and the command in consequence should be reserved for me.'

As little satisfied as Fouché with this ending, I went off at once to Clarck to tell him the news. 'He has not told you everything,' he answered: 'The wretch is persisting in his projects. If it were not for that, instead of going on with the organisation of his National Guard, he would begin to disband it as he has received orders to do; I can prove this to you; your own corps is included in this, if it is not organised so as to be able to enter on a campaign. Go to Marshal Serrurier, and he will confirm this order.'

This was the letter indeed, but not the spirit, which Clarck did not sufficiently consider. The question was how to send back to their homes every one of these volunteers who were already too hostile to the Emperor, without increasing their discontent, which was not an easy matter? But I tried to do more than this; I undertook to alter their frame of mind. It was their officers especially, already uniformed, equipped and mounted at their own expense, and much annoyed at this useless expenditure of money, publicity, and action, who wanted by resigning in a mass, which would have had a very bad effect, to forestall this disbandment which Clarck's officiousness had divulged too early. I dissuaded them from this, and with the help of the administrative authorities, with much civility, fine words and a few dinners, gained time; then going on by degrees, and taking advantage of the fortunate news of the shameful retreat of the English expedition, I held out before them by way of a reward for their now aimless zeal, the hope of being retained as Guards of honour to Napoleon, which they accepted. This was already a return to him, a kind of offer of devotion to his person. At the same time I obtained from Clarck for those whom the pride of a uniform in these glorious days had excited with martial hopes, the prospect of some commissions in the acting army.

Thus by degrees whilst the horses were being sold and the thing breaking up by itself; each of its promoters having been specially gained over, we finished with a grand banquet, where, whilst doing me honour in verse and prose with an enthusiasm which was promoted by champagne, the health of the Emperor was drunk; after which everyone went away mutually delighted.

If, however, peace was re-established with Austria, it was quite otherwise in the Council at Paris. Here the triumphant Clarck and the discomfited Fouché were confronting each other, each striving to damage the other in the mind of the Emperor. According to Clarck, it was certain that Fouché had secret relations with England, and that from Antwerp Bernadotte kept up seditious correspondence with him and other malcontents. The result was that Bernadotte, whose place had been taken by Bessières, was recalled and ordered to travel, or to go to Schoenbrunn, and later to take a command in Catalonia. This marshal's lucky star made him chose the Imperial quarters, and there Napoleon, who was much less vindictive than was supposed, offered him the government of Rome which he first accepted, then neglected as an exile, and finally threw over. We shall see later that the prospect of the throne of Sweden had opened itself to this individual's ambition like a realisation of an Arabian Night's dream.

The quarrel of the two ministers had reached this point when in the middle of the night of the 26th to the 27th October, I was aroused by an order to leave at once to receive the Emperor at Fontainebleau. I got there early in the morning by one door, at the very time when the Emperor, who had just returned from Germany, was entering alone by another; prostrated, however, by fatigue he immediately went to bed and had me called to him at the same moment. The first words he spoke were an eager demand to know what had been the meaning of this National Guard in Paris. I answered: That it had been insignificant, without any aim; and, which was more important, that if it had not been for coercive measures and the rumour that had been circulated as to the possibility of a riot amongst 100,000 workmen of the faubourgs, not a single citizen would have presented himself; and that their disbanding had been effected to the general satisfaction. As to the corps under me I described its composition, making no secret of

its originally hostile spirit, which I palliated on the ground of the
natural discontent of bankers and traders in time of war.

The Emperor interrupted me by recriminations against this class
of his subjects, which he believed to be hostile to him. I calmed him
by speaking of the better feeling with which we had parted. But
as the names of some whom he knew to be against him had been
mentioned, his anger against them broke out afresh and became
even threatening. It is true that these were ardent, aggressive, and
slanderous men, full of self-love, which gave a certain hold upon
them. I commented on this, saying that they could be won over by
a few favours, and that I had taken care to assure myself of this. He
then fell into a reflection of which I took advantage to retire, well
pleased that he had not thought of interrogating me concerning the
quarrel of the two ministers, which, out of prudence, I did not at
all care to be mixed up with. This also saved me from replies which
would have been too much like a denunciation.

The next day, however, during a conversation on this subject with
the Grand Marshal Duroc when I was less on my guard, I perceived by
the manner in which he listened to me, that the conversation might
be carried higher and further than I had any intention of. Indeed the
very next day I saw the two ministers arrive at Fontainebleau: first
Clarck, who left the Emperor's study in a very excited condition, and
then Fouché; whose colloquy with the Emperor had lasted longer. I
knew that in such circumstances it was the Emperor's habit to back
up his own reproaches by citing the names of those whose opinions
or words had aroused his attention. I therefore waited for Fouché's
departure so as to ascertain by his countenance on first catching
sight of me, whether my outpourings of the previous evening had
not made a dangerous enemy of this minister.

This apprehension was not long of realisation. Fouché came
out, and seeing me out of the corner of his eye without appearing
to have taken any notice, he began to walk across the room quickly
with his customary uneasiness. As for me, carelessly leaning against
the marble console which is still opposite to the fireplace, I was
resolutely waiting in silence, when coming straight up at last, he
accosted me, and brusquely proposed a walk in the forest This I

accepted, preferring an explanation, however stormy, to a smouldering grudge, most dangerous in a chief of the police.

This was what he thought fit to tell me with his customary cunning. It is probable that the Emperor, by reason of my confidences to the Grand Marshal, had reminded his minister in the bitterness of his reproaches, of his sorry reputation, without diminishing any of the sanguinary and revolutionary colours which the public and Clarck had laid on so thickly. This was no doubt the reason, that with the view of rehabilitating it, Fouché's first care, while still fresh from this scene, was to relate his entire life to me, a narrative which I found in my notes written that very day, and which seemed to me worth preserving.

'M. de Ségur,' he said, 'many suppositions are originated and many stories are invented about me. It is said that I have been a priest, and that I am married to a nun. The truth is that brought up in the Oratory, I did not even receive the tonsure; and as for my marriage, it took place in 1789, an epoch when priests did not marry and when nuns were not taken in marriage.

Another equally absurd supposition regarding me is that I am said to be a revolutionary. Lyons is given as an instance. There is in all this a share of ignorance, confusion, and anachronism. It may be conceived that it is sometimes needful to run with the hounds, to submit to certain necessities; but the fact is that being sent there, after the sacking of that town, I came back disgusted, with a report against Robespierre, and from that moment up to 9th Thermidor I was his open rival.

Robespierre was installed at the Jacobins; and I in the Committees whence I sent him out; you shall see! I was myself a Jacobin, but there were two kinds. As for us, we were not popular; we talked about equality, but at bottom we were aristocrats. Yes, greater aristocrats perhaps than anyone!

The Jacobins of the opposite party, like Hulin for example, were mere loafers; they shouted from the pit; we looked down upon them from the boxes; it was Robespierre's agents who flattered the populace; Robespierre was their head, their soul, believing he would reign by them and use them to crush the Convention; but we were his antagonists, and I the foremost. He feared me; I had known him from his youth; we were at the same academy; I had then had opportunities of showing him his inefficiency—his relative inefficiency—for he was misjudged. He possessed some talent, a strong and persevering will; a certain simplicity, no greed; but he was swollen with pride which I had humiliated. This was quite sufficient to make him my mortal enemy. His malicious and envious disposition would never forgive it, any more than he forgave Lacuée whom he would have had guillotined but for Carnot. And that simply because once, at Metz, I think, during some academic competition, Lacuée's notes had been preferred to his own. Having been sent for to Paris, Lacuée would have been lost from the very moment of his arrival, if, acting, on Carnot's advice, he had not escaped by one door at the very moment when the gendarmes were entering by the other to seize him and deliver up his head to Robespierre's wounded self-love.

I felt that it would not do to seek out a man of that kind in his club, that he would play me some dirty Jacobin trick; that I should be overwhelmed and crushed and that if I wanted to resist him I must choose some other ground, that is to say the Convention itself and its Committees.

On my return to Lyons I commenced proceedings there by a report on what ought to be done to check the entire disorganisation of this province, of which I accused Robespierre. Everyone was surprised, even terrified at my audacity, amongst others, Carnot, who embraced me in his emotion, praising my courage, but warning me that it would cost me my head. That did not stop me, I still went on; and addressing myself to all the enemies of the Dictator, whether in private, or in meetings which I convoked as the head of public instruction, I wound them up, I encouraged them, and decided the Committee to call upon Robespierre to defend himself before them. This would have placed him in a false position, and he would not do it; he refused to appear, and shut himself up at the Jacobins where I proposed to attack him, have him seized as a rebel, and thrown into the river.

We were consulting as to the means to be employed at the time of the 9th Thermidor, the day when Tallien alone and unexpectedly, without having warned us, and knowing nothing of our own plans, forestalled us by denouncing Robespierre as the tyrant of his colleagues. He quoted me in support of this accusation, to which Robespierre replied, that it was a duel between him and me. You know the rest. But what is not known is that under the Directorate it was I who destroyed the tail of this party after having thus fought its head!

It was still a question of the Jacobins; not those of the Convention to which I had belonged; those had wanted to overthrow Royalty, and substitute a Republic for it; they had a great end in view, whilst these of the Directorate had none at all.

Their club, reconstructed in the riding hall, already comprised 3,000 brothers and friends. They were beginning to settle down, when I made a report against them to the Directorate. The conclusion they arrived at was that in the eyes of Europe, it was humiliating for the Government to allow this vulgar herd of anarchists to impose laws upon them. On this, the Directorate divided and uncertain, and not daring to come to a decision, sent my proposition to the Five Hundred. This caused a crisis, all the more that Bernadotte then Minister of War; Marbot, Commandant of Paris; and Jourdan, President of the Five Hundred, supported these Jacobins. They raised the cry of tyranny, they forsook me, I was on the point of being sacrificed; but I did not hesitate. I sent for Bernadotte, and said to him: 'Idiot! where are you going to, and what do you want to do? It would have been all right in '93 when there was everything to gain by making and unmaking. But what we wanted then, we possess to-day. And as we have got what we wanted and should only lose by going on, why do so?'

He had nothing to answer to this, and yet he persisted. Then I added: 'Do as you please, but just remember this; that after to-morrow when I shall have something to say to your club, if I find you at the head of it, your own shall tumble off your shoulders. I give you my word of honour, and I shall keep it.' This argument brought him to a decision.

'As for Jourdan, the next day at the Council of the Five Hundred, at the moment when he and his partisans were beginning to vociferate, declaring that the Minister of Police was to be put beyond the pale of the law, they were interrupted by a thunder of cavalry. This was a regiment whose chief belonged to me. I had ordered him to execute this manoeuvre, on a given signal to go at a hard trot round and round the hall of the Assembly, making as much noise as possible. This succeeded perfectly. At the sudden and unexpected sound of the clash of arms, words of command, and military movements, the most noisy of the lot were completely terrified; their shouts died away in their throats, those of our friends overpowered them; and that very evening the riding hall was closed to the Jacobins. Repulsed from there, they tried to reunite at the Palace of Salm when I again had them turned out; after which some arrests accompanied by many threats, were enough to put an end to this *carmagnole*.'

In this style Fouché, apparently desirous of proving that he was on our side, and the most useful of friends or the most dangerous of enemies, held forth for an hour. When he had come to the end of this singularly naïve apology, he left me in the full conviction that he had greatly edified me; that between the two shades of Robespierre's Terrorism and his Jacobinism, I should draw a great and flattering distinction in his honour; that this would cause me to overlook in his person the regicide, the proconsul, the signer of so many bloody executions, who had sustained his struggle against Robespierre by making us lose our heads; and that I could not fail to admire the genius with which, as soon as he personally was satisfied with the fruit of his labours, he had known when to stop, to veer round, and associate himself with his victims.

My conclusions were of an entirely opposite nature. If it were possible to recognise in this extraordinary justification, an individual disgusted with the crimes to which he owed his elevation after these crimes had become useless and even harmful to him, I saw over and above this the most audacious of intriguers, always ready to risk revolutionary or other means to render himself indispensable at any price in the position he had won for himself: a dangerous minister to the Government that employed him, ever ready to betray it, and only serving it for personal ends.

XXIX

NAPOLEON AT M. DE CHATEAUBRIAND'S RECEPTION INTO THE ACADEMY

N APOLEON SELDOM DECEIVED HIMSELF AS to the sentiments which he inspired. One day addressing my father, he questioned him as to what he thought would be said about him after his death. My father was beginning to expatiate on our regrets when the Emperor interrupted him with a 'Not at all! they will say:—ouf!' and he accompanied this exclamation with a gesture of relief which expressed in the most significant manner the following words: 'At last we are going to be able to breathe and enjoy ourselves!'

But outside of these private conversations, or the discussions of his Council, in public it was often dangerous to find oneself in Napoleon's road. This may be seen from an incident at this epoch in which my father figured. Chénier had just died, and M. de Châteaubriand had inscribed himself on the roll of candidates who were desirous of succeeding to him in the *Académie Française*, over which my father then presided. M. de Châteaubriand came to ask for his vote and the exercise of any influence that he might possess amongst his confrères. My father answered frankly that he had come too late for this occasion as his vote and influence were held in reserve for M. Aignan, the translator of the *Iliad*; that as a matter of fact, it was forbidden by the statutes that such promises should be made to anyone, although one could keep one made to oneself, and such was his position. M. de Châteaubriand, however, was so actively persistent, he alleged such powerful claims, and so positively promised his vote and that of his friend to M. Aignan for the first place vacant after Chénier, that my father, recognising the just claims of the author of the *Génie du Christianisme* prevailed upon M. Aignan to cede to him a seat of which he had already felt assured.

M. de Châteaubriand seemed particularly desirous of obtaining this seat, and strictly followed out the custom imposed upon every candidate that he himself should solicit the suffrages on which his election depended. He was elected. He knew that in his Reception discourse he would have to pronounce the eulogium of the academician whom he succeeded. Now Chénier had been one of the regicides who had had a seat at the Institute. M. de Châteaubriand composed his discourse with much art. His aim was evidently not to displease any of his new colleagues, not excepting Napoleon. He eloquently praised the Emperor's fame; he exalted the grandeur of republican sentiments, but he said that in Chénier he could only praise the man of letters, remembering in this connection that England for forty years had never boasted of Milton, who had not voted for the execution of Charles the First, but had pronounced its panegyric.

This, like all other Reception discourses, before being publicly delivered, had to be examined by a Commission of twelve members of the French Academy. The opinion of these academicians was equally divided; six thinking that it would produce an undesirable impression; the other six on the contrary, thinking of it favourably. My father and M. de Fontanes were among the latter; but one of the former six, Regnauld de Saint Jean d'Angely, in his too impetuous apprehensions, immediately informed the Emperor of this incident which was in his eyes rather political than literary, communicating to Napoleon his own exaggerated impression of the lecture, but loyally returned to inform my father and M. de Fontanes of this species of denunciation. Thus forewarned, M. de Fontanes prudently forbore for a week from paying his court to the Emperor; but my father the next evening exposed himself to the storm.

It was at St. Cloud where there had been a dramatic representation. The Emperor meeting my father as he came out of his box said to him abruptly: 'You must attend my evening reception, Sir!' My father then followed Napoleon, who, as soon as he perceived him in advance of the numerous assemblage of officers of the Court standing around him in a circle, came straight up to him, saying without any preamble: 'Do these men of letters intend to set France on fire? I have used all my efforts to appease parties, to re-establish quiet, and these ideologists would re-establish anarchy! I would have you know, sir, that the resurrection of the monarchy is a mystery; it is like the ark of Noah, those who attempt to touch it might be struck by a thunderbolt! How dare the Academy talk of regicides when I who wear a crown, and who ought to hate them much more, I dine with them, and sit down by the side of Cambacérès!'

'Your Majesty,' replied, my father, 'is probably speaking of the Commission of the Institute; but I fail to see in what it has deserved such reproaches.' 'It deserves much greater,' retorted the Emperor; 'and you and M. de Fontanes, as a Councillor of State and Grand Master of the University respectively, you both deserve that I should send you to Vincennes!' My father replied: 'I do not believe you capable, Sire, of this injustice. It may be considered a natural thing that the death of Louis Seize should be censured, without thinking it a cause of offence to a Government which has just erected expiatory altars at Saint Denis!'

At these words the Emperor, stamping his foot, exclaimed in anger: 'I know what I ought to do, and when and how I should do it. It is not for you to give your opinion, you are not at the Council of State here. And I do not ask your opinion!'

'I do not give it,' answered my father, 'I justify myself!'

'How?' resumed the Emperor, 'can you justify such an impertinence?'

'Sire,' then said my father, 'M. de Châteaubriand, in his discourse, compares Chénier to Milton, who was a great man: and while condemning him, he only treats Chénier's republicanism and vote as the error of a great soul. I see nothing unseemly in that.'

'In short,' continued Napoleon, 'instead of pronouncing the eulogium of his predecessor, he condemned all regicides, of whom there are some in the Institute. Would you have dared to do the same, to their faces?'

'That is the very thing I did do, Sire,' exclaimed my father, 'in my political *tableau* of Europe, whilst they were still in power during the Republic; and in that I stigmatised as a crime what M. de Châteaubriand only terms an error! These gentlemen bore me no ill-will on that account; they are more accustomed to political arguments than you think.'

'Sir,' retorted the Emperor, 'it is one thing to read a work quietly in one's study, a discourse pronounced in public is quite a different matter; it would have caused a shameful scandal!'

'Allowing that,' replied my father, 'it would have been at the most a twenty-four hours' scandal; by forbidding it, the thing will last perhaps a month!'

'I must tell you again, Sir,' the Emperor sharply replied, 'that I do not ask your advice. You preside over the second class of the Institute; I order you to inform it that I do not choose that politics should be treated of in its sittings.'

'In that case, Sire,' resumed my father, 'I must give up the eulogium of Malesherbes which has been entrusted to me.'

'I do not see any great loss in that,' answered Napoleon. Then he added in his most abrupt, imperious tones: 'Go! and execute my orders, and bear in mind that if the class should disobey, I will break it up like a disorderly club!'

Thus concluding, the Emperor bowed to the company, and each retired, with downcast head, avoiding my father, with the exception of Duroc who came up, and observed that if he had held his tongue, this scene would have passed over in a second.

On the next morning my father, resolved on an explanation did not fail to attend the *levée*, where several looked coldly upon him. When they had taken their departure, he remained, in spite of Rambuteau, then Chamberlain, and now Prefect of Paris, who fearing that he might ruin himself, vainly tried to draw him away into the adjoining room. The Emperor, becoming aware that my father had stayed on alone in his private room, asked him with some gentleness, what he wanted. To which my father replied:— 'To speak to you, Sire, respecting the scene of last night; respect alone prevented me from saying many things which I was anxious to reply. Nothing is more painful for those who are attached to you than to listen to such bitter reproaches. If you will not allow the maxims of your Government to be contradicted, it is necessary, for us at least, that they should not be enigmas. The approbation which you bestowed upon what I wrote on the death of the King, the severe expressions which you recently made use of in the Throne Room against the regicides, and finally, your expiatory ordinance for Saint-Denis, render incomprehensible to me the severe manner in which you spoke to me yesterday, and which has greatly affected me.'

My father then explained to him in detail all that had taken place during the Commission. He represented to him that such a discourse, even allowing it to be mischievous, could only harm its author, whilst, if disallowed, it would turn against the thing itself, the interdiction thus appearing to encourage an act which had been rightly and politically reprobated. He concluded by saying that were literature to be too much fettered, and confined to mere grammatical discussions, one of the most brilliant rays of the glory of his reign would be obscured, if not extinguished, higher literature, like morality, being inseparable from politics.

To all this the Emperor, who had listened attentively, replied thus:—'I am not angry with you. It is a question of policy with me. I said yesterday what I intended to be repeated. There is a good deal of party spirit in all this. If any other than M. de Châteaubriand had made such a discourse, I should not have heeded it; and this you should have known as a statesman. Besides,' he added with a laugh, 'you must admit that men of letters are always aiming at effect, and love to address themselves to the passions. You must also allow that, as a man of letters and a man of taste, M. de Châteaubriand has been guilty of indecorum; for if you wanted to praise a woman with one eye, you would speak of every other feature except the one in which she is deficient!'

My father laughed at this sally, whereupon the Emperor resumed: 'Come now, you are no longer angry, neither am I: but you must prevent the Institute from discussing politics, for it is easier to stop that kind of thing than to moderate it.'

My father then opened the door, and as all saw the Emperor dismiss him in the most gracious and kindly manner, they immediately gathered round him.

Next day M. de Châteaubriand wrote to my father to thank him for the steadfastness with which he had defended him. On the following Thursday the Academy deliberated on the report of its Commission. The conclusion arrived at was that its Director should request M. de Châteaubriand to eliminate from his discourse all that related to the death of the King.

M. de Châteaubriand was waiting in an adjoining room: my father went to convey this decision to him. The first words of the new Academician were that he would not submit to any curtailment. These were also his last words, although modified in form; for my father having answered that he would make no use of this reply until repeated elsewhere, and in a calmer frame of mind, M. de Châteaubriand came the next day to see my father, and not finding him in, wrote at his desk: 'That just now he was not well enough to do any work, and would not send in another Reception discourse to the Academy until his health should allow of his paying sufficient attention to it.'

We all know that this feigned indisposition lasted on to the Restoration.

The Restoration! Meaning thereby conquest and invasion turned back against ourselves! Oh! how far we then thought ourselves from such a catastrophe! or rather we did not think of it at all. How was it possible we should believe in such a complete transformation of so great a fortune and of so many lesser fortunes, in such a thorough destruction of so powerful an organisation, and of so many interests; habits, thoughts, and feelings bound up in it? Yet this year 1811 was to be the last of the ascendant world-dominion of Napoleon and of our Empire. Our star henceforth would only emit brilliant but evanescent and delusive rays, like flickering lights which only shoot up with renewed lustre before expiring altogether, because in dying, they consume with themselves all by which they had up to that moment been sustained and surrounded!

FINIS.

FOOTNOTES

1. Eighty years later, in 1871, General Philippe de Ségur, his grandson, went through the hardships of the siege of Paris and the commune. Does not the following scene recall to us the moving episode of Châtenay. "One day, some delegates of the Commune attired in military uniform made a perquisition in the general's residence. He preserved such a noble demeanour that it inspired them with respect. After a few words, the confused and wavering delegates renounced the search. One of them, however, as he was leaving, suddenly changed his tone and asked the general to give them some money. Upon which the general also altered his tone and demeanour. "Leave this place," he said, "you dishonour the uniform you are wearing." He no longer spoke a resigned victim who braves and intimidates his executioners, he spoke like a general to his soldiers.—The miserable creatures went off with bowed heads. They had recognised the voice of the master, touch of indignant honour had thrilled within them." (SAINT-RENÉ TAILLANDIER.)

2. "The Treaty of Basle (July 22) which does credit to the good sense of Godoï, won for him the honorary title of 'Prince of Peace', the only title which he ever really deserved." (*Translator's Note.*)

3. This Scottish word, and the office it denotes, is the exact equivalent of the French "bailli."—*Translator's Note.*

4. Reille, now a Marshal of France after having been aide-de-camp to the Emperor.
5. The original letter is in the National Archives.
6. The most powerful of the Mongolian tribes.—*Translator's Note*
7. A Spanish gold coin worth about 85 francs, or £3 8s.—*Translator's Note*
8. 1808.
9. The original is in the National Archives.

INDEX

N

ALSO AVAILABLE FROM NONSUCH PUBLISHING

On 23 June 1812 Napoleon and his Grand Armée crossed the River Niemen and entered Russia. This is an eye-witness account of the highs and lows of an expedition which was to terminally weaken the French stranglehold on Europe. In two volumes.
1 84588 021 8 / 1 84588 022 6
£10
288 pages

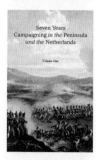

Written by Military and later Ordnance Commissary, Richard D. Henegan, *Seven Years* records the author's experiences in the Peninsula War, from his arrival in August 1808 with Sir John Moore, to the decisive Battle of Waterloo. In two volumes.
1 84588 039 0 / 1 84588 040 4
£10
192 pages

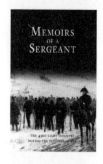

A vivid account of the life of the ordinary soldier in Wellington's army, an anonymous Irish soldier in the 43rd Light Infantry records his day-to-day experiences in the Peninsula until his wounding at Badajoz, as well as his conversion to Methodism on leaving the army.
1 84588 034 X
£12
240 pages

A surgeon in the 2nd Life Guards, S.D. Broughton records his experiences during the Peninsula War from his starting point in Lisbon to his departure from France at Boulogne. An engaging narrative recording details of not only the campaign, but also matters of local interest.
1 84588 030 7
£10
192 pages

For further information please see: www.nonsuch-publishing.com